T0094956

BIKIN' and BROTHERHOOD
MY JOURNEY

David Charles Spurgeon

WESTBOW
PRESS

An Imprint of Thomas Nelson
visit us at: thomasnelson.com

© 2011, 2014 by David Charles Spurgeon.

All rights reserved. No portion of this book may be reproduced, stored in a retrieval system, or transmitted in any form or by any means—electronic, mechanical, photocopy, recording, scanning, or other—except for brief quotations in critical reviews or articles, without the prior written permission of the publisher.

Published in Nashville, Tennessee, by Nelson Books, an imprint of Thomas Nelson. Nelson Books and Thomas Nelson are registered trademarks of HarperCollins Christian Publishing, Inc.

Scripture taken from the King James Version of the Bible.

Thomas Nelson, Inc., titles may be purchased in bulk for educational, business, fund-raising, or sales promotional use. For information, please e-mail SpecialMarkets@ThomasNelson.com.

Library of Congress Control Number: 2011917922

ISBN: 978-0-7180-3035-3 (sc)
ISBN: 978-0-7180-3036-0 (e)

Printed in the United States of America

14 15 16 17 18 RRD 6 5 4 3 2 1

CONTENTS

Having met David Spurgeon back in the day, as well as many of the outlaw bikers he writes about in *Bikin' and Brotherhood: My Journey*, I found this memoir to be factually accurate and brutally honest. A full-throttle ride down the highway of life, David tells his life story without excuse or apology, and I applaud him for doing so. The reader will definitely get a factual glimpse into the world of one-percenters that they won't ever get from Hollywood, or the fiction section of their local bookstore.

—EDWARD WINTERHALDER

Edward Winterhalder is one of the world's leading authorities on motorcycle clubs. His books are published in multiple languages and sold all over the world. In addition to his literary endeavors, Edward is a consultant to the entertainment industry for TV, feature film and DVD projects that focus on the Harley-Davidson biker lifestyle.

To the men and women
who love the thrill of the wind in their face,
and the rumble of heavy metal thunder between their legs.
Keep the shiny side up.

1%er

A 1%er is the one in a hundred of us who has given up
on society and the politicians' one-way law.
This is why we look repulsive.
We're saying we don't want to be like you,
or look like you.
So stay out of our face.

Look at your Brother standing next to you and ask yourself if you would give him half of what you have in your
pocket. Or half of what you have to eat. If a citizen hits
your Brother, will you be on him without asking why?
There is no why. Your Brother may not always be right,
but he is always your Brother. It's one in all and all in
one. If you don't think this way, then walk away, because
you are a citizen and you don't belong with us.

We are Outlaws, and members will follow the Outlaw
way or get out. All members are your Brothers and your
family. You will not steal your Brother's possessions,
money, woman, class, or his honor.
OUTLAWS FOREVER, FOREVER OUTLAWS: O.F.F.O.

PREFACE

In light of the explosion of the biker lifestyle in recent years, I felt obliged to chronicle some of the many events that were part of my involvement with it between 1975 and 1990. My experience began with a pure and simple love of the Harley-Davidson motorcycle. Regretfully, it led me to associations and actions that were detrimental and destructive, both to me and to others.

May this record provide some insight into a misunderstood way of life from one who lived it to its fullest, and then some. I don't know what is more amazing: how some people misperceive how bikers really are, or how some bikers misperceive what they think they are supposed to be.

Though I was heavily involved as a member and officer in one of the largest one-percenter clubs in the world, this book is in no way an attempt to promote the bike club mentality. It is not a how-to book on criminal activity, or an approval, or defense, of illegal pursuits of any kind. It is not a collection of steamy stories of immorality, lewdness, or vulgarity. Nor is it an endorsement of the drug and alcohol abuse that almost destroyed my life, and that often accompanies and is sometimes glorified by the biker lifestyle.

May this book serve as a warning: don't get so caught up with the lifestyle that the love of the machine and the freedom of the road become obscured. I know what I'm talking about. I've been there.

Keep the main thing the main thing. Live to ride. Ride to live.

Chapter 1

The Valley of the Shadow of Death

Live fast, die young, and leave a good-looking corpse.
—common Outlaw saying

As I turned my Camaro Z 28 into the dark alley, I could see the body sprawled out in the gravel ahead of me. I knew it had to be Ralph. He had roared past Kato and me on his motorcycle when we stopped at the light at the corner of Western and Hawley Streets, a block from the clubhouse. It was early Saturday morning, about 3:00 a.m.; now Ralph was dead.

Several hours earlier, Ralph had been relieved of "guard duty" at the Toledo Outlaws Motorcycle Club clubhouse. The rest of the chapter had been in western Pennsylvania for the annual week-long Turkey Day party. We never left the clubhouse unoccupied, especially after dark. Although I was the chapter boss and was never required to pull guard duty, I opted to stay home this time in order to get my bike ready to head south for the

1

winter. The annual New Year's Eve party in Florida was approaching fast, so I decided to take advantage of the week to get loose ends tied up.

When the first carload of our members returned from West Penn chapter's club house, which we called "the Mountain," I was more than ready to head to a local south Toledo bar we often frequented. Kato and I jumped in my car, leaving Ralph behind to wait for someone to relieve him. Though it was late November, Ralph soon showed up at the bar on the only transportation he had, the Harley-Davidson FLH I had built for him.

We had just enough time down at K.O.'s Lounge that night to make up for a long week of sobriety and cabin fever. When I saw Ralph there on the ground, my first thought was that he had lost control in the gravel and hit the fence running along the dimly lit alley. His Harley was lying on its side a little further down. Kato and I jumped out of the car and ran to where he was, but when we got to him, he wasn't breathing. I slid my arm under him to straighten his twisted body out in order to do mouth-to-mouth, but when I pulled my arm out, it glistened with the eerie, deep-red glow of blood in the light of the lone streetlamp. It wasn't due to any injury he incurred going down on his bike. Ralph had been shot to death in cold blood.

This became one of the longest nights of my life. Rage mingled with grief. Apprehension over our newly realized vulnerability mixed with thoughts of severe and immediate vengeance. First I called my regional president, a Detroit Outlaw by the name of Taco, and then I called the police, which in itself was a new experience for me. By dawn, homicide investigators began to scour the crime scene. The cold, hard facts were obvious. Ralph was ambushed as soon as he had turned into the alley, heading to the clubhouse at the opposite end. He had three bullet wounds in his back, and his motorcycle had been hit twice as well. Toledo's finest were unable to find any other evidence during their inspection of the landscape, and club brothers arriving from neighboring cities were making them very nervous. Several of our men began meticulously combing the area as well, going even farther down the alley than the cops did—all the way to the entrance.

At the corner was an abandoned house—not a vacant house or an empty house waiting to be rented or sold and again occupied. It was abandoned, typical of the neighborhood in which our clubhouse was located. It was in a part of south Toledo that had been redlined by the banks and other lending institutions.

In other words, we lived in the ghetto. People here did not call the cops every time a dog barked, or the music got too loud, or a firearm discharged in the middle of the night. People here did not call the cops at all. The neighbors fearfully minded their own business and hoped everyone else did too. It was the ideal place to have a motorcycle clubhouse. As if those factors weren't enough, our enemies stood out like a sore thumb. Not to mention most of the Feds who constantly tried to do surveillance on us.

In the weeds next to the deserted shack, a Detroit brother found nineteen spent shell casings. Of course, the investigator was not happy that one of our guys found the brass that he had missed; that made him look bad. The shells were .223 caliber or, as we used to say in the military, 5.56 mm. The uninhabited structure provided perfect concealment for the assassin. Evidently, the killer had stepped out from behind his cover just as Ralph rode past him and sent the deadly rounds from his fully automatic rifle down the alley after him. Unfortunately for Ralph, three lethal, mercury-dipped bullets found their mark.

Taco arrived later that day. He had been in the club a long time and was highly experienced in every area. He knew the effect an event like this could have on a new chapter like Toledo's, which had just recently turned one year old. All the visions of riding state to state, enjoying the freedom of a life spent "in the wind" also had some very dark realities tied to them. From the beginning of my association with the Outlaws, I was told that years in prison, early death, or both were routinely the cost of "life in the fast lane." I, like so many others, accepted those terms.

Forty-one times in my fifteen years with Outlaw biker clubs, I observed firsthand that death was the consequence of that choice. It was the reality that cut through the bravado of the big talkers and divided the fakers from the faithful. How it was handled is what separated the men from the boys.

By Sunday evening, Ralph's body was in a local funeral home being prepared for the viewing that was to come. Taco took Kato and me there to see him. Kato was the vice president for the Toledo chapter and my right-hand man. The funeral home was closed, so I was surprised anyone answered when we knocked loudly at the door. We were greeted by a mortician who was more than happy to honor our request to see the body. The four of us went downstairs to the embalming room where there were several other bodies besides Ralph's lying on cold, stainless-steel tables. I think the undertaker was hoping we were going to find his work as fascinating as he did and perhaps even compliment him for doing such a good job on Ralph. We didn't—on either count.

We lifted up Ralph's stiff body, cut stem to stern from the autopsy, and rolled him over to look at where the bullet holes had torn through his back. We needed to see for ourselves. We weren't known for taking anybody's word for anything, let alone something as close to home as a fallen brother. That's why Kato and I thought we were there anyway, but there was a much more serious reason to be down there in that room of death. Taco wanted to see our eyes as we looked at our deceased comrade. Taco wanted to see for himself if this violent loss brought anger or fear to his new chapter's leaders. Ultimately, our future would be determined by what he saw that night, revealing whether we had what it took to be true one-percenters or not. He saw the fury of anger with a strong desire for vengeance. He was more than satisfied—he was convinced.

During the course of the next several days, hundreds of fellow Outlaws from all over the United States and Canada began arriving for the first national motorcycle club funeral in Toledo. It was for a dual purpose we gathered there: not only to show respect to our departed brother, but also to declare, "We're here to stay!" to our enemies. It would take a lot more than this to rattle our commitment to the club and to each other.

Death became a way of life for us. In 1979 and 1980 alone, I attended well over a dozen club funerals. The causes ranged from murder, like Ralph's, to drug overdoses and motorcycle crashes. In the next ten years, we buried over two dozen more. There is even a revered section of a rural cemetery near Dayton, Ohio, known as Boot Hill, where many Outlaws are buried. What put them there? Natural causes for those who chose to live in the valley of the shadow of death.

Chapter 2

Love Affair with a Machine

I was twenty-one years old, fresh out of the army after serving two and a half years overseas with the First Battalion 509th Airborne Infantry Battalion Combat Team. I was ready to be free to do whatever I wanted without being told how to dress, when to shave, or how long my hair could be. Growing up in a middle-class family in the Midwest in the fifties and sixties, I had two great desires that, as a kid, I had hoped to see fulfilled one day. One was to own a Corvette, which I eventually did: a beautiful, 1973 candy-apple–red Sting Ray. The other—by far the most important one to me—was about to become a reality.

The closest Harley shop was about thirty miles away from where I was staying at my folk's home. When I walked into the Napoleon Harley-Davidson Dealership for the first time in February 1975, I never imagined I would ever end up in a motorcycle club, let alone a convicted felon. At this point in my life, I just wanted to experience the thrill and freedom of riding down the road on my own Harley-Davidson motorcycle.

Dealerships back then were quite a bit different from the Harley shops of today. The Harley-Davidson Motor Company offered only three basic models. No such thing as Night Trains or Fat Boys existed; no Street Bobs or Softails. There were no Dynas, Ultras, Road Kings or Low Riders. There was the tried-and-true Electra Glide, the newly introduced Super Glide, and the traditional Sportster. The "big twins" had 1200-cc, 74-cubic-inch, horizontally opposed V-Twin engines, four-speed, ratchet-top transmissions, and were all chain driven. The Sportster had recently made the transition from 900 to 1000 cc. All of them had carburetors, and all of them had ignition points.

The Super Glide and Sportster came in kick-start only, as well as combination kick- and electric-start models. My mentality at the time was that if you couldn't kick-start your own motorcycle, then you didn't deserve to be riding it. On several occasions after having to tune a couple of Super Glides because their moronic owners couldn't get them started, I actually started their bikes, in front of their girlfriends, with my right arm. Boy, did that make them look bad! I said something like, "You should be able to handle it from here, don't you think?"

By the way, back then I also thought that only sissies and old guys needed front fenders. That way of thinking changed in the years to come. Some states required them.

The first time I rode in the rain after fabricating a front fender for a run to Oklahoma, I definitely didn't miss the pelting stream of water coming up off the front tire, causing me to sit almost side-saddle to avoid it. I thought to myself, *Why did I wait so long?* I never did have turn signals on any of my motorcycles, though. If you were too lazy to extend your arm out to indicate your intention, you belonged in a car, or "cage," as we referred to the two tons of glass and plastic most people needed wrapped around them to feel safe. Besides, turn signals did not look cool.

The two-page Harley-Davidson catalog of 1975 consisted of pictures of the above-mentioned bikes and that's about all; no jewelry or dog accessories. No nightgowns or underwear. No knives or knick-knacks. No beer mugs, coffee mugs, boots, or jogging outfits—just motorcycles. Imagine that. The dealerships carried two styles of leather jackets: the traditional Marlon Brando style and the citizen-looking café jacket. There was only one T-shirt design available, the AMF stylized #1, but it did come in black or white!

For those Harley lovers who like to talk bad about AMF, allow me to let you in on a little secret about your heritage. If it were not for AMF, the Harley-Davidson Motor Company would have never survived the '70s, let alone become what it is today. Besides, taking those cone-nose, alternator Shovelhead engines apart and rebuilding them is where most of us learned to wrench. Many of the service managers today got their initial experience working the bugs out of those early assembly-line bikes.

These days, Harley-Davidson dealerships resemble mall stores more than the shops of the '60s and '70s. There are many two-story showrooms and even a three-story facility near Daytona. I've been in dealerships that offered lounges for patrons to relax in while they sip coffee, or even shoot pool, before getting back out there to the grueling highway on their state-of-the-art, ultra smooth, nearly problem-free machines. Don't get me wrong. I like going to Harley shops myself, and I love the new bikes. I'm just saying things have changed. A lot.

Back then, the clientele wasn't largely made up of fiftysomething former yuppies. The bikes didn't cost more than cars. Ford didn't offer a Harley-Davidson Special Edition pick-up truck, and you couldn't buy official, licensed products at Wal-Mart. (In fact, I had never even heard of Wal-Mart at the time.) The shops were not strategically located along the interstate highways either. You really had to want to go to one just to find it. Such was the case with Napoleon Harley-Davidson.

I met the proprietor, Marvin Yagel, that cold February day when I walked in to his shop. He was a nice guy who'd lost a leg in a motorcycle wreck some years earlier. He was happy to see a first-time buyer interested in relieving him of one of his "vast" inventory of motorcycles. It consisted of only two "big twins." Harleys were hard to come by in those days. There was no room to be too picky. I was fortunate to find what I was looking for on his showroom floor. I was glad I wasn't going to have to order my bike and wait several months for it, as was often the case in the early '70s. I purchased his only FX model, a burgundy, kick-start Super Glide. Tax, title, out the door, it cost $3,050, and that included a horsehide leather jacket. February 28, 1975 was to become one of the definitive days of my life.

After years of dreaming of actually owning my own Harley, the day finally came for me to take delivery of my brand new 1975 Super Glide FX. I had ridden some dirt bikes in the past and even owned a 1971 Yamaha RT-1B 360 cc Enduro while stationed in Germany. I would take it out to the sand dunes outside of Mainz where the tanks and tracks did their maneuvers. There were some very steep hills, and I learned to jump that Yamaha pretty well. It was also street legal, so it doubled as my regular transportation for about a year and a half. I had never ridden a Harley, though, and now I was about to begin the thirty-mile ride home on my very own.

As Marv was briefing me on this particular model, I was trying hard not to look like the rookie I was. I needed to be shown where the key switch was and then, though I had owned a bike before, I had to be reminded to turn the fuel petcock to the on position. I know they got a chuckle when I nervously pulled out onto Route 6 heading for home. To be honest, although I was enjoying this moment immensely, it was also quite nerve-wracking. Every time I approached an intersection or a stop sign, I tried to make sure I remembered everything I was supposed to remember. By the time I finished my maiden voyage, I was a nervous wreck. When I finally arrived at my parents' home, I was more than ready to get off for a while.

Marv became a good friend who went out of his way to help me learn about the motorcycle I loved but knew nothing about. I really tried his patience when the exhaust pipes on my Super Glide began to turn blue up near the head. I took my bike back and asked him to replace them with bright, shiny ones like it came with. He explained that it was, to some degree, part of the bargain of owning an air-cooled motorcycle. The pipes get hot and discolor.

Looking back, I must have appeared extremely naive, but he put up with me. He checked everything over really well: carburetor mixture, heat range of my plugs, and condition of the exhaust gaskets. Everything checked out to be in fine working order. Then he ordered me a new set of factory staggered duals anyway. They did the same thing. They turned blue up near the head. He knew they would, but he indulged me. By this time I had learned a little, so I just accepted it. I wonder why he put up with me. I'm glad he did. He taught me many good things. I learned plenty of bad things during those early years, but none of them from him. He was a good guy who always treated me right. I wish I could say the same for the way I always treated him.

Marv let me hang out at the shop. I swept the floor and took out the trash. I didn't mind; I just wanted to be around the motorcycles and the people who rode them. He let me bother his mechanic, and he took a lot of time to answer my many questions. He even put in a good word for me at the local Campbell's Soup plant where he worked before taking over Napoleon Harley-Davidson from his father-in-law. Looking back, he probably just hoped to get me out of there a few hours a day.

I got the job at Campbell's as a truck driver, although I had never driven a semi in my life. I had driven plenty of straight trucks on the farm and even a few in the army, but never a tractor-trailer configuration. My brother-in-law took me to a truck lot the weekend before I started and gave me enough pointers for me to bluff my way into convincing them I knew what I was doing. I was even able to make several runs, hauling forty thousand pounds of tomato soup to various warehouses in Ohio and Indiana. My short-lived semi-driving career came to an abrupt end, though, late one night near Napoleon. I was to drop a loaded trailer at a warehouse and bobtail back to the main plant. I hadn't mastered backing up, to say the least, and this night I got one side of the trailer off the concrete. It had been raining all day, and that trailer sunk in the mud and got stuck. Before the tow truck finally pulled that trailer out of the mire, I managed to mangle the dolly wheels, and to damage a buried water line. So much for being a truck driver. Why I wasn't fired I'll never know, but I was reassigned to the warehouse from that night on. I managed to do a pretty good job the rest of the summer driving a forklift. At least I could back it up. It was kind of humbling, now that I think about it.

I wasn't at Campbell's Soup for a career anyway. I took the job because it was second shift, and it enabled me to spend every day at the shop. On more than a few occasions during the summer of '75, as I was enjoying the afternoon ride to work, I just could not seem to be able to force myself to turn in at the plant to begin my shift. The call of the highway and the beautiful scenic drive along the Maumee River refused to be ignored.

One Saturday night in April, on my way home from work, I stopped at the Longbranch Saloon, a Waterville, Ohio tavern. I stayed until closing time, and this particular night, I definitely had one too many. I thought I was fine to ride home, but I wasn't. I roared out of town, quickly attracting the attention of the local Barney Fife, who pursued me as far as he could. I was still living with my parents, and those rural, winding roads along the river had been my training ground. Soon his flashing red lights disappeared in my rearview mirror.

I cut up a secluded road toward home at a high rate of speed, laughing that I had ditched the cop. As I got close to home, out of nowhere a car came up over a steep set of railroad tracks toward me. I probably surprised the driver as much as he did me at that late hour so far out in the country. The combination of my inexperience and the liquor caused me to brake too hard in order to avoid a collision with that car that night. As I went by it, my rear tire began to slide out to the right, and I laid that bike down doing about eighty miles per hour. I went into a PLF as I hit the pavement (that's Parachute Landing Fall for you civilians). Evidently, I bent and flexed in all the right places because after tumbling several hundred feet, I got up with only minor injuries. The alcohol, no doubt, played a major part not only in causing the wreck, but also in my surviving it. Not so for my Super Glide. I'd had my "dream come true" motorcycle for only two months, and now I had all but destroyed it.

The headlight still burned brightly skyward from the ditch where it finally ended up. I limped over to it, turned the key off, and lay down next to it. Although I was within sight of home, I knew this baby wasn't rolling anywhere, and I wasn't leaving it. I thought I was hallucinating when I heard the unmistakable sound of another Harley approaching. It was around 4:00 a.m. by now, and my next-door neighbor, who rode a Sportster, was coming home from shooting pool at my sister's house, so I flagged him down. He couldn't believe how messed up my scooter was, or the fact that I was standing there talking to him at all. If we could have found the driver of that car that night, we'd probably both still be in prison. As I think back and swallow my pride, that car didn't do anything wrong. It was my fault. That was hard to admit back then, so I didn't, not even to myself. I was wrong. I overreacted. I blew it.

My neighbor Tom went to his house and got his pickup, and we muscled my bike up into the back of it. The mangled rear wheel stuck hideously up in the air out of the bed of his truck. That was the first thing my mom and dad saw as they were getting into their car to go to church the next morning. My dad walked over to look at the twisted mass of iron, and my mom peeked into my bedroom to see if I was okay. I was out like a light, but I guess the lack of blood on my sheets satisfied her that I was at least still alive. She didn't freak out or panic. She didn't even wake me. My folks went on to church. There's no doubt about what they prayed about on that Sunday morning or on many Sundays to come.

That afternoon after I woke up and sobered up, I called the local Ohio State Trooper Post and explained what had happened . . . sort of. I told them how the probably drunk driver of the car intentionally tried to run me off the road, and it was only a miracle that I hadn't been killed. I'm sure I convinced them I was just out joy riding at that time of the night—just minding my own business, not doing anything wrong, not under the influence of anything but the cool night air. Yeah, right.

An insurance adjuster came by the next day to look at my demolished motorcycle. He wrote the words "totaled" across the top of his paperwork. I don't know whether he believed my story or not, but there was no way to prove me wrong. He authorized the claim. That afternoon I took my bike back to the Harley shop, this time to get a repair estimate. I made up my mind to do the labor of rebuilding it myself. That decision resulted in my first chopper. This was the beginning of my path to becoming a custom builder, long before anybody was making TV shows about it, let alone earning millions of dollars doing it.

I spent every waking hour at the shop, working on my scooter and learning. I made up my mind: my goal in life was to be a Harley mechanic. I loved wrenching, and I got along well with all the bike riders who came in. They were divided into two groups: the American Motorcycle Association sports-enthusiast types and the rougher, cruder, hard-core types. Being a former paratrooper and a whiskey drinking fist fighter, it would be an understatement to say that I fit in better with the second group.

I built a good-looking scooter out of that wreck, considering it was my first attempt. I picked up a 1956 straight-leg rigid frame and a pair of 1960 three-and-a-half gallon Fat Bob gas tanks. I put together a beautiful "eight-over" Wide Glide front end, added chrome forward controls, Andrews third gear, a Sifton 468S cam, solid lifters, and the newly introduced S&S Super Carb. My bike wasn't quite like any other four-month-old Shovelhead in my neck of the woods. Not to mention the forty-inch drag pipes. Remember, this is rural northwest Ohio, 1975.

Ed Williams was the head mechanic in Napoleon, and he taught me much about working on Harleys. He would blindfold me and put pieces of a disassembled four-speed transmission in my hand one at a time. I had to be able to identify every gear, bearing, spacer, shim, shifter clutch, and so forth by touch before he would teach me how to put it all back together. I did. He was a good teacher.

He also taught me some things about riding, like watching every car, every pedestrian, every little old lady at every stop sign, every stray dog. He taught me how to be ready for people to run red lights, to pull out of parking lots in front of you, or to back out of driveways while seeming to look right at you. He taught me not to lose it when someone did something stupid but rather to expect it. He taught me to have a plan of action ready when they did, not if they did. All that training was for one thing: staying alive.

Something he didn't warn me about was bugs. I'm not talking about the "How can you tell a happy biker? By the bugs in his teeth" stuff. I'm talking about the hazard they can be. On more than a few occasions, I caught up with a bumblebee that wasn't flying as fast as I was riding. One time I went into a restaurant without removing my helmet until I got to my table. When I took it off, a huge yellow jacket was unleashed. It was dive-bombing people and causing quite a commotion. I thought it was hilarious. That time, remarkably, I didn't get stung.

My most memorable confrontation with an insect came late one night on my way home from a night of drinking and playing pool. In the pale light of a street lamp up ahead, I could see something larger than normal hovering in the soft glow. I was doing over a hundred miles an hour, so no sooner than I spotted it, I was on it. I wasn't wearing glasses that night when I collided with that bug, and it caught me dead in my left eye. The impact felt like I'd been hit with a baseball bat. I remember all but my very fingertips slipping from the handlebar grips as I reeled backwards. It hurt really badly, but the realization that I almost went off the back was worse than the pain. How would that have looked in the paper? "Harley Rider, Former Paratrooper, Killed by an Insect." I made it a point to wear eye protection from then on.

One night, Ed and I were riding west on the two-lane Anthony Wayne Trail toward Fort Wayne, Indiana. It was a smooth, winding road running along the north bank of the Maumee River and a perfect road for what he had in mind. Semis would often take this route to avoid the tollbooths and the weigh station on the Ohio Turnpike. We paced ourselves behind a truck until Ed saw one approaching from the other direction. Suddenly, he sped up to about ninety miles per hour and passed between the trucks on the white line just as they were meeting each other. Talk about zero tolerance. There was absolutely no room for error. I really thought he was crazy. As the trucks moved away from each other, I accelerated and caught up with Ed. I looked over at him and he had this big grin on his face, like he'd just done the most fun thing imaginable. Right about then I was beginning to wonder about who I was out there riding with.

It wasn't long before we caught up to another westbound semi. Instead of flying by it like we had the last several cars, Ed slowed us down to match its speed. I knew what he was doing this time. Soon I could see the headlights of an approaching tractor-trailer rig. Ed looked over at me with that grin on his face again and downshifted. Away he went, taking the center line between the two massive trucks as they met. This time I was right behind him. I had made up my mind he wasn't going to be the only one having fun that night (or splattered on the asphalt either). Before the night was over, we did that a few more times. I even went first twice, with him right on my tail. It was fun and scary at the same time.

I spent most of 1975 either at the Harley shop or at the local tavern in Waterville. My good-looking Harley and my reputation for sticking up for the little guy endeared me to the bar's owners and patrons alike. On more than one occasion, members of one of the rinky-dink motorcycle clubs from Toledo would be out riding in the country and end up at the Longbranch Saloon. They just could not help but attempt to terrorize the locals. Several times, I was in the right place at the right time to step in and be the hero. The fact that I liked to fistfight came in very handy. The paratroops taught me not to be controlled by fear, but I learned to fight in the bars—not some dojo or studio, and not in a ring with rules and referees and gloves—on the street, where people really got hurt, where it wasn't a sport or a game. It was real.

Sticking up for people had a lot of benefits too. If you saved someone from getting their rear end stomped, they were grateful. Very grateful. If you prevented some goons from trashing a bar and scaring off all your customers, the owner generally became very generous. I don't think I paid for a drink or a meal at the Longbranch for two years. Not to mention having several old cars bought for me. Life was simple back then.

Somewhere during that summer, I picked up the street name "Cowboy." Big Lou, one of the proprietors of the Longbranch at the time, started calling me that after a pool game one night. I had held the table for a good five or six hours when several rednecks tried to cheat a local out of his turn to challenge me. I stuck up for the guy and the fight was on, but it didn't last long. When the fight was over, Big Lou said anybody that could walk away from laying a Harley down at eighty miles per hour without getting hurt, line dance with semi trucks, and take on four guys to help a stranger had to be a real cowboy. The name stuck for the next fifteen years.

21

That first spring as a Harley owner I met some real losers, but I also met some pretty good folks. I had been gone for three years in the military, so all of my friends from high school were married or pursuing a lifestyle much different from mine. Even Tom, my best friend in high school, was seeing a girl who didn't much like his Harley or me. One night, as I rode past the Longbranch, I spotted a beautiful custom '52 Panhead out front that I'd never seen before. I stopped and parked, but I was far more interested in meeting the owner of that pan than anything else that could be going on inside. I inquired as to who it belonged to, and that's when I met Jay Buck. Jay was a Vietnam vet. He had been with the "Stalking Rhinos" of the 11th Armored Cavalry when our army invaded Cambodia. He was there at the bar with his wife Lana. They were what I would call "real people." What you saw was what you got. They weren't trying to impress anyone; they were just themselves. We hit it off right away and became good friends. I eventually moved in with them and their two dogs: Knucklehead, a boxer, and Freedom, a beautiful silver-and-black German shepherd. We partied and rode together all that summer. It was a good time.

That autumn, an opportunity opened up for Jay and me to buy out a guy who had owned a small motorcycle repair shop. He had many used parts stored in a barn, so Jay rented an old farmhouse with a large workshop and we filled it with the old Harley parts. There were two complete Panhead motors and an alternator Shovelhead motor. There were transmissions to go with them, as well as frames and titles. There were several complete Hydra-Glide front ends, and we ended up with eleven sets of vintage Fat Bob tank sets, complete with emblems. Harley quit using them in 1964, and they didn't reappear from the factory until the Low Rider was introduced in 1977. We had fenders, handlebars, seats, oil tanks, and headlight assemblies. There were crates of engine parts, transmission parts, and disc and drum brake parts. It was like Christmas to a couple of guys who loved the Harley-Davidson. We loved everything about them, you see, not just riding 'em.

It was in that shop, on the corner of Neowash Road and Route 295 in rural Whitehouse, Ohio, that my 1975 Super Glide underwent a major change. This transformation resulted in what would become my favorite scooter of all time. I liked it even better than the brand-new 1977½ Low Rider a bar owner once bought me. I also once built a 1964 88 ci Pan, lower Shovel-top, stroker motor with 4¾ S&S flywheels and an S&S L-block carburetor, which was very, very fast. I eventually had a 1985 FXRS with a 92 ci Blockhead engine, which was even faster, but my favorite remained my first Harley, that '75 Shovel.

In the course of doing a lot of horse-trading, I ended up with a 1973 D&D "Jammer" rigid frame. It had a two-and-three-quarter inch stretch in the down tubes and a ten degree over stock rake. I fabricated and welded Fat Bob gas tank mounts to it. By 1976, Fat Bobs were out, and all kinds of custom tanks were in vogue, from modified Sportster tanks to Easyrider peanut tanks and even coffin-shaped gas tanks. I had always loved the old three-and-a-half-gallon stock tanks and located a 1954 pair with my favorite tank emblems to use on my personal machine.

I had the lower legs of a 1952 Hydra-Glide front end turned down in a ten-step pattern with a fabricated Cle' single-disc brake tab welded on. I had a custom axle made to accommodate a stock Super Glide nineteen-inch front wheel. I removed the stem from the lower triple tree, ground off all the tabs, and re-welded the stem back in with the lower tree inverted. It made for a beautiful custom, disc-brake, wide-glide front end. I added twelve over tubes to make the bike sit level with the custom rake of the frame. When the factory came out with the dual disc narrow-glide front end the following year, several fellow riders asked if I was going to modify my front end into a dual-disc version. This was before Harley built their own dual-disc Wide Glide a couple of years later.

That would have been easy enough to do, but the question reminded me of the time I had asked my dad about an old rusty spur that hung on the pegboard in our garage. When I inquired where it came from, he told me it was his when he was a kid growing up with horses on a farm in Tennessee. When I asked why there was only one, he replied, "If you spur one side of the horse, don't you think the other side of the horse will keep up with it?" That's how I felt about the dual disc. If you slowed down one side of the wheel, doesn't the other side have to slow down too? Besides, with a single chamber master cylinder they used then, the factory's dual-disc brake lever was harder to accentuate than the one I built.

I modified an old Sportster rear fender, welded on and molded in a late-fifties dresser taillight, and mated it to a tall octagon sissy bar. My favorite taillight was the old "tombstone" they used on Knuckleheads and very early Panheads, but glass lenses were few and far between back then. Topping it off with a Corbin Gentry "Widow-Maker" seat and buckhorn handlebars, I had a long, low, custom fat bob with lots of chrome and a beautiful, hot rod flame paint job. At this stage there was no electric starter, front fender, or speedometer. It took me a few years to realize the virtue of some of those luxuries.

More important than how it looked, however, was the fact that it was dependable mechanically, sound geometrically, and comfortable on the highway. It wasn't a show bike or a bar hopper. It wasn't a toy to attract attention. I rode this motorcycle for the next ten years. I rode this very same rigid stroker to Florida and back to northern Ohio at least twelve times. Also, I rode it to Oklahoma City and back three times, and in 1980 I rode it to Las Vegas and back. It was built without unlimited funds or a super-modern machine shop at my disposal, and hardly any aftermarket parts. Back then, you had to do almost everything yourself. There was no place I knew of where you could go and fork over umpteen thousands of dollars for a custom bike that someone else designed and built for you. Custom bike building was far more personal than that. It wasn't a fad, or a rich kid passtime, or a multi-million dollar business. It was truly a passion. It was, without a doubt, a love affair with a machine.

Chapter 3

MC Stands for Motorcycle Club

On a late September weekend in the fall of 1975, while I was still hauling tomato soup around northwest Ohio, Jay met a biker by the name of Wayne Hicks. He was starting his own motorcycle club and talked Jay into joining. I had not seen Jay for about a week, so when I ran into him one night at the bar, he told me all about it. Hicks had been a member of another motorcycle club in Toledo called the Clansmen, but they had kicked him out. I later found out why. His club name had been Scrounge because he was always scrounging around to see what he could get for himself. It should have been Weasel. If ever anyone was only out for number one, it was Hicks. He proved that on numerous occasions throughout the years—definitely not an attribute that lends itself to the concept of brotherhood.

The Mongols was the name of this new club. It was to be a Toledo, Ohio extension, or chapter, of

27

the Mongols MC just across the state line in Monroe, Michigan. Monroe happened to be the hometown of General George Custer of Little Bighorn fame. That should have told me something. I must say here that there was no affiliation with the Mongols Motorcycle Club of southern California. I had never even heard of them at the time. The only club I had ever heard of outside of some of Toledo's rinky-dink bikers was the Hells Angels. Everyone had heard of them. They had made movies, and they had made history. I had never seen even one at this point in my life and did not really expect I ever would.

Jay became a charter member of the newly formed Mongols MC Ohio, and wanted me to join too. There was only one catch. He apologized for not being able to reach me in time for the "charter meeting" and explained, "Anyone who wants to join now has to prospect." When I asked what that meant, he told me it was a probationary period in which you had to prove yourself worthy of membership to the other members. I wasn't worried about proving myself. At eighteen years old, I became a light weapons specialist in the infantry. I turned nineteen at the Airborne School at Fort Benning, Georgia, where I earned my parachute badge. I spent over two years in Europe with an elite airborne combat team. I had experienced laying down a Harley at eighty miles per hour and walking away. I had been victorious in plenty of fistfights with no brothers to back me up.

As far as I was concerned, I was plenty man enough. I was not worried about anything they could throw at me. To be honest, I wanted to check them out to see if they were worthy of me.

In reality, I had no idea what a motorcycle club actually did. I assumed they rode together. I found out that they also hung out together, partied together, and expected 100 percent participation at every function, whether it was an official meeting, a Saturday night party, or a Sunday afternoon ride. Attendance at everything was mandatory, especially from their first prospective member, which was me. Soon there were several more, and I quickly learned to take advantage of my seniority. I worked my way right into the newer prospects' chain of command. Because I had known the full patch members longer than they had, they would ask me what was expected of them in certain situations. On numerous occasions I had them taking advice, if not orders, directly from me.

I had a problem with one lazy opportunist who did not like that one bit. He made sure the others knew we prospects were all equal and answerable only to the five charter members. I got him off to the side and reminded him that 100 percent of the membership must vote in favor of any proposed new member. He said, "So what?" Then I told him I was going to be voted in long before he would ever be considered, and he was never going to get my vote. He and I were never going to be "brothers." I had seen his type in the army. I was not going to trust my back to him, and I told him the best thing he could do was to quit before he got hurt. I made sure he knew I was very serious. Common sense prevailed for the bum. He turned in his prospective colors (the patches worn by MC members). If I had been smart, I would have quit too. I would have saved myself a lot of trouble later on, but quitting was not in my blood. Besides, I really had no idea what I was getting myself into.

I discovered how serious they were about not missing any functions when I did not come to a Saturday night get-together at the Longbranch Saloon. Wayne chewed me out at the next meeting for it. I did not like that, especially when the one doing the chewing out couldn't whip my sister without a sucker punch, a weapon, and two people holding her down. I should have been able to see through him, but I didn't. Before it was all said and done, I was not the only one he fooled. He conned smarter and tougher men than me before he became a full-blown snitch and traitor twenty years later. Hindsight is always twenty-twenty.

I was still doing what I loved the most, which was hanging out at the Harley shop every morning. I was working at Campbell's Soup on second shift, and I usually made it to the bar before closing time, wanting to get to know the people I was anticipating joining up with. The problem came when the warehouse supervisor told me that I would have to work weekends until further notice. As far as I was concerned, I had an important decision to make. Obviously, I was not going to be able to meet my obligations to the club if I could not be there. I thought it all over before going to the next meeting.

When I got there, I told the members about my situation. This was not a social club. It was a brotherhood. More was required than just paying dues and coming when you could. Dedication was expected and required. I was okay with that. That's what I wanted: something to be dedicated to, something to live for besides the humdrum, boring, nine-to-five citizen lifestyle everyone else I knew was living.

The members were disappointed when I explained my dilemma. I was the best prospect they had, if I do say so myself. I had already learned to ride and wrench during the year since I had gotten out of the Army. More important than that, the concept of brotherhood appealed to me more than I can put into words. After letting the charter members hang in suspense for a few minutes, I told them I had decided I would not be missing any functions because of any citizen job. I announced that from then on I would be making my living as a freelance mechanic. I was now self-employed and was going to be doing what I loved, working on Harley-Davidsons.

The shop Jay and I put together at the farm provided the perfect place for me to work. Jay worked a regular daytime job, so I labored in our garage all day, every day. As with any motorcycle club, you had plenty of members who had no real interest in wrenching. I built eleven transmissions and two engines for the guys in the month of October alone. Most of the brothers just wanted to ride. My love for my motorcycle involved riding as much as possible, but when it was not feasible due to the weather, I had to have my hands on the machine somehow.

The minimum prospective period to be eligible for a membership vote was thirty days. The last Saturday in October 1975 was my thirty-day mark. They voted me in unanimously of course, and I became the first member actually to earn his colors. The five original members had just given each other theirs. I was glad I had earned mine, even if it was so easy. Looking back, I have found that just about anyone can be on his or her best behavior for thirty days. Had Toledo's law-enforcement community been aware of the scope of what was unfolding in their midst and what the future held for this rag-tag group of novice "clubbers," they could have infiltrated us pretty easily back then.

Our first clubhouse was a rented commercial building in the Wood County suburb of Perrysburg, Ohio. It was not much, just a vacant warehouse. We boarded up the windows, built a bar, and rented a pool table. It had a bathroom and a small office that I claimed for my own. I put a mattress on the floor in there and moved in. The building had a garage, so I routinely worked on other member's bikes right there at the clubhouse.

It was from this clubhouse that I attempted to cash in on one of my Veterans Administration benefits. I had been accepted at Bowling Green State University prior to joining the Mongols, so I decided to give college a try. Classes were in the morning; there was no real conflict. I would just go to the Harley shop from college every afternoon. If all this sounds like a contradiction, it was. Think of what it was like to try to live in a biker clubhouse at night and attend classes in geology, American history, and philosophy during the day. It was a challenge just trying to locate my books in the morning after club members had been up all night drinking and getting high. It was interesting, to say the least.

I started attending classes in January 1976. I would drive my old '62 Chevy pickup truck twenty miles down to the campus wearing a black leather jacket with my pants tucked into knee-high engineer boots. I did not wear my colors, but only because I was not riding my bike. We did not wear our colors while driving cages. I intended to ride to school in the spring, and I was going to wear them then. I am sure that would have gone over really well. It was the transition age of hippie versus disco, and I did not fit in either category. I did not fit in at BGSU either.

I loved American history, but I had a professor who talked down to his class of about two hundred as if they were little children. He was a jerk. Granted, most of them probably were eighteen-year-olds just out of high school, but I was not. I was twenty-two years old, a former paratrooper, and a member of a rough, tough motorcycle club. One day I stood up in class and told him what I

33

thought of his style of teaching in no uncertain terms. The students loved it. The professor didn't. Needless to say, there was no need for me to go back in there. "Withdrew failing" I think it said when I got my grades for that class at the end of the semester.

I liked geology and philosophy, though, so I decided to give it another try and signed up for the next semester. This time I had a political science instructor who had just received her teaching credential the previous year. Guess what? She talked to all her freshman students as if they were little children. I didn't even attempt to finish that semester. I went back and gave all my energy and attention to the club and my brothers. College interfered with my lifestyle as a club member anyway. Anything that interfered with that did not last very long, be it jobs, girlfriends, or a shot at a free college education. I was really smart, wasn't I?

At the next meeting after I was voted into the Mongols, I was made an officer. I went from being a prospect, to a patchholder, to the road captain in thirty-seven days. How about that? The reason I was so quickly promoted probably had a lot to do with the fact that I had a good running bike, a working knowledge of custom Harleys, and a toolbox.

In my capacity as road captain, I got to ride at the rear of the pack and stop to help anyone who had a problem. There were always plenty of breakdowns, especially if the Monroe chapter was along. We would usually have a truck or a van following the pack, which carried my tools, some spare parts, and a ramp. When a member fell out of the pack because of a mechanical problem, I would pull over with him and fix the problem, if I could. If I couldn't, we'd load that member and his bike into the back-up vehicle. In those days, if you rode a chopper, you owned a pick-up or a cargo van, or knew someone who did. Not some velvet-interior, shag-carpeted, hippie van, but a heavy-duty truck capable of holding at least a half ton of motorcycle iron.

The negative aspect of riding in packs as we did was that it could get boring, especially if you were in the middle. It's more difficult to enjoy the scenery when you have a rear fender directly in front of you. You have to really be on your toes for any braking, or changes in speed, or lane changes, or parts falling off the guy's bike in front of you. Add a wide variety of substance-induced buzzes to the equation and you had great potential for disaster. It was imperative to pay attention.

As road captain, I enjoyed being in the back. That way I rode in the center of the lane, with the two uniform ranks of bikes extending out before me. That vantage point made it easier for me to keep an eye on everyone and spot possible problems early on. It also allowed me to better see the leader and anticipate lane changes. Part of the fun was pulling out into the fast lane on a four-lane highway to block traffic for the pack to change lanes. I did not allow cars to disrupt my pack. It was my job to make sure they didn't. The handle of a fifteen-inch Crescent wrench stuck up out of my left saddlebag in plain sight of contrary motorists. It was placed strategically so that I could get a hold of it if necessary to help dissuade any driver from attempting to get by me and endangering any of the men who trusted me to cover their backs. It worked too, on several occasions. When the pack had made the lane change back into the slow lane, I would be the last to file in, thus allowing traffic to resume its normal flow. Motorists hated being cut off by us, and their faces would often reflect their disdain, though most had enough sense not to display it too openly. Road rage wasn't nearly as prevalent an issue back then as it is now, and when it was an issue, we were the masters of it.

The best part of being road captain was that after I got a broken down brother either up and running or loaded, I could ride as fast as necessary to catch up to the pack. The back-up truck had a map and was on its own. Eventually, it always caught up. Depending on the length of the time of the breakdown, I have ended up many miles behind the rest of the group. Catching up was fast and fun. Speeds of well over a hundred miles an hour or riding the white line through slowed traffic were common occurrences.

White-line "dancing" used to make some drivers very angry, which only added to the excitement. One time a Mercedes-Benz began to drift over toward the center line to cut me off as I approached, riding down the center of the two lanes. The rich boy probably couldn't stand the thought of being stuck in slower traffic while a low-life biker on a chopper whizzed by without a care in the world. As I maneuvered to avoid him, I lifted my right foot, with a heavy, double-soled engineer boot on it, and kicked the left side mirror right off the door of his fancy foreign car. As I looked back laughing, I could see it banging against the side of his vehicle from its remote control cable. He was visibly upset, but I didn't care. I gave him the one-finger salute as I sped away to rejoin the pack. I bet he never cut a Harley rider off again.

In the early days of custom motorcycles, there were always breakdowns. The process would repeat itself until we got to where we were going. By the time we would arrive at our destination, I would be the dirtiest one of all, due to the oil and road grime that I would accumulate from all the leaking Harleys I had been following, sometimes for several hundred miles. Back then, a Harley-Davidson with no oil spot under it was a sign of no oil in it. On many occasions, I spent much of my time fixing other brothers' machines so they could make the trip home. I missed some of the partying because of that, but my first love was the motorcycle. No doubt, the responsibility of my office probably kept me out of some trouble at least.

Just prior to one of our weekend runs, my trusted Shovelhead developed a lower-end vibration that demanded immediate attention. I began by removing the primary cover and inspecting everything from the clutch hub to the nut holding on the twenty-three-tooth rigid engine sprocket. Nothing was loose. Every locking tab was installed correctly, but something was very wrong. Upon closer scrutiny, I was horrified to see a fluctuation in the sprocket shaft itself as it spun at a thousand revolutions per minute. To me, it meant the sprocket shaft nut on the inside of the flywheel had come loose. On this particular model, the sprocket shaft was held in place by a tapered press fit instead of a key and keyway like the older models. A locking tab washer prevented the nut from backing off, and I was positive I did not assemble those flywheels without locking the tab on both shafts. With only twenty-four hours to go before pulling out on a mandatory ride, my engine was officially down. I could not stand the thought of riding in a truck, watching my brothers enjoy the highway. If someone broke down, I'd still be able to help them, but I'd miss all the fun of riding. If that was the way it had to be, so be it, but I wasn't giving up without a fight.

Though the exact cause of the problem was still unknown at that point, the next step was clear. I began by preparing my workbench for a complete engine tear down. Every tool was put in its proper place. Projects that were already under way were moved carefully so that nothing would be misplaced. I began by doing all the preliminaries for engine removal: disassembling the primary drive train, dismantling the exhaust system, and disconnecting the applicable wiring. In just under an hour, I had the motor sitting on my engine stand, ready for tear down. I had to take it completely apart before I could even begin to know what parts to try to locate. I knew I'd need rings and gaskets. Those things I had, or was confident the Harley shop would have.

Some would take this occasion to rail on American Machine and Foundry, which had bought Harley-Davidson. I entered into the world of Harley-Davidson during the "dark years," when they were owned by the infamous producers of boats and bowling machines. It's true: many problems resulted from the changes AMF implemented, including an undeniable lack in the quality control department. For me it was an asset because it provided a lot of warranty work for the dealership where I worked occasionally. The rest of the Harley-Davidson world might want to consider this: had not AMF bought Harley-Davidson in the late '60s, there probably would not have been an American-made motorcycle company to buy back in 1981.

I took that motor apart, pulling the heads and the cast-iron jugs that Shovelheads still had back then. I carefully removed the wrist pin keepers and slid the pins out so I could take the pistons off. Looking down into the lower-end and slowly rotating the flywheels, I tried to detect any abrasive feel or sound that shouldn't be there. Everything seemed fine. The wheels turned smoothly, and the rods showed no reason for concern, but there was reason for concern. There was no way around that wobble in the sprocket shaft. I split the cases and continued my careful inspection. The Timken bearing on the sprocket shaft looked good, as did the caged roller bearings on the pinion side. The crankpin nuts were tight, and the keepers were locked. The main races in each case half looked and felt fine. So, the flywheels needed to be separated and the investigation needed to go further. Finally, after removing the crankpin, unlocking the sprocket shaft nut keeper, and pressing out the shaft, I discovered a hairline crack at the base of the threads. I shuddered to think about what could have happened had that shaft broken all the way through and the nut dropped to the bottom of the cases at 2000-plus rpm.

I immediately called the closest Harley dealer and confirmed he had the parts I needed, including a new sprocket shaft. It was around 5:00 p.m. on Thursday, and I needed to be leaving in a pack the next morning, so I got the parts and put my beloved Shovelhead motor back together that night. In less than twenty-four hours, it went from running, to complete engine rebuild (minus headwork), to reassembly. I took it out in the pre-dawn hours to put some gentle break-in miles on the rings before putting it to the rigors of "road captaining." As happy as I was to be up and running, the satisfaction of locating and resolving the problem, under the pressure of that time constraint, gave me as much pleasure as the run itself.

Our first big run with the Monroe, Michigan, Mongol chapter was in May 1976. About thirty of us left Toledo together, heading for the Indianapolis 500. As far as I knew, no one had any particular interest in auto racing. On the other hand, we all had an interest in what was going on all weekend in the infield of the legendary speedway. One big, nonstop, anything-goes *party*.

Many in our group couldn't wait to get there to drink, get high, and do what bikers do. Use your imagination. As I checked over the bikes to head off any obvious problems before they happened, I detected an interesting attitude among many. They couldn't wait for this ride to be over so they could party. It was apparent by their machines that riding was not even close to the most important thing to them. The motorcycle was just the means that enabled them to reap the benefits of the motorcycle-club life.

I made up my mind that day, that (for me, at least) the party started when I let the clutch out; in other words, when I pulled out onto the highway. I joined the club for riding and for the camaraderie that came with being with men who felt the same way about bikin' and brotherhood. Many, however, were just thugs who used the Harley to get girls, or wimps who needed the club to finish the fights they started by running their mouths. I had no respect for either type. Still don't.

That first run to Indianapolis was a great success overall. It was a miracle none of us went to jail that weekend. There were some pretty serious fistfights. That was inevitable when you had so many people drinking and getting high in one place. The Indiana State Police, with their mattock handles and riot helmets, did not play well with others, especially troublemakers from out of state. Our guys were notorious for hitting on women, even if they were with their boyfriends or husbands. This usually led to the girl dumping her companion and going for a ride, or a fight with the guy. Either were acceptable outcomes to us.

Soon after our arrival at the Speedway, I pulled into a gas station outside the track to fuel up after being separated from the rest of our group. Four good old boys stood with arms crossed, intentionally blocking my way. Real brain surgeons, these guys. I plowed my Harley right into them. They cursed me as they jumped out of my way. That gave me all the invitation I needed. The biggest loudmouth of the quartet threatened me with what *they* were going to do to me. I told him he had the "easy part done"—in other words, the talking about it. With that said, I offered him the first punch. It surprised him so much he didn't know quite what to do. I told him I figured him for a coward, and I dared him to take a swing. He did. He gave me his best shot. It wasn't a bad punch, but I just smiled and told him he hit like a girl. That made him so mad and embarrassed that he did not even see my haymaker coming that knocked him to the ground, spitting blood and teeth out of his mouth. I turned to the next candidate and told him to take his best shot. I guess the loudmouth was the toughest of this little crew because none of the other three wanted any part of the action. Such was life in the motorcycle club. Riding, partying, *and fighting*.

In February 1977, I got the chance to go to Reynoldsburg, Ohio, for a Harley-Davidson factory authorized service school for two weeks. I was still hanging out and doing some work at the Harley Shop in Napoleon, and though Marv did not approve of me being in a motorcycle club, he sent me to the school. I learned some things for sure, but the most memorable thing about that trip was meeting the Renegades MC in Columbus. By the way, these Renegades were not affiliated with the ones in Dayton, Virginia Beach, or Tampa Bay. They were, however, a sister club of the infamous Renegades MC out of Buffalo, New York.

One of our guys knew one of them from back in their hippie days together and got a contact number for me. I made the call and got the invite to come over. Their clubhouse was on Cleveland Avenue just south of the Ohio State Fairgrounds where the famous Old Time Newsies charity motorcycle races took place annually. They were not the most formidable bike club I had ever met, but they were friendly. We hit it off okay, and they said I could crash there for the time I was in the area for the service school.

These Renegades were more into drugs and drinking than bikin' and brotherhood. Their bikes were nothing to brag about because of it. Several of them were seriously into a powder called T, or THC. We used to call it "rubber medicine." It would not only turn your body into rubber, but your mind also. Many bad decisions were made by folks who chose to party with this drug. I have seen a few seriously maimed from trying to ride a motorcycle high on T. There were many, especially females, who later regretted ever getting anywhere near this poisonous nose candy.

One night after service school, while hanging out at their clubhouse, one of their members got to talking about a dead person in a warehouse downtown. He had been there for years, he said. When I asked him how he knew about him, he said his old lady's dad was a wino who slept on the fire escape in the back of the Central Chemical Company, where they made embalming fluid. Supposedly, the story went like this: sometime in the forties, Central Chemical got the idea of doing an innovative field experiment to study their product. They requested, and got permission, to get the cadaver of an inmate who died while in custody at a nearby prison farm. He had no known relatives and was to be buried on the prison grounds. Central Chemical got this man's body and embalmed him. They kept him in a zippered body bag at the chemical plant and occasionally would open him up and document his rate of deterioration.

I told him I did not believe for a second that anybody had a dead body lying around in a warehouse for thirty years. Bob said he had seen him himself. They kept him on one of the upper floors, lying on a couch. He swore he had seen him with his own eyes. I told Bob he had better lay off the dope for a while; it was melting his brain. Then Bob said he could take me there to see him for myself. Of course, I jumped at the chance.

When the Harley-Davidson service seminar ended, everyone went home except me. I went to the Central Chemical Company. When Bob and I entered the front office, there was a distinct aroma about the place, which I did not recognize. Reminiscent of a high school chemistry class, there were glass bottles around the room that contained different colors of liquid: embalming fluid, to be exact. The look on the proprietor's face when he asked, "May I help you?" was like something out of an old, cheap horror flick. Bob said, "We're here to see the dead guy." Just like that. The man gave us a morbid smile and said, "This way."

He directed us to a freight elevator and told us which button to push to get to the dead guy's floor. When the gate opened on the elevator, you could see several large rats scurrying across the floor. We turned a corner and there he was, lying on a couch, just as Bob said. Actually, it was one of those psychiatrist type couches with no back. He was in a body bag all right, but the zipper had long since broken and the bottom had rotted away. The rats had pretty much chewed his toes off, but overall, he looked good considering he had been dead for so long. He was naked except for a napkin covering his privates.

His skin had a yellow tint to it that made it somewhat difficult to tell what race he was originally.

The experiment to see how their embalming fluid worked was probably considered successful. I still have a hard time believing it was legal to have a dead body just lying around. I felt sorry for the dude. His value had long since passed. He probably ended up in the dumpster eventually, or he might even still be on the couch. Who knows? I offered to buy him. With all the morbid stuff we surrounded ourselves with, he would have made a great conversation piece, sitting down at the end of the clubhouse bar or hanging in the corner with a noose around his neck.

The Toledo Mongols went to Columbus several times that summer to party with the Renegades. They were not what I would call hard-core bike riders, their bikes pretty much being held together with bailing wire, hose clamps, and "hundred-mile-per-hour tape." That is what we called duct tape. It was amazing how much of it they used to hold their bikes together. It worked for them, though, probably because none of their machines were capable of going a hundred miles per hour. I will give the Columbus Renegades this, though: they were hospitable. They opened up their clubhouse to us, and they shared everything. About the third time down there, we met some members of their Buffalo, New York, chapter who had come for the weekend. They were a different breed altogether. They were much more serious about everything, from their machines to their brotherhood, to maintaining their composure when they were around people they didn't know. In other words, they controlled their buzzes around us. No T for any of them, or for any of us either. Several of us hit it off pretty well, and before the weekend was over, we were invited to Buffalo to party with them at their clubhouse.

Chapter 4

Genghis Khan Rides Again

L ife was simple in the early years as a patch holder in the Mongols. We weren't rich by any means, but then again, we weren't trying to be. We wanted to have fun. Ride. Party. Be free. If we could get to the bar and buy our first couple of rounds, we were often set for the night. Some idiot would usually get stupid and cause someone else to need rescuing. We were the cheapest rescuers around. We'd fight your fight for you for beer and bar food.

That first winter in the club, almost every night found me at the Longbranch Saloon. It was where I hung out, but it was also where I ate supper. Jay's old lady, Lana, fed us once in a while, but she made it clear that she married Jay, not the rest of us. That was fair enough. The bar in Waterville had a pretty good menu, and the price was right: free. Big Lou sold the Longbranch to a lady named Cookie, who happened to be a great cook. Go figure.

Not long after she took over, a bunch of members from the Iron Coffins MC in Toledo stopped by one afternoon when none of us were there. They were being their normal selves, intimidating old people and women, when someone told them they better cut it out. This was the Mongols hangout, and we wouldn't like it. In response, they trashed the place. Not that bad really, but flipping the pool table over had a tremendous psychological effect on the easygoing patrons. I got a frantic call over the incident and immediately went down there, but of course, the Coffins were long gone.

Cookie and the locals were terrified, and she begged me to be there every night to make sure it wouldn't happen again. I assured Cookie it wouldn't, confident that a call to their boss would obtain an apology, whether he meant it or not. She made it clear to her help that "Cowboy doesn't pay for anything anymore. Everything is on the house." At the time, that seemed like a pretty good deal. After all, I spent a lot of time there anyway.

One cold January evening, Termite and I were on our way to Longbranch in my '67 Buick Deuce and a Quarter when it decided to quit running on me. I had been "borrowing" some of our landlord's tractor fuel and mixing it with gas to save money. It made the car smoke and run a little rough, but who cared? It was just a winter cage. Besides, who wanted to waste money on gas? It had gotten really cold the night before and, best I can figure, the fuel must have gelled enough that it wasn't mixing properly. Regardless of why, it quit running, and we had to hitchhike the rest of the way to the bar. Catching a ride home would be no problem, so I didn't give the big black-and-white Buick another thought.

Hours later on the way home, we had to go right past my car and, low and behold, someone had smashed the windshield out of it. I wondered if someone I had beaten up had done it, or some jerk whose girlfriend had decided to go for a little ride with one of the bikers. Either way, it was no big deal. I went back the next day, wiped all the glass off the dashboard, poured in some 260 Sunoco, and it fired right up. When it came time to head back to the Waterville bar that evening, Termite and I donned motorcycle helmets, goggles, and winter coats for the very cold ride. Actually, it was comical. It was going to take more than a broken windshield to keep us out of the fast lane.

One of the problems with living way out in the country was it took a while for our roads to be plowed after a winter storm. On several occasions, we were snowed in for a day or so, but rarely did the weather prevent me from making it to the bar. It started snowing one night that winter of '77, and it literally snowed for days, not hours. I wasn't able to go out the first night of the storm or the second. I was starting to get cabin fever, and there wasn't much food in the house. To make matters worse, what food there was had kind of a "healthy" slant to it that I sure wasn't used to. Jay and Lana both drank,

51

smoked, and got high, but then would lecture me about eating greasy foods or using too much salt. By the third day of being snowed in, my body was craving bar food. To make matters really worse, the only dope we had was a pound of "homegrown" Lana had cultivated in the corner of the backyard. It tasted lousy, it would barely get you high, and worst of all, it gave you an incredible case of the munchies. If that wasn't enough, we were down to our last pack of cigarettes among the three of us.

While the wind was still blowing and the snow was still coming down on the third day, we got a knock on the door. Jay, Lana, and I all thought the exact same thing: *Hopefully it's someone with cigarettes!* It was Termite. He looked like the abominable snowman. His long beard was solid ice, as were his eyebrows. We let him in and begged him for his Marlboros before even thinking to ask him if he was okay or how he got out to where we were stranded. We had a snowdrift over twelve feet high in our driveway. No vehicle of any kind had made its way so far down Neowash Road during what turned out to be the infamous blizzard of 1977.

Toledo's main streets had been plowed several times, and Termite took the opportunity to come rescue us. The phones had been out, and he had gotten worried about us, so he borrowed his rich dad's Lincoln Town Car and headed out for no-man's-land. Even with the National Guard assisting the Ohio Department of Transportation road crews, they still hadn't cleared Route 295, which ran near our house. Termite actually made a heroic effort, getting within a few miles of the house before getting that Lincoln stuck up on a three-foot drift. Luckily for Termite, a farmer came along on a tractor before he froze to death and brought him to within a couple of hundred yards of our house. As noble as his attempt was, he really made matters worse because he was one more mouth to feed. Also, he loved the cheap homegrown pot, which made what little food we did have go even quicker. At least he had some cigarettes. What a relief it was when the snow finally stopped. The snowplow made it down our road at last, and we shoveled our driveway for an entire day, determined to make it to the bar that night. We did, and we had some great stories to tell about our ordeal.

In the spring of '78, we welcomed the opening of the first Wendy's restaurant on our end of town. It was the only drive-through I'd seen since going through a Jack in the Box back in California a few years before. Back then, the Jack in the Box drive-through had the speaker in the clown's mouth. I hated it. I didn't talk to clowns. I still don't. This Wendy's in south Toledo was very convenient to some of the places where we hung out at the time, so several of us would frequent it often. Bar food was okay when we were drinking, but when we weren't, we needed a little better quality of food, not to mention some variety. You can't do much better than cheeseburgers and chili. For some reason, almost every biker I ever met loved chili, and Wendy's chili wasn't too bad. Not as good as Steak N' Shake's, but pretty good just the same.

The speaker/microphone system wasn't as sophisticated as they are today, so often there would be communication problems. One afternoon I pulled up to order while driving Jay's big Chevy van. The girl on the inside misunderstood my order and asked me to repeat it. I did. This went on two more times before I ran out of patience. I unleashed a stream of profanities that punctuated every other word of my order in a volume loud enough to be heard at the cash register without a microphone. As I pulled up to the window, there was no girl there, but rather an unhappy manager. The ordering system did not include headsets back then, but rather a speaker for the cashier to listen to the customer giving the order. When I unloaded my frustration in no uncertain terms, everyone in the dining room could hear me. That was evident by the look on their faces as I looked past the nerdy manager who was about to read me my drive-through rights. I could also see the order girl crying behind him.

Jay's van made the manager and me eyeball-to-eyeball, so as he began to threaten me with the police because of my behavior, I reached out and grabbed ahold of his tie. He hadn't even seen a token of my behavior. I never said a word to him. I just let my foot off the brake and let the van creep forward slowly. He had no choice but to come with it. Right out the window. Soon his hands were on the roof of the van, and he wasn't threatening anymore.

When his ankles were on the windowsill and his entire body suspended between the van and the building, he was begging for mercy. I showed him some. I goosed the van just a little and he fell straight down on his face onto the pavement. The only thing hurt was his pride. I thought it was hilarious, until I realized I didn't get my food. Oh well—I thought that kind of entertainment was worth it at the time.

Wayne, our chapter president, committed us to go on a run over to Sandusky, Ohio, with the same Iron Coffins that terrorized our bar. I don't know why. We used to make fun of them because some of their tennis-shoe-wearing members didn't even own motorcycles. I guess you could join them as long as you promised to get one someday. Many of their members who did have bikes didn't even have Harleys. That was a major problem for me. We were 100 percent Harley-Davidson. None of us looked forward to this ride except Wayne, which meant he had something to gain. That's the way he was.

From my vantage point as road captain, the pack before me was a sight to behold. By no means were the Mongols professional high milers, but these Iron Coffins made us look like it. I couldn't believe how many times the pack had to pull over or the number of people that dropped out in one measly fifty-mile ride. As we neared our destination, some bar we'd never been to before, I was glad that our clubs wouldn't be riding back to Toledo together. I was tired of the irritating sound of the Suzuki in front of me.

We were less than a quarter of a mile from the crest of a small hill when one of the Iron Coffins on the 750 Kaw dropped back next to me. My scooter had a reputation for being pretty quick and I knew he wanted to see if that was accurate. Three-cylinder Kawasaki 750s were very fast if the rider knew what he was doing. This wannabe goosed that Kaw and I remember thinking, *What a ridiculous sound.* I dropped down into second and we were off, neck and neck at first, but as my Sifton cam, S&S Super Carb and Andrews third gear blended together to generate heavy-metal horsepower, I pulled away from him.

I was doing at least one-hundred miles per hour when I approached the top of the hill and could finally see our destination. I could also see the railroad tracks that bordered its gravel parking lot. The street we were racing on was a dead end. I began to downshift and brake, but I knew I'd never be able to stop in time. As I neared the bar, I applied the rear brake hard and brought the rear wheel around to the right. At about twenty miles per hour the bike began to slide out from under me, and I pushed off of it. My scooter eventually came to a stop, wedged under a parked car. I got up, dusted myself off, and yelled for a couple of the prospects to get my bike out from under that cage. I wasn't hurt, and my scooter didn't suffer any serious damage either. Most importantly of all, I won the race. That incident gave me even more bragging rights that day. Crazy goes a long way in the fast lane.

As our reputation moved from the country towns out in the county to the city of Toledo, I noticed something very interesting. Part of establishing yourself in the biker world involved being challenged by the various local legends and earning their respect. As more and more fistfights in the bars resulted in the cops being called, I found the Toledo police not nearly as excited as the bar owners about this new problem called the Mongols. There were occasions when I expected to go to jail but didn't, only to learn that many of the cops were glad to see some of the city's lowlifes, who were traditionally pains in the neck to the cops, getting what they deserved at last. As long as innocent civilians weren't getting hurt, the police didn't treat us that badly at all.

One time a Toledo police sergeant was moonlighting as a security guard at a local nightclub, and one of our guys, Ralph Tanner, happened to be there with a girlfriend. Ralph and the officer recognized and acknowledged each other. Soon after, the sergeant got involved in an altercation with some yuppie punks who started to gang up on him. There was Ralph to his rescue, going back to back with the officer. That act proved to be very beneficial in the years to come. That officer not only treated us more than fairly from then on, but he also didn't let any of the other cops get stupid with us either, as long as he was around. One night he stopped Kato, who was drunk as a skunk, heading to the clubhouse at 3:00 in the morning. Kato assured him he could make it home, and the sarge let him go. Another icy, winter night, I wrapped a beautiful '68 El Dorado around a telephone pole on Hawley Street and almost tore my right kneecap off in the process. I handed my Colt .45 and a bag of dope to Kato, and he ran up the street to the clubhouse for help. I was drunk, high, seriously injured, and deserving of jail that night for DWI, but this same cop showed up and talked the others into letting me go. I heard him tell them, "He's totaled his Cadillac, and his leg is messed up. That's enough. Let him go home."

There was an infamous bar in north Toledo back then called the Seaport Lounge. We hung out there quite a bit, and one night Wayne got some folks stirred up over nothing, which is what he was good at. He was famous for starting fights someone else had to finish. He was giving one of his old Clansmen MC buddies a hard time, and the guy had all he was going to take. There was no doubt in my mind that he could've whipped Wayne. I couldn't let that happen, though, even if Wayne did deserve it. This poor sucker and I exchanged a few blows before he began to panic. His best blows weren't affecting me very much, and my punches were beginning to rattle his brain. He grabbed a handful of my hair as I drilled him square in the jaw. He went down, but he didn't let go of me, so he dragged me down with him. He had both hands full of hair by now and was afraid to let go. I told him to, but he wouldn't. He was too scared. I told him I would let it be over if he'd just let go of my hair. He had known Hicks for years, and he knew he couldn't be trusted, so I guess he figured I couldn't be either. Too bad. If he would have let go, I would've let it be over, like I said. I turned my head to the side just enough to bite him on the shoulder very hard. He let out a scream reminiscent of a starlet on a black-and-white horror flick. He let go then, but I spun around and drilled him several more times. Why? A half dozen people heard me say I'd have ended the fight if he would have done what I told him. They needed to see what had to happen because he didn't.

In 1976, ABATE (A Brotherhood Against Totalitarian Enactments) was very active in its effort to repeal Ohio's mandatory helmet law. I never joined them officially, but I supported many of their events. There were several runs to the courthouse in Lucas County, many fundraisers (parties), and even a run to the state capitol in Columbus. In 1977, our efforts were rewarded with the repeal of the "Lid Law." I was ecstatic. I never liked wearing a helmet. Once I was in a Kmart and tried on one of those full-face helmets like the professional racers wear. I flipped the visor down and felt like I was in a Star Wars movie. The sound of my own breathing reminded me of Darth Vader. I couldn't see. I couldn't hear anything. I hated it. I thought to myself, *If you have to wrap this much plastic around your head to feel safe, you might as well be in a cage.*

The old football-type helmet, in my opinion, was almost as bad. I had one in the early years, but I felt it also severely hindered my peripheral vision and my hearing. I heard a horn honk one time and was not able to tell exactly where the sound was coming from because of the helmet. That almost caused me to change lanes into the path of a speeding car. I never wore that type of helmet again. I got myself what was called a half-helmet, which did not prohibit any of my natural senses. My sister, Anita, painted a very cool looking pair of Harley wings on it, and I had the best-looking helmet around. As I stated earlier, back then we had to do everything ourselves. There was no 150-page accessory catalog around from which to order gear, not that I am knocking the availability of stuff nowadays. On the contrary, I actually find it quite interesting. I am just saying it took more than a pocketful of money to be cool in the '70s. You had to be creative.

We had our clubhouse in Perrysburg for a year when the lease ran out. It's not hard to fool a landlord into leasing you a building when he has no idea what you're really going to use it for, but after a year of complaints and police reports, the owner of the property wanted us out. The other tenants in the area wanted us out, and the Perrysburg Police Department wanted us out. We spent the next year or so hanging out at various members' houses, including the farmhouse Jay and I had before we rented a dive on Montrose Street, near the intersection of Dorr Street and Detroit Avenue. It wasn't a clubhouse as much as it was a "flop house"—in other words, a place to crash after partying in the city. This shack was in the heart of Toledo's ghetto, but it was cheap and close to some of the bars we were frequenting at the time. It was so bad that the bathroom sink fell completely off the wall one day while someone was washing his hands. We simply disconnected the water lines to it and that was that. We never did fix it. We didn't care.

It was while at this address that one of our guys hopped into an open boxcar of a slow moving train on Toledo's east side. He began to pitch out boxes, of what he had no idea, over the course of a mile or so and went back later with an old van to retrieve them. One evening when I arrived at the Montrose Street house, there were thirty-eight boxes stacked in the kitchen. The spoil from the infamous Toledo train heist consisted of food products, all from one manufacturer: the Campbell's Soup Company. Imagine that.

There were large boxes full of tomato and chicken noodle soup. Cases of Swanson boned chicken dominated one corner of the kitchen floor. I never saw so many cans of tomato juice in one place outside of the Campbell's warehouse where I used to work. Every member went home with grocery bags full of the stuff. The cupboards were packed from top to bottom with cans. It was a miracle that the cupboards didn't come off the wall like the bathroom sink. For weeks, there was a huge pot of chicken soup on the stove, supplemented with boned chicken to thicken it up. If the Feds could only have seen us then! Organized crime? Yeah, right.

In the spring of 1977, the old Crescent Raceway in north Toledo came up for rent. It consisted of a one-mile asphalt track behind a huge building that once housed a go-kart business. It was located in a commercial district on Toledo's North Detroit Avenue, not far from the Michigan state line. It was ideal for a clubhouse. The property was composed of about five acres, with the nearest neighbor being an auto junkyard. There was plenty of room to play loud music, shoot guns, rev motorcycles, and party. It had a good-sized shop area with a steel ramp leading up to a garage door. The main room of the building had ample space for a bar, a pool table, pinball machines, and a couple of picnic tables. They were our furniture of choice because of their durability. Flimsy stuff didn't last long around us. Neither did flimsy people.

The main party room had a small office off it that I claimed for a bedroom. I moved my tools, my parts, my bikes, and myself into the Crescent Raceway. When I got involved with something, I got in all the way. I didn't play around. I wasn't a weekend warrior. If our club life centered around the clubhouse—and it did—then that's where I wanted to be. I painted the walls of my room black, put a hefty lock on the door, and became the only official resident. Crescent Raceway became my address. Rent free, of course.

It was from this clubhouse that I went to jail in Toledo for the first time since I was in the army. Toledo's Finest was unaware that we had taken possession of the property, and when our first big party took place one Friday night, they invited themselves. They made up some charge about an illegal drinking establishment and began making people leave. They also loaded all the beer and liquor as evidence and confiscated the substantial gun collection from my room. They had to charge someone, and since I was the only one who claimed to reside there, they decided it would be me. Go figure. I was out on bond the next morning, and when the case came to court, it was thrown out. The judge determined that we had a legal right as lawful tenants of the property to have a party there if we wanted to. The judge made them return everything they had confiscated. The cops were not happy about being made to look so foolish. The icing on the cake for me was pushing a four-wheel cart loaded with beer, liquor, and weapons out of the Safety Building in broad daylight with a police escort.

In August of that year, six of us rode to Buffalo, New York, at the invitation of the Renegades MC there. They were much different from their Columbus counterparts, who had also arrived that week, only they showed up in vans. These New York guys were not drooling "T-heads." They had a much more serious air about them. Even their motorcycles were different. They were built for riding, not just to fulfill a requirement for membership as so many clubs had. The Buffalo Renegades were extra somber when we were there because of the death of one of their members earlier that week. Bernie died in a motorcycle accident several days prior to our getting there, and his funeral was going to be the next day. Another unexpected surprise for us was the arrival of the Rochester chapter of the Hells Angels Motorcycle Club. None of us knew much about how club politics worked at the time, but the Renegade chapter in Buffalo was being courted by the Hells Angels for membership into their international organization. Although the Hells Angels would have loved to have a chapter in Columbus, the Ohio chapter of the Renegades was definitely not included.

We rode in the funeral procession with the "Red and White" and later partied together with them at the Renegade's clubhouse. These Hells Angels were the first one-percenters I had ever seen, let alone partied with. Everything about them was different from what I was familiar with, from their motorcycles to their demeanor when it came to watching each other's back. They were "professional," for lack of a better term. Their club was not a social organization to them. It was serious business. It was their life. I never saw those particular guys again, and it was years before I saw another Hells Angel, but the impression they left on me never left. From that week on I knew there was much more to bikin' and brotherhood than I was experiencing, and I longed for it. We invited the Buffalo Renegades to come to our clubhouse in

Toledo someday to party, but they never made it. That was probably a good thing, because our destinies were to go in completely different directions, though neither of us knew it at the time.

Chapter 5

Broadening Our Horizons

We had many parties during the year and a half we were at the Crescent Raceway clubhouse. One of the most memorable, and saddest, was the going away party for Jay and Lana Buck. They had decided to move to Phoenix, Arizona. Jay was a good motorcycle mechanic, and he hoped he could make a living wrenching out there in Arizona where he could ride twelve months a year. I was not especially happy about his decision. Jay was my sponsor in the club, and I certainly didn't want to see him move two thousand miles away. Besides, he was one of our most respected and dedicated members, not to mention the vice president. It would be a great loss to our chapter, to be sure. No one could talk him out of it though, and some of us promised to go out during the winter to visit and ride at least part of the cold season away with him out there in the Southwest.

The void in the officer ranks was quickly filled without conversation, nomination, or vote. I went from road captain to vice president the day Jay pulled out of the driveway for one reason and one reason only: my loyalty and dedication were unquestionable. We didn't have elections or debates. We just did what was best for the club. I was the natural choice, and even I agreed.

In February 1978, Wayne and I went to visit Jay in Arizona as we had promised him. We put our bikes on a homemade trailer, hooked it to a '65 Chevy van, and headed west. I'd been out West before. I had moved to northern California after being discharged from the army in '74. I'd seen the wide open spaces, the mountains, and the desert. Wayne had never been anywhere, so this would be a new experience for him. As we headed out to Arizona together to see Jay and Lana, we anticipated riding our Harleys while all our friends were snowed in back in Ohio.

The trip went remarkably well and was uneventful until we were within one hundred miles of Phoenix. On Interstate 17 coming down the mountain from Flagstaff, that old van developed the high-speed wobble that the short wheelbase vans were famous for in the '60s. Of course, that's why you weren't supposed to drive them at high speeds, especially down a 70 percent grade. I guess Wayne didn't know that. In an effort to correct the wobble, Hicks overcompensated. We were soon all over both southbound lanes of the Interstate 17. The flatbed trailer with our Harleys strapped to it almost came around to pass us, or so it seemed. As I looked down the deep chasms on either side of the road, my greatest fear was that my bike would come loose and become an airplane. Somehow, disaster was averted. He got it stopped, and we got out to tighten the tie-downs securing our scooters. That experience called for a couple of long swigs of Old Number Seven, which I always kept handy. I took over driving the rest of the way to Jay's trailer, which was not far from Oceanside Harley-Davidson in North Phoenix. I spotted the Harley shop easily enough, but I never did figure out what ocean it was near. All I'd seen for hundreds and hundreds of miles was sand and Saguaro cactuses.

In Arizona, it was legal to carry a handgun unconcealed, which was both different and fun for us Ohioans. We rode out into the desert northeast of Phoenix with our pistols strapped on our sides, and every once in a while we'd stop and do some shooting. There were plenty of targets. Wayne especially liked the tree-like Saguaro cactus. He proved that a .44-magnum round could effectively blow the arm off one of those majestic cacti. It wasn't until later that someone told him it was a major no-no, as in federal offense, to damage the protected plant in any way. Whoops. Honest—we didn't know.

The problem with carrying an unconcealed weapon was that you could not go into a liquor establishment with it on your hip. Regular people would lock their firearms in their trunks or their pick-ups. My dilemma was, I didn't have a trunk. I wasn't about to put my Colt .45 SAA revolver, with its custom quick-draw rig I'd just bought in San Luis, Mexico, in an unsecured, leather saddlebag. I felt pretty stupid wrapping the hand-tooled leather gun belt around that pistol and sliding it under a dumpster on the side of some dumpy bar. I would not have even been able to do that if it hadn't been dark outside. From then on, I went back to carrying my Colt .45 automatic in my belt, completely concealed, as I did in every other state.

Although we went out to Arizona to ride, we soon learned that it was often too hot to do a lot of pleasure riding, while the sun was up anyway. One day I did ride up to the top of South Mountain, where the view was fabulous. There were days, however, when we just sat in the bars, waiting for the temperature to drop. The extreme heat radiating up from the asphalt would be harmful to our air-cooled engines. It was during one of these long afternoons that I acquired my first pair of cowboy boots. My club name was Cowboy, but it wasn't because I wore a cowboy hat, or boots, or was from Texas, or anything like that. It was because of how I carried myself, and how I dealt with problems.

At this particular watering hole, there was an idiot who considered himself to be the local bad boy. I watched him as he harassed customers, and knew he was obligated to check us out because we were out-of-towners. As I kept an eye on this fool, I noticed he had on a beautiful pair of

70

boots. I was really trying to be on my best behavior since I was so far from home, but a man can only tolerate so much. When he finally worked his way over to give me a hard time, in response to whatever stupid thing it was he said to me, I answered with, "What size are those boots?" He said, "Ten and a half," and before the "half" was all the way out of his mouth, I hit him upside his head with a right hook hard enough to knock him out cold. He hit the floor with a thud, and I walked over and yanked those nice boots off his feet. I pulled up a chair next to his motionless form, took my engineer boots off, and tried on his. Perfect fit. I took my old boots out to my scooter and strapped them to my sissy bar, then went back inside to drink. I was still there drinking when the clown woke up. He looked at his bare feet and then at his boots on my feet. Right there he had a decision to make. He made the right one. He left. I wore those boots for the next six or seven years. As a matter of fact, I've been wearing cowboy boots ever since.

Jay took us to a bar often frequented by a local motorcycle club called the Dirty Dozen. They were definitely the most notorious bike club in Arizona. I'd heard their name whispered in the bike shops we had stopped at, and they were considered bad news by most of the local loners. One of the reasons was that they stuck together. What kind of idiot would expect club members to do anything else? Truth of the matter was, Phoenix was full of idiot bikers.

Most of them seemed to be from back East somewhere, and they all tried to convince each other that they were the toughest of the tough back there, having only moved to the Southwest for the weather. Yeah, right. What I found was a bunch of losers who had earned no respect in their hometown, moved out West, and made up their own history. Kind of like starting over, only with every detail based on a lie. Several other areas of the country attract that crowd: California, Colorado, and Florida, for example. They seem to have more than their share of idiots. The ones I met in Arizona didn't like the Dozen, because true bikers can see right through that crowd.

Jay, Wayne, and I went to an annual bike rally held out at some Salt River party spot. There were a hundred-plus bikers there, but no colors except ours. It wasn't too long before the liquor loosened up the brains of some of the pseudo-tough guys. They surrounded us, wanting to know our intentions and making sure we knew colors were not welcome at this run, or in Arizona. I could tell by looking at them they were all a bunch of wimps who had probably been slapped around by real bikers or had had their girlfriends run off with real bikers back East. They got their courage from their beer and each other, and the false belief that there was strength in numbers. There isn't. Not in our world. Strength comes from unity.

I told them what I thought about them and their questions and told them where they could put them. We didn't go there looking for trouble, but we weren't backing down when trouble came. The three of us positioned ourselves so that we could cover each other's backs and invited them to come and get it. They could not conceive of how three guys would be willing to take on so many of them. They couldn't comprehend why we weren't afraid of them, because they had lived most of their lives in fear. They could not fathom that there were men who simply refused to live that way.

In reality, three guys with colors on intimidated them. Just about the time it looked like it might get real interesting, two Dirty Dozen MC members we'd met earlier pulled up. Perceiving exactly what was going on, one asked me if there was a problem. They knew we were not out there to infringe on their turf, so they weren't threatened by us. I replied, "No problem that won't be over in a couple of minutes." When they asked the other guys if there was a problem, they tucked their tails between their legs and backed off as usual. Twenty against three, they were considering it. Twenty against five? No way. Sissies.

We spent the rest of February enjoying the weather and partying with Jay and Lana, but as the first of March rolled around, we headed east. We weren't heading home though. Our destination was a small town on the Georgia-Florida border called Valdosta. Bikers from all over the North would assemble at the campgrounds in and around Valdosta for the Run to the Sun. It was approximately 215 miles from there to Daytona Beach, Florida, the home of the world famous Bike Week. Professional motorcycle racers from all over the world converged on the beautiful beach city for the famous race at the Daytona International Speedway. Simultaneously, bikers of every sort from the "snow country" would invade Daytona Beach to get a jumpstart on spring and to party.

There were literally thousands of bikers from all over the country assembling, partying, and preparing to converge on Daytona Beach for the most famous event in bikerdom. We arrived at the KOA campground in Valdosta and linked up with two of our Michigan Mongol brothers. Kato, a brother from our chapter in Toledo, jumped in with them at the last minute, and we were glad he did. He drove our van down to Daytona while we all rode in the famous run.

After riding down to Daytona and getting our tents set up at a local campground, the four of us with bikes headed to town while Kato stayed with the gear. I had never seen so many motorcycles in one place in my life. They were everywhere. We just followed the flow over the intracoastal waterway and down onto the legendary beach where you could ride your scooter along the Atlantic Ocean. Although Wayne and I had been riding for weeks already in Arizona, most of the bikers in Daytona that week had been snowed in up North for months. They had been working on their bikes in preparation for spring, saving their money and vacation time to kick the season off early in Florida. Sounded like a good plan to me.

We eventually located Main Street and looked for the renowned Boot Hill Saloon. We found it. It was easy because it really was across the street from a cemetery. We parked our bikes, went in, and I ordered my favorite whiskey, Old Number Seven. That's Jack Daniel's Black to all you beer heads. It did not take long before our colors attracted exactly the same kind of attention they had at the Salt River Run in Arizona. I wondered if those guys could have called their relatives back East and warned them about us. They didn't want any fighting in there though, not during Bike Week. They were far more interested in cashing in on the snowbirds. They simply threatened to call Daytona's Finest, who liked colors less than anyone did, if we did not leave. Discretion being the better part of valor, we moved on. I wasn't interested in going to jail the first day. Such is the life of a patchholder. We found plenty of places to party where we didn't have any problems, and I was having a great time looking at all the Harleys.

As the four of us turned west onto Volusia Avenue from Atlantic Boulevard, there were two bars across the street from each other that immediately captured our attention. On the south side of Volusia was the Shark's Lounge and directly across the street was Broadway Sam's. Many good-looking bikes were lined up in front of each one. There was nothing odd about that in and of itself, but these scooters were all backed in at the same angle, spaced pretty much evenly; they were all Harley-Davidsons, and there were over fifty of them. It was obvious they did not belong to your average Bike Week hodgepodge of citizen bikers. You could tell that these bikes all rode in together. We rode down to the end of this group of beautiful, glistening machines and backed up to the curb. As we walked up the sidewalk toward the door, I had no idea that what I would find inside would change my life forever.

As we approached the door of Broadway Sam's, we could see two men, one on either side, obviously scrutinizing anyone who wanted to enter. Each of them probably easily weighed in at four hundred pounds. Their shirts were off and both were heavily tattooed. They sported very similar tattoos on their chests: "Outlaws MC."

It became obvious why the bikes had a different appearance than the hundreds, maybe thousands, of other Harleys scattered all over town that night. These scooters belonged to members of the infamous Outlaws Motorcycle Club. That meant, of course, that Broadway Sam's would be full of them, as would the Shark Lounge directly across the street. We had managed to stumble across the Bike Week hangouts of one of the most notorious one-percenter motorcycle clubs in the world. Upon realizing this, the two Monroe Mongol brothers made it absolutely clear they were not only not going in, but they also weren't hanging around out front any longer either. They turned and headed to their bikes before even waiting to get a response from Wayne or me. Wayne looked at me with a "what-do-you-want-to-do?" look. The two tattooed sumo wrestlers seemed to be giving me a similar look too, so I said, "Let's go in." As far as I was concerned, we were committed beyond retreat. Besides, I was intrigued by these striking, custom Harley-Davidsons. *What are they going to do to us anyway?* I thought to myself.

As we entered the long, narrow, dimly lit building, the first thing to catch our eyes were two stages, one at each end, both occupied by dancers gyrating to the deafening music being pumped out of the juke box. As the strobe lights flashed and flickered, they revealed an eerie glimpse of the clientele. The place was packed wall-to-wall with long-haired, bearded bikers, just like every other bar in Daytona that night. These guys were different. These guys were together. They all had colors on, the same colors. These men were Outlaws.

No sooner had we got past the huge doormen, when Wayne and I were challenged by a South Florida Outlaw who was obnoxious by nature and drunk on top of it. As the attention of several of his brothers nearby turned to the only two wearing colors other than theirs, I recalled my thought at the door, *What are they going to do to us anyway?* I realized the answer to my question was, "Anything they want to do." Nevertheless, we stood our ground and prepared for the worst. I knew if this drunk could make one of us mad enough to swing at him, it would have been a trip to the emergency room for us at best . . . and the morgue, at worst. My thinking at the time was that it would be better to have been beaten to death in there, while putting up a fight, than to back down and leave with our tails between our legs. That was not an option.

The tension continued to build between our self-appointed host and us. Many of his brothers, who knew he was being a jerk, were watching intently. Right, wrong, or indifferent, they were still going to side with him. To make matters worse, an undercover cop let a pistol fall out of an ankle holster not far from us. I could not believe he and his partner had to be in there at the same time we were. Outlaws get very edgy around strangers, and it was a miracle that those two cops, and us, were not shot when that revolver hit the floor. After the cops showed their badges to diffuse their situation, the attention of our welcoming committee turned back to us. All of a sudden, a tall, dark-haired Outlaw made his way toward us and saved the day. He obviously commanded much respect in the club. He told his brothers he had heard of us, and that we were his guests. Everyone accepted that. No more questions. No more head games. He invited us back to his table and offered to buy us a beer, but after all the excitement, I told him I'd rather have whiskey: Jack Daniel's—straight. Make it a double.

This Outlaw's name was Kraut, and he was a member of the Detroit chapter. Detroit was a tough city, and its Outlaw chapter was tough right along with it. That's why the situation changed so quickly, so completely. Kraut had an impeccable reputation. We couldn't have been rescued by a better brother. We talked for a while as he explained that Bike Week was a national run for them. Outlaws from all over the United States and Canada would converge on Daytona for the biggest, most famous motorcycle event of the year. It was an opportunity to leave the snow country far behind for a while, see the brothers, and ride. It was also important for them to make a powerful showing here because Florida was an Outlaw state.

I asked him how he knew about us. He told me they had heard about the confrontation between the Ohio Mongols and a Detroit Federation club called the Bikers United. It took place in April 1976 in front of the Zulus MC's Michigan Avenue clubhouse on Detroit's West side. Several of us had ridden up there with our Monroe, Michigan, chapter. A jerk from the Bikers United gave one of our guys a hard time and got decked. Some Vigilante MC members attempted to butt in on behalf of their DFMC comrades, but their reputation didn't mean anything to us. We weren't from Detroit. They were sufficiently checked, just as anyone else would be. The problem ended without further incident, other than us getting a bad name among the Detroit Federation of Motorcycle Clubs. They didn't like the thought of Ohio bikers coming to Detroit anyway, let alone not kissing their rear ends while they were there. To the Detroit Outlaws, that was a plus. They respected people who stood for what they believed in, especially when the odds were against them.

Because of that incident in Detroit two years earlier, we were delivered from a potentially very serious problem that night in Daytona Beach, Florida. We were a thousand miles from home, in an Outlaw bar, in an Outlaw state, and we found a friend in the nick of time. Kraut invited us to the campground site of their gathering, but we respectfully declined. I could envision dealing with about fifty more drunken Outlaws wanting to challenge the outsiders while they got drunker as the night got later. I wanted no part of that. We did exchange phone numbers with Kraut and invitations to each other's clubhouses. When we left there that night, I knew I had just been around a bunch of guys that were doing everything I'd ever wanted to do. Riding good-looking, custom Harley-Davidsons all across the country and dedicated to something in which they truly believed: brotherhood.

Toward the end of the week, my rear brake caliper went out on me. Being in Daytona with all the traffic that Bike Week generates was not the place to be with faulty brakes. It was an expensive item, even if you could find one, and money wasn't very abundant, especially in light of the fact that I'd been on the road for over a month already. On Thursday night, Kato and I headed to town in the van, not to party, but to get me another caliper. People and motorcycles were everywhere, so we found a bar where many Harleys were parked far from the door. Citizen bikers didn't keep an eye on their machines like we did. If we were in a group of any size, someone stayed outside at all times, watching. Usually prospects took turns, but if there wasn't a prospect along, members assumed the responsibility. If there were just one or two of us, we checked on them regularly. Those scooters were important. They were our life.

It was beneficial to us that most didn't think that way. Their Harleys were just another toy, another possession, another status symbol. That made for an endless supply of spare parts for us in the years before Harley-Davidson made their product much harder to steal. Back in the '70s and '80s, many Harleys were "liberated" from owners we deemed "undeserving" of their ownership. All that meant was that if we could get it from you, you didn't deserve it. That mentality came back to bite us years later when Ralph's bike was stolen from under some girl's bedroom window in Point Place, Ohio. I helped him build another bike, but the thought of someone laughing about getting away with ripping off one of us was much worse than the actual loss itself.

This particular night in Daytona, Kato and I weren't looking to steal a motorcycle; we were out scouting for an H&H rear disc brake caliper. They were very common. We spotted several Harleys pulling into the crowded lot of a bar and parking where there was very little vantage point from the door. We had picked the spot knowing that as the lot filled up, and it would, any machine parked in this particular area would be easy pickings. As the owners strolled inside, Kato made his way over to a nice, new Super Glide with a 3/8 inch, twelve-point socket on a ratchet and a sharp knife. In less than a minute, the four bolts were out and the brake line cut. He even retrieved the new brake pads for me. I feel sorry now for the guy that came out to a puddle of brake fluid under his scooter. I hope he discovered his loss before he got out on the road. But I didn't feel sorry for him that night. I didn't care one bit. Within an hour, Kato and I drove to our camp, repaired my bike, and rode back to town to party. Kato was riding one of the Monroe bikes. Its owner had a headache . . . and cold feet.

As Bike Week wound down, we didn't see the Outlaws again. Our Monroe comrades wanted nothing to do with them. They were at this famous run to ride their bikes, drink, and ogle at the biker chicks. We rode around the city for a couple of more days doing those things, but that night at Broadway Sam's never left my mind, especially during the long trip back to Ohio.

I tried to imagine our little ragtag club taking the trip up to the Outlaws MC clubhouse in Detroit. I couldn't picture it happening. Here's why: As Wayne and I recounted our adventures out West to see Jay, followed by Bike Week in Daytona, and, finally, meeting the Outlaws, it was obvious our enthusiasm wasn't shared by all of our Ohio Mongol brothers. Some were very much opposed to our partying with them at all. They were bad hombres, I was told. Exactly.

We didn't have to debate about partying with the Outlaws very long. Early in April, just weeks after returning from Florida, Lenny, the Detroit boss, called to inform us he was bringing a crew down to party with us for the weekend. I can't remember it being put in the form of a request or suggestion. For good reason. It wasn't. We were subtly reminded of Kraut coming to our rescue and our invitation for them to come by *anytime*. When you tell an Outlaw something like that, you'd better mean it because he'll hold you to it.

Our club was divided when it came to looking forward to the upcoming weekend. Some were frantically looking for places to strategically hide guns, just in case things got out of control. This wasn't the Iron Coffins or the Clansmen who were coming. It wasn't the Brothers MC or the Pride of Lions either. It was the Outlaws, and they were a far cry from any of the local bike clubs most of us were familiar with. On the other hand, several of us very much looked forward to meeting them, seeing their bikes, and hearing about their chapters in so many cities and states. It was hard for us to comprehend. We'd pretty much ridden every road in our little world of northwest Ohio and southern Michigan. We looked forward to hearing their tales of riding clubhouse to clubhouse all over what they called the Outlaw Nation. The only thing I was worried about was not having enough whiskey and beer.

About a dozen of them arrived early the following Saturday afternoon. I wasn't disappointed. They looked every bit as professional as I'd hoped they would: from their machines, to their appearance, to their attitude. These folks were not weekend warriors. They were one-percenters. The club was their life. They had come to take us up on our invitation. Besides, Toledo was a major interstate crossroad and very close to Detroit. They were there to check us out.

In spite of some of our guys being noticeably nervous, the weekend went great. They were used to getting that reaction, and they were on their best behavior. The Outlaws were there to possibly make new friends and to perhaps forge a new alliance in a strategic Midwestern city. They went out of their way to make sure there were no problems. There were no problems, other than that several of our guys saw the handwriting on the wall. On the other hand, about a half dozen of us, including myself, were fascinated by their stories of making runs from Michigan to Fort Lauderdale, stopping at many other chapters along the way. One Detroit Outlaw had a tattoo of the Interstate 75 shield on his forearm and told us that that highway was the official "Outlaw Trail."

As I looked over their motorcycles, I was impressed by the way they looked, but even more by the fact that they were built to be ridden. The show-bike craze, where elaborate choppers were built and then trucked to bike shows, didn't impress me one bit. I knew of a bike that won a first prize trophy at the Toledo Sports Arena one year that didn't even have internal engine parts, like flywheels, rods, or pistons! I guess the owner wanted to save money so that he could use it on that fancy metal-flake paint job and lots of chrome.

For those of us who showed great interest in the kind of riding the Outlaws did, a challenge was offered. They would be riding through Toledo the following Friday on their way to their spring up-date run in Western Pennsylvania. The up-date run was the first official function of the northern chapters who were coming out of winter. It would be about 220 miles for us. We only made one run a year that long and it took two months to prepare for it. I knew only a few of us would even seriously consider going with them. Personally, I couldn't wait. These guys were right up my alley. They didn't sit around talking about riding; they did it. About a dozen of them showed up early Friday morning, just as they said they would. Four of us joined them, both apprehensive and excited at the same time.

Seeing a large group of long-haired, bearded, tattooed ruffians rolling down the highway on thunderous two-wheeled machines is a remarkable sight. It can be an intimidating sight. The two-by-two, militaristic, column formation in which the Detroit Outlaws rode was a formidable thing of which to be a part. In the Mongols, we rode two by two as well, but these guys had it down to a science. No changing lanes unless the guy in front of you did. No stopping to relieve yourself or to smoke a cigarette until the whole pack of motorcycles stopped. I'd seen all these things go on in our little club, and as road captain, it was my job to police the lollygaggers. It was frustrating to say the least. These guys had a road captain too, but he was focused on making sure the passing lane was clear so the boss up front would know when it was safe to change lanes. His responsibility this particular day also included keeping an eye on the guests—namely, us.

The unity with which they maintained their close proximity to each other at high rates of speed spoke of their dedication to riding and to each other. Not just in a straight line on the interstate, but while changing lanes too. Even on the rural, two-lane roads of Western Pennsylvania, the precision with which they maintained their formation was amazing. That's why you can spot a club coming down the road as opposed to a bunch of weekenders out for a joy ride, yo-yoing back and forth, jockeying for position.

On this particular Friday in April, the weather was very cold and nasty. It was overcast and rainy, and as we got into Pennsylvania, it even snowed some. It was quite a day to become acquainted with this group of professionals, all the while trying to impress them, hoping we didn't do anything too stupid. The lousy weather made us look forward to arriving at the West Penn chapter clubhouse.

The road up to the fifty-plus acres the Outlaws owned on top of a mountain was as formidable as the ride had been. It was a mile up a twisting, turning, muddy lane, complete with huge ruts left by pickup trucks and vans that hauled supplies to the top for the weekend regional party. Once I finally made it to the top, I was not only cold, wet, and tired from the long day, but now I was very muddy too. It didn't matter though. I was glad to be there and looking forward to getting to know these guys better. Bikes were everywhere, and there were at least sixty Outlaws already there, plus a handful of invited guests, like us.

We were on our best behavior, and they treated us very well. No doubt the word had been put out that we were guests of Detroit, and that in itself carried a lot of weight. I gladly took the responsibility of policing our crew, mainly because I didn't want one of us doing something that would make me look stupid. Everything was going fine until eventually one of the Youngstown Outlaws, who evidently didn't get the memo, had a little too much to drink and couldn't resist giving the non-Outlaws a hard time. He wandered over to where several of us were hanging out near our bikes, and I knew he was trouble when I saw him coming. His intention was to trick bag one of us into a situation in which we could not prevail. After all, he definitely had the "high ground," being on Outlaw turf, surrounded by so many of his brothers. Even if they didn't approve of his behavior—

and most didn't—they would still back him up. That is what brotherhood is all about.

"Death before Dishonor" was more than just a catchy saying or a tattoo on an army ranger's arm to me. This drunk, Outlaw or not, was not going to make a punk out of me or any of my guys just for the fun of it. It got pretty tense for a few minutes, but in response to his comment about there being plenty of room to bury us up there on that mountain, I informed him there was room for him too. (Just like the old question, "How many square feet are there in Lake Erie?" The answer is, "Always room for two more.") He thought better of his challenge and backed down. When Lenny had been made aware of what had transpired, and how close they were to losing any chance of an alliance in Toledo, he had this brother taken out behind the clubhouse for a serious talking-to. . . and a black eye.

Chapter 6

The Times, They are a Changin'

Running along the back of the Crescent Raceway clubhouse property was a set of railroad tracks. One hot mid-June morning in 1978, a tie gang was busy at work on this particular section of track while several of us sat out behind the clubhouse, nursing hangovers. There were odd-looking machines pulling spikes, lifting the rail, chopping rotten ties, and inserting new ones, while several men kept busy working the track the old-fashioned way. They are the ones who got our attention. They were driving spikes with hickory-handled implements called "spike mauls." The men were strong and their biceps bulged as they swung those eleven-pound hammers repeatedly, sometimes two men driving the same spike in unison. Four hits and a huge railroad spike would disappear into the tie, securing the plate in place that held the rail itself. They were good at it, and they were fast; they had to be because the machine that pulled the cart with their wooden barrels of spikes didn't stop. It constantly moved ahead, maintaining its pace behind the rest of the work crew.

As we watched them for lack of anything else to do, something possessed me to say, "I could do that." What I meant was, I was able to do it physically. Though these men were big and obviously very strong, I was confident I could keep up with them. Railroad-labor-gang members had a reputation of being roughnecks, so that presented a challenge that intrigued me too. Wayne said, "No way," so that provoked me even more. Because of my veteran status, I knew I had an edge at the employment office. Shortly thereafter, I applied, was accepted, and assigned to the very crew that worked the track behind the clubhouse that day. That's where I met Ralph Tanner.

Ralph had been with this particular crew for five years. He had worked his way up to the position of ballast regulator operator. The ballast regulator was a huge machine that graded the stone along the track and in between the ties. Its place was at the rear of the gang, behind the "spikers." Ralph would travel up and down the rail, pushing the gravel around that supported the track, as well as the train that would ride on it, while smoking a big fat joint. I, on the other hand, had been assigned the very position I'd observed that day at the clubhouse: driving spikes in the heat of the summer sun, at the end of the work crew.

Ralph was strong, tough, and as able to fight as any of the men on the crew, but he also had a unique sense of humor and an outlook on life I found interesting. We became fast friends, and he taught me many things about how to make my job easier and more efficient. Once, he put a Styrofoam coffee cup on the rail plate, pushed a spike through the bottom of it, and tapped it slightly into the tie. He then stepped back and with three swings drove that spike into the tie without touching the cup. By the time Ralph was done teaching me, I could do it too. He also taught me how to "double spike." We would stand on opposite sides of the rail and take turns driving the same spike. That was against the company policy because the potential for injury was greatly multiplied should either spiker lose his rhythm. We never did, though. Rules weren't the biggest priority in either of our lives anyway. Having fun was. We made a great team.

When our tie gang moved from the city to the open rail in September, our gang headquarters was relocated to Bryan, Ohio, about seventy miles west of Toledo. Rather than sleep in the camp cars the railroad provided, Ralph and I opted to carpool daily so that we could be with our families. His was a wife and two daughters; mine was the Mongols MC. We worked four ten-hour days and spent three hours a day together traveling back and forth. We would smoke pot coming and going and got to know each other very well.

Ralph had a million questions about the club I rode with and eventually met all the members. Everyone liked him. The only problem with Ralph was he didn't own a scooter. He had always wanted one, but as of this time, he had never owned one. Other than that, he had all the makings of a good brother. He was no wimp, he was loyal—but still, he didn't own a motorcycle, and that was mandatory. It could not be just any motorcycle, mind you; it had to be a Harley-Davidson. As important an issue as that was to us, it was also easy to rectify. Easier than making a man out of someone who wasn't. What I mean is, anybody can buy a bike, but that doesn't make him a biker any more than buying a hammer would make a carpenter out of a man who couldn't drive a nail. Ralph was already a man, so I built him a bike.

First, he bought a brand-new 1978 Shovelhead motor from Lammon's Harley-Davidson dealership in Wauseon, Ohio. They were giving substantial discounts on new motors that year if you brought in an old motor to exchange. That was it; no title was necessary. I came up with an old set of cases, cylinders, heads, flywheels, rods, pistons and threw them all in a crate. Ralph took the mismatched parts and $750.00 in to Lammon's and walked out with a brand-new Shovelhead engine. I wish I'd have bought twenty at that price. I supplied everything else Ralph needed and built him a 1978 Harley-Davidson, complete with a certified State of Ohio self-assembled builder's title. I thought we were never going to get the smile off his face.

My job with the railroad and my newfound friendship with Ralph were taking place at the same time we were getting to know the Outlaws. Soon after that trip to the Mountain, we were invited to the Detroit clubhouse for the first time. Six of us rode up there on a Saturday late in April. It was a fascinating weekend for me. I spent a lot of time talking to them about their bikes and all the riding they did. They had chapters and clubhouses every two to three hundred miles not only throughout the Midwest, but all the way to South Florida. As we drank and got high together, I listened to their tales of bikin' and brotherhood at a level I had previously only hoped existed. Now that I knew it did, I'd never be satisfied with bar hoppin' around Lucas County again. My world was well on its way to becoming a lot bigger.

Toledo was actually located in a critical part of the Outlaw Nation, situated at the crossroads of Interstate 75 and the Ohio Turnpike. Detroit was fifty miles to the north, and Dayton, Ohio, the next closest Outlaw chapter, was 150 miles to the south. Word got around fast that the Outlaws were partying with a local club there. One night we got a call at our clubhouse from a man who called himself Hambone and said he was the Dayton Outlaw boss. I'd heard his name mentioned up on the Mountain, although he wasn't there. He was in Orlando, Florida, soaking up the sunshine and enjoying the riding weather at the time. He was a hard riding, hard drinking, hard partying, and hard fighting one-percenter in the truest sense of the term. His entire life was dedicated to the club and had been for over ten years.

It seems one of his Florida brothers had run across a guy at a bar in Kissimmee who claimed to have ridden with the Mongols MC in Michigan. This didn't mean much to the Florida Outlaw, but when Hambone heard it, he got our number from Lenny and called us. That's how it works. Running is not hard, but hiding is. Rick, this Michigan Mongol, had decided to leave the club, but in so doing had made two mistakes. His first mistake was not telling anybody; that's not how brotherhood operates, even at the amateur level. By far, his greatest transgression was his failure to turn in his colors before he left town. I knew Rick personally and he never struck me as the type to wimp out. Evidently, something transpired in Monroe that I knew nothing about to cause him to break this unforgiving code.

Whatever the case, the colors had to be recovered immediately. I hadn't met Hambone yet, but he assured me we would be welcome to come to the Orlando Outlaws' clubhouse and would be put in contact with our wayward member. Though it was primarily a Monroe Chapter issue, none of the Monroe Mongols seemed to be very interested in dropping everything to jump in a car and drive the eleven-hundred-plus miles one way just to get their colors back. Besides, they weren't too keen on partying with the Outlaws in the first place, let alone going to one of their clubhouses in Florida.

Conversely, Kato, Wayne, and I were ready to leave that very night, which we did. Wayne and Kato were blood brothers as well as club brothers, and they somehow talked their dad into loaning us his big Chrysler for the trip. One Monroe Mongol, Rocky Cole, was so ashamed of his home chapter's lack of courage that he reluctantly did go with us. We had a blast on the way down. We had Rocky pumped up about meeting the Outlaws, and we were all looking forward to finding Rick, getting our colors back, and partying with even more Outlaws.

Arriving early the next afternoon, we had some time to get to know Hambone and a few of the others before it was time to take care of business. Hambone and I hit it off really well. He was a Vietnam vet who loved his scooter and loved to ride. Those two don't necessarily always go hand in hand, though they should, and they did with Hambone. He gave me the phone number for the Dayton clubhouse and an open invitation to come by, meet the "family," and party. I knew I'd be seeing this guy again.

Hambone introduced me to the Orlando Outlaw who had come across our wayward member. He agreed to take our recovery crew to the bar where Rick hung out as long as we promised not to do anything in public that would make him or his club look bad. We promised. By now, I was more concerned about this growing bond with the Outlaws than I was with Rick anyway. Besides, in the back of my mind I kept wondering what happened in Monroe to make him go AWOL in the first place. If Rocky knew, and he probably did, he wasn't saying. It most likely had something to do with a female, but I never did find out. We weren't there to sort out Monroe's business, anyway. We were there to retrieve a Mongol patch and to thump Rick for making us come after it.

The four of us spread out in the large, dimly lit barroom. I watched Rick enter the establishment, make eye contact with our Outlaw host, and smile. As he approached him with his hand out for the customary biker handshake, I stepped up behind him and said, "Hi, Rick." The smile left his face immediately as he nervously said, "Hey, Cowboy. What brings you all the way down here?" As he spoke, he glanced around the bar and spotted Wayne, Kato, and Rocky heading toward us. In answer to his question, I replied, "You, Rick. You're the reason we're here. We've got a little problem that needs to be worked out." Rick was no idiot. He knew what I was talking about. He knew the only thing that would bring three Ohio Mongols to Florida over a Monroe incident was the patch. The colors. He knew exactly why I was there.

With every intention of keeping my word to the Outlaws, I "suggested" we take a table in the corner to talk. Rick informed us he was staying at his mother's trailer and his patch was there in his bedroom, safe and sound. Our host left us at that point, confident we had things under control. Rick soon found himself between Rocky and me in the backseat of that big, borrowed Chrysler, on our way to his mom's house. The customary threats toward friends and family were made just in case he entertained any thought of trying anything stupid once we got inside. Only I went into the trailer with him. I was courteous and respectful as I met his mother, and then accompanied him into his room. His Mongol colors were neatly folded in the bottom of the locked wooden box he kept his valuables in. My interest was only in the patch. I now had in my hand what we had come for.

His bike was still at the bar, so we headed back there. Once in the car again, I informed Rick there was an issue about getting an "outdate" put on his club tattoo that needed to be attended to. He said he'd been meaning to take care of that but hadn't gotten around to it. We got around to it that night. We had arranged for one of the Outlaws who was a tattoo artist to be standing by for this purpose. He was more than happy to accommodate. I could see he enjoyed inflicting pain when he got the chance. I'd never seen the voltage on a tattoo gun turned up so high, and Rick's outdate addition to his Mongols MC tattoo looked pretty painful. It didn't have to turn out that way, if only he'd have left right. Contrary to popular belief, it is possible to leave right. People who don't think so watch too many movies and have misconceptions concerning a lifestyle about which they know little or nothing. They would appear more intelligent if they just learned to keep their mouths shut.

With a sore arm, Rick once again climbed into the backseat for what he hoped would finally be a ride back to the bar and back to his bike. It was around three o'clock in the morning by now; the bar was closed and he was worried about it. We drove past the front of the place to confirm his scooter was safe, but to his chagrin, we didn't turn in. One more stop had to be made. I directed Kato to turn down a grassy lane into a remote wooded area and then informed Rick it was time for him to take his lumps. I told him how it went depended on him, and that if he'd take his punishment like a man, it would go better. At that point, we all got out of the car, and Rocky began to work him over a bit. I didn't feel any need to lay a hand on him myself. Besides, somebody had to keep a cool head to make sure it didn't get out of hand. Kato and Wayne both had a tendency to get a little carried away.

I always liked Rick anyway, and in the back of my mind, I still wondered what had happened in Monroe to run a good man like him off. It was a shame when things like that happened, but it did happen occasionally. He took his beating like a man. He didn't whine, cry, beg, or try to run. Satisfied with Rick's black eyes, bloody lip, and sore ribs, I stopped it. It was done. We had in our possession what we went for, and we did what was needed to satisfy our code.

Detroit had so many bike clubs that they formed the Detroit Federation of Motorcycle Clubs. They even wore a little peanut-looking patch that had the letters *DFMC* on it. Although the twenty-plus clubs that belonged to it maintained their individual identity in every respect, there was an unwritten rule about loyalty to fellow Federation members. That presented a minor problem for the Toledo Mongols when we were invited to participate in some of their events as guests of the Detroit Outlaws. They were members of the Federation, but they didn't wear the "peanut patch." Their allegiance was to their own organization, period. Their membership in the DFMC was strictly political. It gave them an advantage in keeping up with what was going on in the world of bike clubs in the Motor City.

In June 1978, the DFMC had a run an hour or so north of Detroit, and the Outlaws invited us to come along. It seemed every event the Federation had was within an hour north of Detroit. They sure limited themselves. The country, which was theirs to enjoy, was much bigger than Michigan, but most of those guys never made it very far away from their jobs. A seventy-five-mile ride and a weekend party in a field was living it up for most of that crowd. Not so for the Outlaws, though. They were much more interested in expanding their kingdom beyond the boundaries of any state line and took advantage of this party to further determine if there was any one-percenter material in Toledo.

Several clubs that we had butted heads with in the past were there, and they were not happy to see our little group from Ohio on their turf. What made it worse for them was that we were guests of the Outlaws, the most feared and respected club in the Federation. They weren't the biggest by far. Some of those clubs boasted over a hundred members, but power isn't about numbers— it's about unity. I watched fourteen or fifteen Outlaws intimidate literally hundreds of other bikers that weekend, and I was glad I was on their side.

I met an Outlaw at that party whose influence helped shape the destiny of the next twelve years of my life. Harry Bowman was his name—the Detroit chapter vice president. The reason I hadn't met him previously was because he'd been in prison. At the time of this run, he had just been released, to the chagrin of many. He was introduced to me as Taco, but I eventually came to refer to him simply as T. He was highly respected both on the street, and within the ranks of the Outlaws Motorcycle Club. He seemed to be the epitome of the outlaw biker. He was extremely streetwise, fearless, and loyal. He was a brother who would literally give you the shirt off his back if you needed help, but he was also unpredictable, alternating between comical and deadly serious. He intimidated people and he knew it, and he used it to his advantage. Don't get me wrong. He wasn't a jerk or an idiot. He was smart, and he was dedicated to his brothers. He went out of his way to make us, as guests, feel comfortable.

It was a riot walking around with him as he introduced us to other Federation club presidents and members. They had to act as if they were glad to meet us and have us there. What a bunch of liars. I learned a lot about motorcycle clubs that weekend. It reinforced in me what I didn't want to be—a pretender, a poser. What I longed for was something real, something worth living for. The Outlaws had found it for themselves and were willing to show others. Few could measure up, though. I was glad to be their friend. I was almost afraid to dream my relationship with them would ever be anything more than that. However, it was good in itself to be a friend of the Outlaws.

This friendship had already begun to take a toll on the membership of our little club in Toledo. Some were threatened by their commanding presence, others by the dedication of their "old ladies." The ladies' colors sported "Property of Outlaws" on the back, which many outsiders chose to believe meant they belonged to no one specifically, or in other words, to everyone at the same time. How ridiculous. Nothing could be further from the truth. The "property patch" was to let other bikers, including Outlaw brothers, know that a particular female did indeed belong to someone, and that she had earned enough respect to be given the privilege of wearing a cutoff vest with the club's name on it. The women's libbers hated that. I watched the Mongol's wives and girlfriends as they observed the Outlaw women, who were almost as dedicated and tough as some of the men were. Some were fascinated, others intimidated . . . *very intimidated.*

One time at the Detroit clubhouse, a citizen guest had one too many. One too many of what was difficult to determine. It could have been one too many shots of whiskey or one too many pills. It could have been one too many snorts of anything from THC to speed to cocaine or any combination thereof. It's hard to tell when you're in the midst of a party where everyone is doing something and some are doing everything. One thing was certain. Whatever this guy was on had robbed him of his brain and almost cost him his life. This idiot made a lewd gesture as he took the liberty to cop a feel from the Detroit boss's old lady as she walked by. Bad move. She was a small, pretty girl, but upon being touched by this jerk, she turned and violently pushed him off his barstool.

As she stood over him, she let him know, in no uncertain terms, that he was never to put his hands on any Outlaw old lady ever again and that he would answer severely for it if he did. Here was this guy, laying on the floor with a 110-pound go-go girl reading him his rights while everyone else laughed at him. I won't attempt to quote what he said next, but it earned him a double-soled boot in the teeth, not from any of the brothers defending her honor. She kicked him herself, and as he tried to grab her leg, another boot caught him in the temple. A club sister wasn't about to let this guy drag her down, so she attacked as well. So did two others.

From my vantage point, it was hilarious. He was bleeding from his mouth, his nose, from gouges in his face, and he was helpless to do anything about it. He saw his chance to escape and bolted for the door, but the girls followed him out and brought him down again in the yard. They continued to kick him and curse him, while many of us had made our way outside to continue enjoying the spectacle. Out of nowhere, the girl he originally accosted appeared standing over him with a huge concrete block, about to crush his skull. That's when her old man stepped in and put a stop to it. Did he deserve to be humiliated? Absolutely. Was it fair for four girls to gang up on him? Who cares? Did he deserve to die for his crime? No. He learned a great lesson that day. So did the rest of us. As I said, even the Outlaw women, many of whom were petite and feminine, were tough as nails. They had to be.

In July of '78, Wayne got wind of a big party out in Holland, Ohio and wanted us to attend. Miraculously, this was a weekend when no Outlaws were visiting. By midsummer, we were continually getting guests from Outlaw chapters all across the country. I'm glad none of them were with us when we went to the birthday party of a man named Thomas Polaski. He was throwing a big shindig for himself and a couple of hundred guests on some wooded property he owned out in the county west of Toledo. There may have even been a band; I don't recall. I remember enough about that disgraceful night as it is.

We arrived just after dark and were, as I found out later, uninvited. Wayne wasn't well liked by many people who had known him very long, so he would use the club to make an appearance where he would have otherwise been unwelcome. When he heard that members of the Iron Coffins MC and the Clansmen MC were going to be there, it was no longer about going to a party for him. It was about saving face. He had to make a showing. The rest of us just went along to drink, get high, have a good time, and try to get some of the local girls to go for a ride.

That fantasy didn't last very long. As soon as Wayne located the other clubs, he had to start running his mouth. He began by insulting a Clansman and then he ridiculed an Iron Coffin who attempted to stick up for him, all within about fifteen minutes of us getting there. Finally, one of them said the wrong thing to Wayne; I blasted him in the teeth, knocking him to the ground. When the other one tried to come to his rescue, I nailed him too. I wasn't looking for any trouble that night, but I wasn't going to let anybody besmirch a Mongol, especially our president, even if he was acting stupid. As it turned out, this was Wayne's last night as my boss.

I had a reputation as a fair fighter, and my people knew I didn't want any interference. I wasn't dumb enough to think I couldn't be whipped, and I never insinuated to any of my guys that they should ever stand by and allow that to happen. It's just that I was so sick of hearing about bike club members piling up on people. Many clubs were feared when they were in a group, but their members had no respect on an individual basis because they were nothing but punks. Sad to have to admit it, but that was the case with Wayne. He did have some leadership potential, but he used it to accomplish his own agenda. He was always out for number one, as the saying goes. Number one to him wasn't the club. Number one was him.

While I was involved in this fistfight, the guest of honor made his way over to see what the problem was, seeing as how this party was supposed to be fun, not a forum for club issues to be disputed. I had never met Tom Polaski and wouldn't have known him if I saw him. He had a nickname too. It was Big Boy. I was aware he had a reputation as a bit of a rounder himself; in other words, he wasn't a coward. He had a lot of friends because he was a good guy, and like me in the early years as a loner biker down at the Longbranch Saloon, he had stuck up for some folks when they needed help.

Wayne, on the other hand, did know him and when he saw him coming to break up the fight, sucker punched him. That was Wayne's style. Blindside the guy, try to get him to the ground, and then put the boots to him. Problem was, Big Boy didn't go down so easy. When he did, he was on top of Wayne, punching him in the face. Wayne deserved it, but still, two of our guys grabbed Big Boy by each arm to pull him off. What happened next came as a complete surprise to everyone, especially to our guys who were trying to break it up. As they pulled Big Boy away to stop the fight, Wayne pulled a knife and slit his throat. Big Boy was killed at his own birthday party while he was being constrained by two men, totally helpless. He didn't deserve that. It was totally unnecessary. Wayne's life was not threatened in any way when he murdered this man in front of at least thirty witnesses. Of everything I was ever involved with in my fifteen years as a motorcycle club member, there is nothing I am more ashamed of today than being anywhere near this tragedy.

While in the midst of my own fight, one of our guys grabbed me and said, "We have to go." I had no idea at the time what had actually happened. All I was told was that Wayne had cut a guy and took off, leaving it up to me as VP to get our guys out. I rounded our crew up and led them out of there, through the midst of some very angry people. As the ambulance screamed past us on its way to the party site, I knew it was serious whatever it was. I had no idea how serious until we got back to the clubhouse and got the details. It was not until the next day we learned for certain that Big Boy was dead. By then, Wayne was long gone. We didn't see him again for many months, until he finally turned himself in.

As we tried to regroup in light of what had happened, several charter members took this opportunity to turn in their colors. They were the very ones who'd tried to help Wayne from getting beat up too badly and ended up charged as accomplices to murder. That was the straw that broke the camel's back for them. They had been apprehensive about the way the club had been heading since the Outlaws came into our lives anyway. They wanted to be a small, local, beer-drinking fraternity without all the pressure that came with the big-time. I didn't blame them really. They had been good brothers, and we'd been through some stuff together, but times were changing rapidly, especially after this night. Looking back, I probably should have gone with them.

Wayne had run south to the Dayton Outlaws to hide. Of course, when he told the story about what happened, it made him sound like a hero. If they'd have known what a punk he really was, they'd have thrown him out. That's the problem with a good con artist though: by the time you find out how they really are, the damage is often done. Dayton brothers shuttled him over to Indianapolis, to get him across a state line to complicate the extradition process. That's where he was when Lenny, the Detroit boss, called for me to come to fill him in on what in the world was going on. He was no stranger to this sort of stuff. What he really wanted to know was the effect all of it was having on the rest of us. I told him some had quit, but eight of us were more committed than ever.

I made up my mind about one thing that night: Wayne would never be my boss again no matter how this thing played out, and I told that to Lenny. Lenny was then careful to explain that a situation had occurred at the Indianapolis Outlaws' clubhouse that involved Wayne. He was careful, because Kato, Wayne's little brother, was with me. Lenny was a wise man and he didn't want the progress of establishing an Outlaw chapter in Toledo to suffer any setbacks. He told us Wayne had showed up in Indianapolis without telling anyone he was on the run and then proceeded to get very drunk. It wasn't long before he forgot all about where he was and who he was with. He was abruptly reminded, but because he didn't heed the warning, he also got himself beat up and handcuffed to a water pipe. Why would I be surprised? Lenny was apprehensive about delivering this tidbit of information, but Kato and I made sure he knew the incident in Indianapolis didn't affect our decision to continue down the road to becoming closer to the Outlaws MC. With Wayne on the lamb, I was now the acting president. If there were no objections from the remaining members, I would officially take the responsibility of getting us through this mess. There weren't. I was unanimously voted in as the Ohio Mongol chapter president upon returning from that meeting with Lenny in July 1978.

I had some serious decisions to make. We no longer had enough members to maintain the Crescent Raceway clubhouse, nor did we need it. We weren't very popular anymore—with anybody. The heat was on from the cops, and the locals shied away from us as if we had leprosy.

After two and a half years as a club in the city of Toledo, if it hadn't been for the Outlaws, we wouldn't have had any friends at all.

The "rescuing-the-underdog" image was now totally shot. The reputation of sticking up for the weak and helpless was out the window, or perhaps better said, down the toilet. Now we were the club that would hold you down while we slit your throat; the gang that would pull a lethal weapon if it even appeared as if you might get the best of one of us in a fistfight. That was the last thing I wanted to be known for, with the exception of being a quitter. I signed up for this lifestyle willingly, and I was raised to take the bad with the good. Right now it was bad. That's life.

Termite had purchased a run-down shack of a house on Toledo's south side earlier that same year. It was at the end of an alley that ran down to the railroad yard. The house sat high on the hill overlooking the traffic on Hawley Street, as it went in and out of the tunnel the trains went over. As our membership eventually whittled down to six, I decided to move the club to this location. We built a fence around the place, partitioned off the attic into bedrooms, and moved everyone in. We put up a makeshift bar and knocked down a wall to make room for our pool table. It wasn't fancy, but we wouldn't be entertaining much for a while. We weren't trying to attract any new members either. We were trying to determine how we were going to weather this storm while being courted by the Outlaws for consideration as a chapter of the American Outlaw Association. They were watching us very closely to see how this was all going to play out. Who would leave, and who would stay?

When all was said and done, more had left than stayed. Our Arizona brother, Jay, was needed more than ever. In February of 1979, Kato and I went to Phoenix to try to persuade Jay to come home to Ohio and join the Outlaws with us. We told Jay the Outlaws had offered us an opportunity to become a prospective chapter. We would continue to operate our local chapter, business as usual, with the exception of attending all mandatory Outlaw events. We would even be allowed to retain our Mongol colors, with the addition of an AOA Prospective patch sewn on the upper right front of our "cut-off." Kato and I partied with Jay and Lana for a week or so, even crossing the border into Mexico on my birthday. I had a little Mexican kid so intent on shining my cowboy boots that he wouldn't take no for an answer. He actually shined them while I was walking down the sidewalk! He didn't do a bad a job either. We all laughed at his tenacity as I gave him a dollar.

As the time approached to return to Ohio, we sat Jay down for a serious heart-to-heart talk. The thought of being able to ride all over the eastern United States with brothers and a clubhouse every couple of hundred miles was what got him. I understood; it's what got me. Jay promised to sell his trailer and move back to Ohio as fast as he could.

Chapter 7

Entering Life in the Fast Lane

The Regional shakedown run of 1979 marked the origin of the Toledo Outlaws' prospective chapter. I pulled my knife and began to cut my Mongols colors off the back of my cut-off when Lenny reminded me we didn't have to do that until we became official full-patch members. That way, if we didn't make it, we'd have something to fall back on. I told him most people I had known who had left something to fall back on usually ended up "falling back" and that I had no intention of not making it. If for any reason the attempt to put an Outlaw chapter in Toledo failed, I would be moving to either Detroit or Dayton to probate for membership myself.

Our term as a prospective chapter began in the spring of one of the Outlaws' bloodiest years. The president of the Warren, Ohio, chapter was intentionally run down by a drunk outside a local tavern in April. Soon after, a brother in Montreal was killed when a bomb exploded as he started his motorcycle. Four Outlaws were shot to death in their clubhouse in Charlotte, North Carolina, on the Fourth of July. One of them was to be buried somewhere near his original stomping grounds outside Tallahassee, Florida, and the Ravens MC there had graciously allowed us the use of their clubhouse for the solemn gathering.

After the funeral, as several huge packs wound their way through rural North Florida heading for Interstate 10, the leader of my pack pulled into a small convenience store so we could fuel up. Back then, many Outlaws rode choppers with small gas tanks, so we had to stop often for them. It was the most hilarious gas stop I have ever witnessed. The cashier was literally overwhelmed by the starting and stopping of the pumps, filling up, then pulling away, making room for the next guy. There was no way they could keep track. To make matters worse, the little store filled up with members who not only shoplifted, but also made absolutely no attempt to conceal it. They walked around the store drinking beer, eating potato chips, or whatever else struck their fancy. As I turned a corner at the end of an aisle, I saw one of the Dayton brothers spreading mustard on a piece of bread with his huge Bowie knife, an open package of bologna under his arm. Another reached into a cooler, opened a jar of pickles, stuck his filthy fingers inside to grab one, then re-sealed the jar and put it back on the shelf. The look the cashier got from the men was a defiant "I dare you to call the cops." No one did. We laughed about it the rest of the day.

In August 1979, Magilla, a much-loved Detroit Outlaw, died. His funeral brought much of the Outlaw Nation through Toledo. We had met a lot of them at the funerals we had already been to, but now many of them were going to see our clubhouse for the first time. It was exciting for us. The local biker community became acutely aware that our little club had survived the tragedy of Hicks murdering Tom Polaski, and was still alive and well. On the way back to Toledo from the wake, the Michigan State Police pulled over a group of us on Detroit's South side. There had been the traditional gun salute at the gravesite, and the authorities were definitely not happy about it. The gun salute consisted of hundreds of Outlaws pulling handguns and emptying them into the air as a final, defiant sendoff to a departed one-percenter brother. To make matters worse, Detroit was being negatively publicized as the "murder capital of the world," and its concealed weapon laws were very strict. The idea that we publicly and blatantly disregarded those laws made them furious. As the six of us pulled over and dismounted, we were accosted by officers brandishing shotguns—locked and loaded—and screaming, "Step away from the vehicles! *Get down on the ground now!*" I have argued with my share of cops over the years, but not on this particular occasion. These guys were serious. It was August, and their squad cars had been running all day long. The barrel of a riot pump was pressing against the back of my head, forcing it down onto the scorching hood. It was so hot it burned second-degree blisters on my elbows as I tried to keep my face from being singed. I never, ever took my helmet off during a traffic stop again. Live and learn. They searched our gear and found three handguns. A beautiful 1911A1 Government Model .45 happened to be in my saddlebag, and I was arrested, along with two Tennessee Outlaws. The three of us were taken to different precincts to await transportation to the Wayne County Jail in downtown Detroit the next morning. As I was being physically inserted into the back of a cruiser, I felt the familiar *click, click, click* of the handcuffs tightening around my wrists as I leaned back in the seat. They had not set the little lever that kept the cuffs from collapsing, and they were cutting off the circulation to my hands in no time. I learned something else that day. Never tell an angry cop you need to go to the bathroom. They drove me around for at least an extra hour, all the while telling me the back seat better be dry when we got to the First Precinct stationhouse. It was.

Being charged with carrying a concealed weapon within the city limits of Detroit was a definite no-no. Fortunately for us, the Outlaws had lawyers and bondsmen standing by for this kind of thing, especially in light of the great influx of out-of-towners due to Magilla's funeral. I was released on bond the next day, and my case was eventually thrown out for illegal search. The judge did not feel, however, the need to have my precious Colt returned to me. My lawyer said, "Be happy with what you got and go back to Ohio." I took his advice. I also bought another Government Model when I got there.

The year of 1979 was so bloody that three of our original eight members ended up quitting. They just did not have the stomach for all the violence. That was the purpose of the prospective period: to sort out potential members who were not going to stick through the rough stuff. Better to do it before they actually became patch members. These three leaving put us below the required number needed to start a new chapter, but I reminded Lenny of Wayne. He had eventually turned himself in, copped a plea for involuntary manslaughter, and was sentenced to five to twenty-five years at the reformatory in Mansfield, Ohio. Because he was technically a member, we still had the six necessary to continue the process. Besides, I reasoned, we also had Ralph.

I left the railroad in December 1978 to pursue bringing Toledo into the Outlaw Nation, but my friendship with Ralph continued. I saw him often, and he spent a lot of time at our clubhouse. He loved riding the scooter I built for him, and he loved being around the club. As he spent more and more time with us, he spent less and less with his wife and daughters. He also began to miss a lot of work. As I was beginning to bring our little club into the Outlaws, he made up his mind that he wanted to be more than just a friend, associate, or hang-around. He left his excellent job with the railroad and asked me if he could join up with us full time. I was elated. I knew him pretty well by now, and I knew he could be trusted. Kato sponsored him immediately. He would have to start on the ground floor, that is, as a probationary member. He was already well accustomed to being around us, and his friendship and support for the club had weathered the tragedy of Big Boy's murder. Not only that, but he had also met many of the Outlaws who had passed through and partied in Toledo. He knew what he was getting into, as much as any of us did anyway.

As we began the prospective process, so did the Oklahoma City Chapter of the Rogues Motorcycle Club. They had become acquainted with the Outlaws MC in much the same way as we had. They were not rookies by any means, and in some ways, they were more experienced than we were. The eleven funerals in 1979 gave us, as prospective chapters, a chance to get to know each other, and gave both of our chapters much exposure to the American Outlaw Association.

Besides the funerals, there were also several National Runs each year. They were mandatory gatherings of the membership, and they often revolved around events such as Bike Week in Daytona Beach, Florida, or the Black Hills Classic Motorcycle Races in the little town of Sturgis, South Dakota. One of the nationals in the summer of 1979 was to Oklahoma City. The Sooner state capitol was not accustomed to seeing the one-percenters for whom they were about to become a host city. As it turned out, they did not like the idea at all, and they made sure we knew it.

The ride out to Oklahoma was to be the longest I had been on thus far, and I was excited about going to this destination over a thousand miles from home. The Detroit chapter came through on their way, and we left with them the next morning, riding south to Dayton. Hambone's crew was ready to go when we got there, so we all headed west toward Saint Louis together on Interstate 70. It was a great day to be in the wind, with no problems that we could not easily remedy. The end of the day found us in a little Missouri town called Pacific. We found a city park and zeroed in on it to camp, oblivious to the fact that locals were more than a little freaked out by our presence.

A lone, local police officer had enough sense to approach us without trying to act like Barney Fife or treat us as if we were some menace to the community. We had ridden well over five hundred miles that day and were only interested in a place to bed down for the night. We were not there to cause trouble, although we were accustomed to it. This cop made the wise suggestion that a rock quarry on the edge of town might be more to our liking, for privacy and security reasons; not to mention that moving us out of town would stop the telephone from ringing off the wall at the local police station. We were quite a ways from our own turf and security was always an issue, so we agreed to follow him. The secluded spot to which he escorted us was perfect for our needs and was actually very close to the highway we were going to need in the morning.

Several carloads of young locals took note of the motorcycle procession being escorted out of town and followed it. They had never seen this many outlaw bikers before and most were just curious. They were friendly enough, and I will never forget one fellow who went by the name of JR. He must have watched *Scarface* one too many times. He tried to impress his girlfriend by making a marijuana deal with the big, bad bikers. Bad move. Before the night was over, he had lost his marijuana, his reputation, and his girlfriend.

We were on the road early the next day, enjoying the beauty of central Missouri for the first time via Interstate 44. The highway rolled gently through those picturesque hills and we made good time, heading for the Oklahoma border. Shortly after crossing the state line, a Dayton brother named Bear had a minor problem and needed to pull over. I motioned to the road captain that I would stay back and help him. We were a long way from the Outlaw Nation by now, and no one was going be left alone, for any reason. Bear and I got his problem squared away easily and proceeded to catch up with the rest of the pack. We needed to top off our fuel, so we pulled into a travel plaza on the Will Rogers Turnpike north of Tulsa. Bear decided he wanted a cup of coffee, so we went into the crowded café and ordered some. As soon as Bear took a drink, he spit it out on the floor and in a loud voice said, "This tastes like truckers' coffee. Don't you have any coffee fit for a man to drink?" I could not believe my ears as I watched every trucker in the place turn their attention toward us. You have to understand something—Bear was a 6'6", 350-pound, highly decorated former Marine sniper, and he feared nothing. He just smiled at the drivers and said, "Just kidding, fellas. What's the matter? Can't ya take a joke?" About that time, I was wondering if they would be thinking the same thing about us out on the turnpike, while staring down at us from their eighteen-wheelers.

The run to OKC went well; it was an especially great ride for me. I enjoyed the sense of accomplishment that came from building my own rigid-framed, stroked, Shovelhead chopper and having it perform flawlessly on a two-thousand-mile road trip. One of the main things that attracted me to the Outlaws in the first place was the talk of these long rides. Now I was out there on the highway with them myself, many miles from the very limited world of the Toledo Mongols. I was finally in the "fast lane," and I was having the time of my life.

During that prospective year, back on Hawley Street, a curious thing began to happen. Some of our neighbors decided to move. I cannot imagine why. Surely, that end of the alley was safer than any other part of South Toledo. I suppose our late night partying, incessantly barking dogs, bikes roaring in and out all hours of the night, not to mention the occasional discharge of large caliber firearms, was a bit more than they could handle. The owner of the property next door to us saw the handwriting on the wall. He knew his days as a slumlord in that part of town were coming to an end. He correctly discerned that no one was ever going to rent his shacks anywhere near these crazy white boys. He offered the two adjoining properties to us at an excellent price, so we bought them both. Now our little domain consisted of three addresses—numbers 32, 36, and 38 North Hawley Street—and included three houses and two garages. We chose number 36, the center structure, to be the actual clubhouse. I purchased number 38 for my own personal residence. I liked to be close to the action anyway, and one of the garages was located on that lot. I was still building custom motorcycles at the time, and I had a large inventory of parts and plenty of tools. The garage behind number 32 would become the club garage.

Number 36 was nestled between the other two-story houses and was going to require a lot of work to be turned into a clubhouse. For starters, the forty-year-old electrical service was only rated at thirty amps, which would never power the coolers we required, let alone the air conditioners we planned to install. As I compiled a list of materials we needed, it was obvious we did not have the money in our meager treasury to do much right away. At the same time, we were an American Outlaw Association Prospective chapter, and it was important for us to have a functioning clubhouse as soon as possible.

Security was priority one. As much as we enjoyed the tales of bikin' and brotherhood, we were also made well aware of the many enemies we would now acquire. For the Outlaws to feel comfortable at our place, and indeed for us to become Outlaws ourselves, safety had to be at the top of our list of main concerns. The first thing we did was to put a seven-foot fence around all three lots, wire the perimeter with listening devices, and accumulate the meanest guard dogs we could find. Spotlights, and eventually closed-circuit cameras, added to our fortress's defenses.

In between obligations to the Outlaws, we worked on our garrison. Whatever building material we needed would miraculously appear. I did not ask questions. I had an idea about where some of the stuff came from, but I really did not want to know any specifics. For example, one night we discussed the need for installing a nice shower for our guests when one of the brothers suggested we steal a baptistery he had spotted outside a church under construction. He said it would be easy pickings, and we could convert it into a giant hot tub. I nixed the idea. I told everyone not to be stealing anything from any churches. We had enough problems with people who did not like us, not to mention the cops. I did not want God mad at us too. After the security issues, the first thing we did was get the electricity up to par. Once that was finished, we paneled the entire inside of the place with three-quarter-inch exterior paneling. The plaster was looking pretty shabby, and I never did like drywall. It was too easy to put someone's head through it.

When Detroit and Dayton both showed up for the housewarming party, it became evident that we needed more room, both in the yard for bikes and in the actual clubhouse itself. One night while I was visiting Hambone down in Dayton, I got a call informing me that the house at 32 North Hawley had caught fire. No marvel really, with the antiquated, overloaded wiring and a half dozen residents who drank, got high, and often fell asleep with lit cigarettes in their hands. It is a wonder that every building we had didn't burn to the ground. Fortunately, all the members but one were out at the bars at the time, and no one was injured. As they returned to the clubhouse that night, the alley was full of fire trucks. The brother on guard duty was in the middle house and, unfortunately, the blaze was out of control by the time he noticed. Arriving back in Toledo I was told that the night of the fire one of our members was staggering in the alley, drunk as a skunk, asking a fire chief if we should call the insurance man yet. He suggested we wait until the fire was out at least.

The building burned almost completely to the ground and ended up being a total loss. Now our compound had a gaping hole where the house had been. We quickly extended the fence to fill the breach and began to demolish the wreckage of number 32 ourselves. We kept a fire burning 24-7 for over a month, burning every piece of the old house that was not salvageable. When we were informed we needed an expensive permit to have a "sewer kill" and a "water kill" done by a city-approved, licensed contractor and the whole deal would cost thousands of dollars, we simply ignored it. We cemented the sewer and water lines closed ourselves, and before long, you could not tell a house had ever been there. We sowed grass seed, laid some gravel down, built a huge bonfire pit, and could soon accommodate sixty motorcycles instead of twenty.

With the $10,000 we did get from the insurance company, we built a twenty-four-by-thirty foot, two-story, concrete block addition onto number 36. It was very impressive. We mixed cement and poured it down through the holes in the block every five courses and, when it was finished, it was solid concrete. We even put in a few narrow, bullet-proof, double-pane Plexiglas windows, but we kept them above head level so that no one would be able to see in from outside. Barrier walls concealed the hefty oak doors and steel plates so that a sniper could not get a bead on anyone walking out. We used the massive floor timbers and the actual two-by-four oak studs from number 32 to make the inside as "Outlaw proof" as possible. In other words, it was built tough. It was constructed to accommodate hard partying without us having to be constantly worrying about damaging anything. In the basement, we put in a large bathroom, complete with urinal and huge shower, as well as a washer, dryer, and a big freezer my parents donated.

123

We also built a huge room and filled it with mattresses, so the out-of-towners could crash and feel secure.

One of the advantages with an inner-city ghetto clubhouse was our enemies all stuck out like a sore thumb. It was a predominantly black neighborhood, with just a few older white couples here and there. If adversaries came sneaking around our area, they were generally easy to spot. Feds were the same way; they never figured out that new Crown Vics were even more obvious than police cruisers. As a matter of fact, they would have done better in regular squad cars. We were used to seeing them.

Rats, on the other hand, were a disadvantage in our neighborhood. Not that we were so fainthearted they freaked anybody out, but they were a nuisance. Our guard dogs were no help: the rats easily outsmarted them, and most of us couldn't stand cats. For a while, we even had rodent problems inside one of the houses. We made a sport out of eliminating them. We would bait the pests by putting bread, cheese, or whatever on the floor in the kitchen and wait in the living room for them to come sniffing around it. When one did, the loud ring of a .22-caliber pistol would echo through the house as another rat bit the dust. We would dispose of the carcass and then we would patiently wait for the next one. There was always a next one. It provided good entertainment at a time when there were only three television channels that all signed off by one o'clock in the morning. I saw *Quincy* so many times I think I had every episode memorized. Shooting rats was much more fun.

It was so much fun, in fact, that a couple of us decided to take the sport outside. We had spotlights all along the perimeter, some of them eerily lighting inside the compound. The filthy rodents could be seen scurrying from building to building on a regular basis. Ranger One, a Vietnam Vet from the Detroit Chapter, and I would compete to see who could get the most in a single night while on guard duty. Gunshots ringing out in the middle of the night were no big deal on that side of town. I don't ever remember the cops coming in response to a call from any of the neighbors. They knew we were just having a little fun. Besides, our reducing the rat population benefited them too.

The record for the most rats killed in a single night was twenty-one. Ranger One killed eleven and I bagged ten. Carcass disposal became an issue, so we devised a solution. Our property overlooked Hawley Street as it came out of the railroad tunnel, so we decided to hurl the dead rats by their tails onto the street forty feet below. They would hit near the center of the roadway and slide over against the opposite curb. That worked well for a while, and it made it easy to keep accurate count of how many we killed.

A problem finally arose when the dead rats lining the sidewalk started to freak out the neighborhood kids as they walked to school in the morning. Some of them must have mentioned it at school because it wasn't long before Toledo's Finest served us with a paper requiring one of us to attend a meeting with the head of the school board. I felt like I was in the principal's office in high school all over again. Some idiotic social worker tried to insinuate throwing rats in the street where the schoolchildren had to walk by them might have some racial ramifications. Give me a break. Most of those kids had seen more rats, alive and dead, than we had. I told her to get a life.

The truth was we never considered the kids one way or the other. We were like everybody else. We generally were only thinking about ourselves. I promised those folks I would get to the bottom of this "crime of the century" and gave them my word there would not be any more dead rats in the street because of us. I kept my word too. From then on, we just threw them over the south fence onto the railroad's property. That worked out pretty well, and Conrail never accused us of being prejudiced.

One day I did have a problem with shooting a rifle in the middle of the afternoon. I had been working on a .30-caliber M1 carbine and needed to test fire it, so I put a whiskey bottle against the fence at the far end of the property and blew it to smithereens. What I did not know was that there was a police cruiser down by the tracks manned by two relatively new officers. They started calling for backup as if they were under attack, and soon police cars filled the street below, as well as the alley behind the clubhouse.

Cops were having a problem climbing up our hill because of all the barbed wire we had intertwined throughout the dense brush. I stood on the catwalk overlooking the alley, as some very upset police officers demanded that we open the gates and let them in. The two rookies were fuming mad, claiming to their fellow officers that they had narrowly escaped death. I told them they were nuts and denied any shots were fired from within our premises. They didn't buy it and remained adamant about coming in. I demanded to see their search warrant and informed them that our attorney had been notified, which was a lie. The truth was, that .30 caliber round I fired went into a ten-by-ten oak beam and it never endangered anyone, but of course, I didn't tell them that. One of the rookies suggested to his buddies that they ram our flimsy wooden gates open with one of their cruisers. I said to him, "You don't want to do that." Then he asked, "Why not?" I replied, "Then you'll be in here with us, and you're not ready for that, Junior."

While I was stalling them, fully expecting them to enter one way or another very soon, my people were locking up guns, hiding drugs, and stashing money in anticipation of the impending raid. Just as things were about to get seriously out of hand, a "white shirt" pulled up and took charge of the situation. He sensed emotions were high with his officers and wanted to make sure they did not do anything that would facilitate our lawyers getting an illegal search thrown out of court, which happened often. We had learned that if we could agitate the cops just enough to get them to forget, or skip, just one necessary step in the process, our lawyers could run with it.

This particular sergeant was a big, black fellow who had been around for years. He was no rookie; he was not excited, and he was not nervous. He was calm, cool, and very professional. In fact, he was the same officer who had been moonlighting as a security guard the night Ralph had to come to his rescue. The two of them, back to back, had brought the potentially dangerous situation quickly under control, and this sergeant never forgot it. He had always made it a point to treat us fairly, even letting a few of us go on home to the clubhouse in spite of being obviously under the influence a time or two. He spoke to his fellow officers to get their story. Then he turned to me and said, "What's going on, Cowboy?" I assured him that no one had shot at any of his men. He knew me long enough to know we knew better than that.

He said, "We're going to have to come in and take a look around." I had received the signal from one of my men that we were ready, so I told him, "I know, Sarge. You can come in and look around all you want." I pointed at the other cops and said, "They're going to need a warrant, though." You could see the anger in the faces of those rookies, who were looking forward to coming in and throwing their weight around. What they were mad about was that they thought I was supposed to be intimidated by them. They had uniforms, badges, riot pump shotguns, and even shiny, new police cars. They could not figure out why we were not intimidated. Here is what I think: men who get their backbone from all that stuff probably were slapped around in school when they were kids. How did I know? We had guys like that too. To them, the club was their source of power. We were constantly weeding out jerks like that. They made us look bad. I would think police departments probably had to deal with that as well.

I let the sergeant in and escorted him around the property. He had no interest in going in any of the buildings. He walked along the south fence and noticed glass fragments on the ground. He was no dummy. He cautioned me it was against the law to discharge a firearm within the city limits. I thanked him for the reminder and told him I would make sure everyone was clear on that at the next meeting. That was it. I respected him, and he respected me. That's how it works, sometimes anyway. I did decide to replace those rickety, wooden gates after that incident, though. We concreted railroad ties four feet into the ground and hung boilerplate from them, complete with wheels to handle the immense weight. Thanks to those inexperienced rookies, we now had a pair of gates you could only get through with a bulldozer.

Chapter 8

Outlaws MC, Toledo

Fall finally arrived and the annual Outlaw National, the Punkin Run, was fast approaching. It was so named because it fell on the last weekend of October every year. We had been a prospective chapter since the shakedown run in April and had hopes of being awarded our charter at this last big run of the year. The Oklahoma City Prospective Chapter was in the same position. Both clubs had attended every run and had been represented at every funeral. That in itself was no small thing. There were eleven funerals that year.

Ralph and I had left several days early for the run, so we'd have a few days to hang out with the Dayton brothers. We had become very close to them, as we had the Detroit chapter. It was particularly cold the night Ralph and I left heading south, and we were so bundled up we could hardly look over at each other going down the interstate. I could barely feel my clutch lever or my throttle through my two pairs of gloves. The plan was to shed as much of our cold weather gear as we could at the Dayton clubhouse, 150 miles down the road. When Jay, Kato, and the rest of the Toledo crew finally arrived, we all pulled out together for the 350-mile ride down to Tennessee.

The Punkin Run was going to be held at an old, dilapidated antebellum mansion on the outskirts of Nashville, Tennessee, which was the clubhouse of the Rolling Thunder Motorcycle Club. They had thoroughly trashed it themselves, to the degree there was not much danger of us doing it any damage, outside of burning it to the ground completely. Outlaws from all over the country and Canada were steadily arriving. It was exciting to see so many Outlaws we had made friends with during the year, as well as meet new ones. Taco had become the boss of the Detroit chapter, and he personally took me around to meet every other chapter boss. It was his way of reminding them that Toledo was sponsored by Detroit. He was one of the most respected men in the organization, so his approval carried a lot of weight. I had no way of knowing for sure that there was going to be a vote taken, but he did. On Saturday night, October 27, the Toledo chapter of the Outlaws Motorcycle Club officially came into existence. Moreover, so did the Oklahoma City chapter. We were welcomed into the American Outlaw Association with reactions ranging from hugs to chest punches. It was one of the most memorable days of my life. We had already shed our old colors, as did OKC, so we took our pocketknives out and cut the prospective tabs off from underneath our AOA patches. Both Toledo and Oklahoma began this journey with every intention of successfully completing it, and we had. We were no longer prospectives but full-fledged Outlaws.

Two chapters being added to the Outlaw Nation was definitely cause for celebration. Ralph was very happy for us and proud to be associated with us. His status changed from being a probate for a prospective chapter to a probationary Outlaw for a sure enough real Outlaw chapter. As Ralph looked on while we were being congratulated, someone yelled "Probate." Any probate within hearing distance of that call was required to respond to see how he might be needed. As Ralph turned to respond, I stopped him and called him over to share in our accomplishment. One of the other probates could answer the call this time. Ralph had been an integral part of making this occasion possible. He was as good a brother as I had ever known, except for one thing. He was not a brother. He had gone from my friend on the railroad, to official club hangaround, to probationary member. He had worked for us and with us. He had forsaken his job and his family to prove his loyalty to us. He had fist-fought alongside us and had partied with us for two years. Tonight, he would become one of us. The night I became an Outlaw, so did Ralph. I had brought him up for a vote in Toledo in the event that we received our charter at this run. The vote was unanimous. This brisk, autumn night not only saw the Outlaw Nation increase in membership, but also the newly formed Toledo Outlaw chapter.

Perhaps I should address a grave misconception about motorcycle clubs at this time. It has to do with initiation into the club. I have heard many foolish stories in my time. It is a shame that so many of them are believed and taken as fact when there is often little or no truth to them. I cannot speak for every club, but the two I was a member of for fifteen years had no initiation ceremony that involved humiliation of any kind. I have heard of prospects being required to perform unspeakable acts in public before being deemed man enough to wear the colors of the club for which they had been eliciting membership. That is a concept born out of some B-grade Hollywood biker movies. Some clubs may have fallen prey to it. Let me assure you, we did not.

Here are my thoughts on the subject. If I had to sacrifice my self-respect to prove I was "man" enough to wear a particular club's colors, I would not want their colors. I would not want to be around them at all. Clubs like the Outlaws, the Hells Angels, the Mongols, the Banditos, and a few others are not college fraternities who get their kicks out of humiliating each other. Nor was it a requirement to commit a murder, or even a felony for that matter, to gain membership, as I have heard folks say. I have read transcripts from court proceedings in which men testified to these sorts of things. Granted, things got way out of control for some. Many individual members committed, and were convicted of, horrendous crimes. That is a matter of record, but that was not what the club was about. Our policy was, what people did on their own time was their own business, and the safest way to live was to mind your own business. It is a proven fact that it is easier to repeat the truth than a lie, so the principle of the need-to-know basis was adamantly ascribed to when it came to a brother's personal affairs. It *was* a requirement, however, to prove your love for bikin' and brotherhood.

Motorcycle club history was made that cool October evening of 1979. Two cities had been brought into the one-percenter brotherhood of the Outlaw Nation. Although Toledo and Oklahoma City both received their official charters, being afforded full rights of membership, neither had yet been awarded their colors. The coveted symbol of the ominous skull with large red eyes in front of a pair of crossed, connecting rods, complete with pistons, the OUTLAWS top rocker and, in our case, the TOLEDO bottom rocker, had yet to be made. The embroiderer in Detroit was running behind this particular fall. She probably had a back order of bowling-league shirts to catch up on. Though disappointed, we got over it quickly and began to party for the first time, not just with Outlaws, but also as Outlaws. Exactly four years from the weekend I got voted in to the Mongols MC, I was now a full-patch member of the most respected, and notorious, motorcycle club that ever existed.

Several weeks after returning home from that memorable run, I got a call from up north that several Detroit members would be coming down on the upcoming weekend. We all hoped this visit had to do with our finally receiving our patches, and it did. They were delivered by Speed and Ranger One. Our old ladies were standing by with sewing machines ready in anticipation of their arrival. By early evening, everyone's colors had been sewn on, and we were on our way to the bars to celebrate. It was mid-November and very cold that night. We had to pile into cars, but we didn't care. It was time for "Charlie," as we affectionately referred to our patch, to make his debut with a Toledo rocker under him for the first time. Our colors were black, white, and obviously brand-new. No one was going to be able to miss them anywhere we went.

We got very drunk that night, as friends and bar owners alike helped us celebrate. They knew it was in their best interest to be on our good side, and they were right. We had re-earned a reputation for taking care of folks that took care of us and for sticking up for the underdog again. It had taken a while for the dust to settle because of Big Boy's tragic and needless murder. The fact that Hicks was off the scene helped a lot. It helped us, and it helped the community in which we lived.

By midnight, we were all pretty well wasted. Last stop of the night was the Exotic Lounge on Sylvania Avenue. Everyone had gone in except me. I stayed outside talking to my old lady when four men piled out of their car not very far from where we were standing. It was obvious they had been at it for quite a while themselves. I remember thinking there was going to be trouble when they got inside the bar where my brothers were, but trouble did not wait that long. As they walked by us, one of these idiots stuck his nose where it did not belong, so I bloodied it for him, and he went down. The fight was on from there. As I squared off with two of them, the third reached into their car and grabbed an unopened wine bottle. He snuck up behind me and clobbered me on the back of the head with it. Having a very hard head is a virtue in the world of thugs and street fighting, so after punching the two in front of me a few times, I turned to the coward behind me. With a liter of red wine mingled with my own blood streaming down my back, my brand-new colors were getting broken in fast.

A squad car cruising Sylvania Avenue saw the ruckus and skidded to a halt right where we were, so I commenced to pound this punk's brains out right on the hood of the cruiser. The cop started ordering me to stop, my old lady had run into the bar to alert my brothers, and soon the sidewalk in front of the place was crowded with onlookers, as well as more police. The policeman handcuffed me, but before I was officially arrested, the white shirt in charge noted that the vehicle the four chumps pulled up in was one they had been looking for already that evening. It seemed they had started trouble in several places earlier that night and had beaten up a young man who attempted to stick up for his girlfriend in light of their lewd remarks. The sergeant in charge told his officers to release me because they had it coming. I have to hand it to the Toledo Police Department. On more than a few occasions, they let us slide for taking care of punks they would have liked to have pounded themselves. Toledo's Finest loaded three of those jerks into a paddy wagon, while the wine bottle bushwhacker got a free ride in an ambulance. For us, it was a great night to be an Outlaw.

The first opportunity for the newly chartered Toledo Outlaws to attend a club function as full-fledged members came the following month. The Windsor, Ontario chapter was hosting a party the weekend before Christmas, and we were excited about the chance to get over into Canada to party with those brothers. We had met a dozen or so Canadian Outlaws during the course of our prospective period, but none of us from Toledo had ever been over to their side of the border. There was much heat involving the club by the Ontario Provincial Police, as well as the Royal Canadian Mounted Police. Since several chapters of the Canadian Satan's Choice Motorcycle Club had joined the Outlaws MC in 1977, there had been much violence between the motorcycle clubs there, and Canada was very sensitive to it. All but one or two of the Detroit Outlaws had been either deported or denied entry due to convicted felon status and/or association with the Canadian chapters.

Taco strongly encouraged me to take a crew to this particular party. Though it was just across the river from Detroit, no one from that city's chapter was going to be able to attend, and it was important to have a showing from the USA. At that time, none of us new guys were felons, except for Hicks, and we were not in the computer as being associated with the Outlaws yet either. It was a Christmas party, so we would have the perfect opportunity to sneak over the border wearing winter coats with no club colors visible.

Five of us drove the fifty miles up to the Ambassador Bridge that spanned the Detroit River into downtown Windsor and proceeded to enter Canada. It was about 7:00 p.m. when our turn came at the border-crossing booth. I answered the usual questions: "Do you have any weapons? Do you have any contraband?" To both, my response was "No, Sir." Then he asked why we wanted to come into Canada on this particular night. I replied that we were interested in visiting some of their go-go bars. Many young men drove up from Ohio to frequent such clubs in Windsor, so it seemed like a feasible explanation. The guard looked at all of our drivers' licenses for a few moments, then handed them back and said, "Maybe some other time." He then directed us into the U-turn lane that would take us back over the river into Michigan.

Discouraged but not defeated, I headed into downtown Detroit to where the Detroit-Windsor Tunnel was. The tunnel entrance was only a mile up river from the bridge, but it was a good four-and-a-half-mile drive for us. I pulled up to the booth and went through the same initial question-and-answer routine before the guard said, "Pull over there." Several other agents suddenly appeared to make sure we had no questions as to where "over there" was. They were very polite. They even opened the van doors for us before escorting us into the building. On our way in, we passed the crew that was going to do a thorough search of my van, including a beautiful German Shepherd "sniffer" dog. I was glad I was honest when I had told them we did not have any weapons or drugs.

The problem was not with the van. It was clean. The problem was the personal search to which we were subjected. As soon as we removed our coats, it became apparent that we were not attempting to cross so we could see the sights. Each of us, beneath our jackets, was wearing a brand-new set of Outlaw colors. So much for the new members not being in the computer; they documented our attempt and turned us back. I started to get angry; this was becoming a challenge. I really wanted to make a showing at this get together in Windsor. Taco had personally asked us to go, and I did not want to let him down.

There was one more shot, as far as I could see. It was now about 10:00 p.m., too early to give up. I sent my two roughest-looking characters to the old Mt. Elliot Avenue clubhouse with the van after being dropped off near the bus station. I took Jay and Hobbit with me to try to get across on the bus that ran regularly through the tunnel, as well as the automobile and commercial truck traffic. Boarding the bus, the three of us spaced ourselves out so that it was not apparent we were together. We did not make eye contact, let alone speak to each other. We were already in civilian clothes so as not to alert the Canadian authorities of any affiliation to the notorious AOA chapter in Windsor.

I figured at this point perhaps at least one of us, maybe even two of us, would make it through the gauntlet of border and immigration officers to be able to represent our new chapter at this party. The bus pulled out, and soon we were once again below the Detroit River on our way back into Canada for the third time that night. I was determined to do everything within my power to try to make it. As the bus pulled into the customs station, I was optimistic. This terminal was far enough away from the auto crossing that I was not worried about being spotted by any of the cops who had kicked us out earlier. Slowly, the passengers began to disembark and head toward the lone agent who looked at the ID of each one.

I noticed he never even looked up, did not seem to scrutinize anyone at all. He just motioned for each individual to proceed on through to where the taxis and city buses were waiting to take them on to their destinations in Windsor. Six or seven passengers were waved through ahead of me without so much as a grunt out of the officer. I was elated, convinced I would make it and that we had beaten their system with our perseverance.

My heart sank as I handed him my Ohio driver's license and heard him say, "Stand over there." I had been through this twice already tonight. I knew I was not going to make it now and realized there may indeed be some legal complications because of my relentless persistence. I did not care about that one bit at the time. My hope of getting to this party was dashed, but I still believed Jay and Hobbit had a good chance of making it in.

About fifteen more passengers filed past the guard without a hitch. He never looked up at anyone; he never spoke to anyone else. That is, until Hobbit handed him his license. "Stand over there" again resonated in his monotonous, uninterested tone. Hobbit made his way over to the brick wall where I was standing, but we still did not acknowledge we knew each other. We just stood there with dumb looks on our faces, as if we had no idea what possible problem there could be.

Jay was our last hope of getting a representative to this annual Windsor Outlaw Christmas party. It was important for us to be there, at least one of us. He was near the rear of the bus, about twenty passengers behind Hobbit. All of them came up to the immigration official, showed their identification, and were admitted without as much as a grunt. As Jay took his place at the gate and brandished his ID, again, without even looking up, we heard the familiar words once again escape the Canadian's lips, "Stand over there." The entire bus had unloaded and all but three of its passengers entered the country that night with no problem at all. All except Jay, Hobbit, and me.

I determined it must have had something to do with shoes or, in our case, boots. Canada must train its law enforcement personnel to do criminal profiling according to footwear. That is all the guard ever looked at. Extremely clever, those Canuks. The three of us stood along the wall of the tunnel, waiting for whatever was going happen next. We no longer attempted to conceal the fact that we were together. By now, it was nearing eleven o'clock, and the shift change was beginning to get underway. Lo and behold, here came several of the guards who had detained us at our previous tunnel-crossing attempt several hours prior. It seems they had to come to the main office near where we were to clock out. They informed the lone agent of our determined, though unsuccessful, endeavors to enter their beloved Canada. They all got a good laugh at our expense as they directed us aboard another bus heading back under the Detroit River to the United States. "Better luck next time," they said as they waved goodbye to us. In a little over four hours, we had been denied entry into Canada three times. Even though we never made it, no one could say we did not try.

On our way to find a payphone, a car pulled up next to us and this hippie looking dude asked me for directions to a certain Detroit club. I noticed the Ohio front plate, and realizing they thought we were locals, I gave him directions into one of the worst ghettos in the city. He said, "Thanks, Man, I owe ya," as they sped off. We laughed. We needed to laugh. I hope he kept his windows up and his doors locked. He and his fellow Buckeyes were going to stand out like a sore thumb if they followed the directions I gave them.

When your life revolves around a motorcycle, winter always seems especially long. I spent much of the time working on my bikes, but not because they needed a lot; it's just that if you could not be riding them, you ought to be improving them. My scooter got a new paint job, as well as anything else it needed, every winter. It was imperative it be roadworthy for the upcoming riding season. The garage behind 38 North Hawley, where I lived, became my personal shop. The rest of the chapter shared the one behind number 32. That structure somehow escaped the devastating fire without any damage at all. In my shop, I poured a concrete floor and rewired it so I would have plenty of electricity for lighting and power tools. I removed the garage door, boarded it up, bullet-proofed the alley side with quarter-inch steel plate, and put a door just wide enough for a Harley dresser on the clubhouse yard side. Inside, I built a heavy-duty table to set my frame on. It was designed so that the front end could be put on, as well as the rear wheel, while up in the air. That made it easy to work on, wire, and get creative with. I have heard that nowadays they have hydraulic lifts that accomplish the same thing and then lower the bike to the ground for you. I used to have to get a couple of brothers to help me lift my bike down off the table. It worked just as well and was a lot cheaper.

In the spring, the property next to number 32 came up for sale. It had a two-story house on it that had sat vacant ever since we moved into the neighborhood. It was not likely that anyone would purchase the property that bordered the Outlaw clubhouse, but we were not going to take any chances. We did not need or even want the house, but the quarter-acre lot would allow us to expand our compound. I found the owner and expressed interest in purchasing the property. Greed got the best of him and he said he had to have $6,000 for it. I informed him he was out of his mind.

To our amazement, someone actually did buy the property at 28 North Hawley Street. The new owner began cleaning the yard up, apparently oblivious to who his neighbors were. Before he had the chance to move in, his newly acquired "piece of the rock" mysteriously burned to the ground. One of the engineers on a Conrail locomotive watched the fire from the rail yard at the end of the alley, right next to number 28's property line. He swore to arson investigators he saw lightning hit the building, causing it to start on fire. Fires in this neighborhood did not exactly get the fire department moving quite as fast as some other parts of town, and the building was a total loss. The original owner had to let his purchaser out of his contract, and he decided to offer the parcel to us as is for $1,000 cash. I told him I would think about it while we tried to figure out how to get the money. If we were the organized criminals we were later accused of being, we shouldn't have had any trouble coming up with a lousy grand, but alas, we never seemed to have very much money. We did, however, have a lot of fun.

The garage at number 32 had no electrical service because of the earlier fire. We had run a heavy-duty extension cord over to it from number 36 for the lights and light power tools. That worked okay until someone brought home a used arc welder. There was no way the building had the electricity to run it, so I decided we would bury a 220-volt cable from number 36. The problem was, the ground between them was what had been the driveways of the two properties. It was very hard, consisting of compacted gravel, rock, and chunks of asphalt. The idea of digging that trench by hand was not very appealing to any of us. Ralph, who had been a machine operator on the railroad, suggested we rent a Ditch Witch to do the job. That sounded good to us. The treasurer gave Ralph some money so he could to get the trencher the following Saturday morning.

On Friday, Ralph showed up at the clubhouse with his hair dyed blonde. It was still long and wavy, only now it was yellow. He looked like a California hippie or maybe even a rock musician. The rest of us laughed and made fun of him. He didn't care. What I didn't know is that he had gone to the Department of Motor Vehicles and got a phony driver's license, complete with his "new look" on the picture.

Ralph devised a plan to get our trench dug for nothing and obtain the $1,000 needed to buy the lot next door. He rented the trencher, but after he dug the trench, he didn't return it. He had worked out a deal with a brother in Pennsylvania to sell it to him for $1,200. That was enough to recover the deposit, pay for the gas to and from Pennsylvania, and still have $1,000 cash to turn over to the chapter treasurer for the property. He did exactly that. Nobody asked Ralph where the money came from. What a brother did on his own time was his business.

We immediately began tearing down our newly acquired, fire-ravaged structure. The lumber we salvaged allowed us to build a formidable solid oak fence around the entire lot. We never obtained the required sewer or water kills on that property either. In fact, we never got permits to demolish numbers 32 or 28. We just tore them down, board by board, burning the scrap in the yard. As I said, neighbors on this end of town were not very prone to calling the law. Soon we had spotlights lining the new extension of our perimeter, and a couple more junkyard dogs giving us the sense of security we needed.

In 1978, the Mongols MC of Ohio moved into a rundown shack at 32 North Hawley Street because of a needless murder that nearly destroyed the club. Within just a few short years, we had become the Toledo Chapter of the Outlaws Motorcycle Club, with a concrete fortress for a clubhouse and property that encompassed half a city block.

Chapter 9

Back to Normal

It had been two years since we began to party with true one-percenters. In that time, we survived the ordeal of Tom Polaski's murder and the subsequent changes that went along with it. We endured an apprehensive year of being an Outlaw-prospective chapter, which included losing several more of our original members. Finally, we were able to get back to the normal routine of being a local motorcycle club.

Not only was winter the time to work on our bikes, but we also had to maintain a high profile on the street to keep up our image. One cold Friday night early in 1980, the new Toledo chapter loaded up in two cars and headed to the Exotic Lounge. It was "our" bar and everyone knew it; that was mainly because several of our old ladies worked there as dancers, so we frequented it often. When we arrived, our girls informed us that four local idiots had been in there earlier. They were harassing them and making comments that they did not care whose bar it was. I recognized who they were by their description and knew they would be at the Seaport Inn just down the street. It had a reputation of being the hangout of some rough characters back in the mid-'70s, and I had personally been involved in some pretty good fights there over the years. Now the Seaport Inn was a hideout for many of the losers we had been slapping around in recent years.

We were hot about what had transpired and were ready to find, and whip, these punks who talked tough to our women then skedaddled before we showed up. Since there were only four of them, I decided Kato and I could handle it. We jumped in my Z 28 and roared toward the Seaport, assuring the guys we would be back soon. When we got there, I pulled up onto the sidewalk just outside the door, not bothering to park in the lot. I did not intend to be there long. Kato and I went in and quickly spotted the punks, who knew why we were there. We grabbed the two, dragged them outside, and began to put a couple of knots on their heads to teach them a lesson. What happened next I did not expect.

The door to the bar came open and out walked the other two jerks we were going in for next, but they were not alone. A group of about twenty or so came out with them, led by a former bouncer who had recently come back into town. He had been stirring these guys up, convincing them we would not have gotten away with terrorizing them for so long if he had been around. He told them they didn't have to take it from us anymore, even though we were Outlaws now. He had them all pumped up, and this situation gave them a chance to see if he was right. Out they came to inform Kato and me that our days of pushing people around at the Seaport Inn were a thing of the past. As I looked the mob over, nearly every one of them was someone who had been beaten up by one of us at one time or another.

Faced with these odds and this ultimatum, I did the only thing I could do. I hooked the rabble-rousing bouncer in the teeth with a right and began to punch as many of the others as I could get my hands on. Kato did the same. It was their turn to be surprised. One fool finally grabbed me from behind while another punched me in the face. I told him to let go, but he was too scared to let go, afraid of what I would do to him. Another guy took a free shot while I was constrained, and I was starting to get mad. I slowly pulled a double-edged dagger from my belt and told the one holding me that if he did not let go of me, I would carve him off. He could not see my knife, and I guess he thought I was bluffing, so I "gently" poked him in the arm, just enough to let him know I meant business. He let out a scream and released me. I knocked him off his feet and then lit into his buddy who had sucker-punched me. He left a couple of teeth on the pavement that night. Then I started looking for Kato. Kato was a lot smaller than I was, so more of the mob went after him. When I spotted him, he was down on the concrete. I decked one of those jerks just as he kicked Kato in the ribs. When I pulled Kato up, he had a black eye, a bloody lip, and a big grin. We were having a ball. Riding and fighting was what we did best. In that order.

Just about that time, an old station wagon pulled up and out jumped Ralph, Jay, and Termite. A girl we knew had seen what was going on outside, and she ran into the Seaport and called down to the Exotic Lounge. It did not take long for this fight to be over after the cavalry arrived. Twenty against two were their kind of odds, and they still were not doing very well. Twenty against five was way out of their league. They began to disperse like cockroaches when you turned the lights on. We chased them a little ways, thumped a couple more in the parking lot, and then went back down Sylvania Avenue to the Exotic. We got a big laugh out of the whole thing.

When several Detroit brothers came down the next day to party, I told them the story of the night before. They felt these losers needed to learn a lesson once and for all, Outlaw style. We decided eleven of us would go back there incognito. The six out-of-town brothers would go in first and spread out inside the bar. One even grabbed a hatchet from my garage to cut the phone lines in the bar. He never got the chance. The moment I walked in, they called the police. The cowards at the Seaport were so paranoid; they had warned the cops there may be trouble with us in the near future. Toledo's Finest got there fast, averting the rumble before it could begin. The biggest disappointment of the night was that my hatchet was ditched when the cops showed up. I had had it since I was a Boy Scout. I wonder what they thought when they found it. When the bouncer realized how many of us were actually in there, he quit his job, and we never had any more trouble in there again. In fact, it got downright boring even to go there. The Exotic Lounge and the Seaport Inn were on the north side of town, closer to the old Crescent Raceway clubhouse than to Hawley Street. We still regularly made the rounds there, as well as the Raceway Lounge on LaGrange Street, but what we really needed were some places to go on the South End, where the clubhouse was now. Heading west down Western Avenue a little ways past Libby High School was a bar called KO's Lounge. KO as in "knockout," I assumed. The temptation was too great. We had to check it out.

It turned out to be owned by the father of an elementary school classmate of mine. John Swing was his name. He was a ten-year-old kid, new to the school, and he stuck up for me on the playground one time in the fifth grade. I never forgot it. I took that heavily into consideration when I found out it was his dad's place, and I told the fellas we would try to respect the bar itself, although we were not going to take any guff from the locals. We were not going in looking for trouble, but we weren't backing down if trouble came.

153

Trouble always came. There were times when I wondered if I had some sort of magnetic field that attracted pseudo-tough guys. Some of them actually were pretty tough. One of the local South End bad boys knew early on that his reputation was eventually going to be seriously tested. One snowy, winter night he had just enough to drink to make it sooner rather than later. I had made a point not to allow myself to get too inebriated at KO's until we knew "who was who in the zoo." This fellow was a pretty good-sized boy and supposedly had some martial arts training. As I saw him getting closer and closer to the point where I knew he was going to go for it, I positioned myself between him and the brother he was heading for. I intercepted him and suggested we step outside so as not to tear up the bar. Normally, that was the least of my concerns, but we wanted to make this place our local bar since it was so close to the clubhouse, plus I wanted to respect John's dad.

As I stepped out the door with him behind me, I saw the sidewalk covered in fresh snow, which would make footing a challenge. Yes, I walked out the door with my back to him. It proved to him and everyone else in the place that I was not the least bit afraid of him. I think it unnerved him a bit too. Besides, Ranger One was right behind him, armed and dangerous, to cover my back. I was bold, but I wasn't stupid. I looked up and down the sidewalk and found a bare spot of concrete where water had been dripping off the roof all day, melting the snow. It was not frozen yet, so I made my way over to it and planted myself squarely on the only dry spot within sight. I put my dukes up, and he did the same. It did not take much of a "fake" before he lost his footing, and I crossed with a solid right to his left eye. He went down. He slipped as he was getting up, and I tagged him again. The fight was over, and he knew it. Was he overpowered? Not really, but he was definitely outmaneuvered.

Handling that local tough guy that way, one on one, earned us respect on that end of town. Bike club members too often had the reputation of ganging up on their victims and "putting the boots" to them. No one respects that. Some clubs may have been feared because of that tactic, but they were not respected. Respect is better than fear any day. It was an absolute necessity that our members be respected when they were alone, because we often were. When you have a reputation of being fair on the street, you stand a lot better chance of getting some help from the local citizenry if you need it. This was better than having the locals happy you are finally getting what you'd been dishing out.

Another death took us back to Florida early in the spring of 1980. Though it was a funeral, we had a lot more fun as full-patch members than we did as prospectives. I knew there would inevitably be run-ins for us as new guys with some other members, especially in light of the fact that every get-together, except for "church," our official mandatory meetings, involved drinking and getting high.

It did not mean anything, though. Rough guys play rough, but it was generally all in good fun. We were brothers. An Outlaw was an Outlaw, whether he had been in the club thirty days or thirty years.

After we had laid our departed brother to rest, a large group of us ended up at the clubhouse in Tampa. As a chapter, they had a reputation for being extremely violent. They even had a patch made up that they wore on their colors that read "Tampa Bay Crunch Bunch," after the Tampa Bay Buccaneers' hard-hitting linebackers. About forty of us were milling around the yard one sunny afternoon, when a guy pedaled his three wheeled vending cycle up in front of the gate. He was a weird-looking character who appeared to be a couple of bricks shy of a full load. Turns out he was selling crab cakes and would occasionally stop by, especially when there was a crowd of out-of-towners around as there were on this particular day. His crab cakes were a dollar apiece; all the Yankees were eagerly buying them up, myself included. I noted the guy who was selling them seemed to have a wild look in his eye. During the tourist season, when the hotels on Busch Boulevard were packed, he would make up a huge batch of his crab cakes and sell them to his unsuspecting victims. When he saw the large gathering at the clubhouse, he made his way over and sold all he had to the big, bad bikers. When I heard about him being busted for selling crab cakes made out of cat food, I remembered that wild look in his eye. This crazy guy had thirty or forty of the meanest men on the planet paying him, and thanking him, for supplying them with cat food. Talk about laughing all the way to the bank.

Though 1980 was a great year as Toledo's first patch members of the American Outlaw Association, it ended tragically with the murder of one of our best. With all the good times, there was always the reality of constant danger. We got a rude awakening that cold, winter night in late November. I'll never forget Kato and I turning into the alley behind our clubhouse and seeing Ralph sprawled out in the gravel. He had passed us less than a minute before, roaring under the tunnel on Hawley Street, only to be gunned down by a rival club's bullets. The murderer most likely was hoping for a chance to kill me simply because I was the boss. The theory was simple. Cut off the head and the body dies. As painful as it was to lose a great brother that way, the intent of shaking our resolve failed. We were more determined than ever to go on, especially after the enormous turnout for his funeral.

Within days of Ralph's funeral, we got a call that Big Red had been shot and killed in an altercation at a bar in South Florida. Big Red was a longtime member and had even held the position of national president at some point in the early '70s. Hundreds of Outlaws were on their way home from Toledo, but their destination changed to Fort Lauderdale to bury this highly respected brother. The funeral went well enough. There was a humongous crowd. Brothers who did not come to Toledo came to

Lauderdale to pay respect to Big Red. Many other clubs, some from as far away as Illinois and Ohio, came to honor him too. Rightfully so. Big Red had been a good brother for a long time, and he had been highly supportive of the formation of the Toledo and Oklahoma chapters. He would be sorely missed.

The Florida Department of Law Enforcement seized the opportunity to crash the party the day after the funeral. Seeing as how it was December, many of the guys were not in any big hurry to head back to snow country. Hundreds were still hanging around when the helicopters could be heard approaching the Southwest Fortieth Street clubhouse just before dark. Soon the street filled up with police cars. Even firefighters were on the scene, placing huge floodlights on the roof of the clubhouse to illuminate the yard. Dogs were brought in and used to locate weapons and drugs. One of our Pennsylvania crews gathered their handguns and placed them above the rear differential of the U-Haul truck they rented in which to bring their bikes down. The theory was that the greasy undercarriage of the truck would sufficiently disguise the smell of gunpowder and throw the dogs off. It actually worked. A few brothers made it out over the back fence or simply were not there at the time, but the police did succeed in herding over a hundred brothers into the backyard of the clubhouse. There they began the long process of trying to photograph and identify each member. They hoped, of course, to detect any who might have an outstanding warrant.

Kato and I were sitting in the back of my old Ford van we had come down in, trailering our bikes behind it. We were parked about four houses down from the clubhouse when the police cruisers began to pull up, so we tucked ourselves into the rear of our van, locked the doors, and tightly closed all the curtains. As we peeked out, we saw a lot of law enforcement officers converging on the CH. All the while the police helicopters were overhead with their spotlights, occasionally lighting the area around where we were. We thought we were going to slide after about half an hour until a car pulled just beyond where we were holed up. The cops immediately surrounded the occupants, and after determining they were indeed friends of the club, escorted them into the backyard as well.

Several officers remained standing outside our van. Noticing our Ohio license plate, they decided to investigate further by beating on the back of van to see if anyone was in it. Naturally, we did not respond. Again, I thought we might skate until suddenly a powerful light was held up to the window. It shined right through the thick black curtains and lit the inside of that van up like daytime. The next thing we heard was, "Open up. We see you in there." I opened the door, pretending not to know what was going on. "What's the problem, Officer? We were just taking a little nap before going back in to party." They didn't buy it. The officer said, "Party's over."

As Kato and I were marched into the improvised holding area behind the swimming pool, we could see we were in good company. There were many Outlaws rounded up back there. Some were giving the cops a very hard time, demanding the opportunity to summon their attorneys. The police were extremely nervous. One rookie cop was visibly trembling at the verbal abuse he was getting. He actually ejected a twelve-gauge round out of his riot pump into the pool.

Some of the officers were manning a makeshift identification processing point, busily taking pictures and checking IDs, while others were intently scrutinizing the motorcycles. Of the several hundred bikes there, they decided forty or so had questionable vehicle identification numbers and called for trucks to take them away. Now it was not funny anymore, especially for Kato. His rigid-frame, 88-ci Shovelhead stroker was impounded. I was with Kato when he bought that engine and transmission brand-new from the Harley dealer in Wauseon, Ohio. That bike was as legal as any police car there that night, but it did not matter. It was all just a harassment maneuver anyway. It took over a year to get all but a couple of those bikes back. For Kato, it involved several expensive trips to Florida for court proceedings, and over $700 in storage fees, just to get his own motorcycle back after it was determined there was nothing wrong with it. To make matters worse, Kato and many of the others who had had their bikes confiscated needed to buy or build another motorcycle. The club had rules. Just because the law impounds your scooter does not mean you don't have to be running by update like everyone else.

On a more positive note, Big Red's funeral did give me a chance to spend some time with Hambone. He had moved to Orlando earlier that year, and we did not see each other as much as we did when he lived in Ohio. It was good to talk to him, especially in light of Ralph's recent death. Since it was winter up North anyway and my bike was in good running order, he suggested I come to Orlando and cool out for a while. I thought it was a great idea. Soon after taking everybody home to Toledo, I loaded my Shovelhead onto my trailer, hitched it to my Camaro, and was ready to leave winter in the rear-view mirror. I left Jay in charge and told him I expected to see everyone in March in Daytona. Termite jumped at the opportunity to go with me, so we loaded his bike next to mine and headed south again.

It never ceased to amaze me how relatively simple it was to go from the dead of winter to the summerlike riding conditions of central Florida. Hambone lived a half block off the infamous Orange Blossom Trail, so we located his house easily. He was glad to see us, helped us unload our scooters, and gave us keys to the place. Then the party was on. Out came the Jack Daniel's, the marijuana, the 'ludes, and the coke. Whiskey and reefer were okay with me, but I never was partial to barbiturates.

I had seen what they did to others, and I was afraid to ever lower my guard that far. Cocaine, on the other hand, was new to me. It was way too expensive up North, and up until this time anyway, was not the party drug of choice. I was willing to try it, primarily because I could control the amount ingested, or so I thought, unlike a pill where you never knew how far it was going to take you. Besides, coke was not a depressant. Like speed, it wired you up. There seemed to be an almost unlimited supply down there in Florida in those days. Between the cocaine and the whiskey, my mind was able to think of other things besides losing Ralph.

While soaking in the hospitality of the Sunshine State with Hambone, I got a chance to party with the Orlando chapter quite a bit. One afternoon, Termite asked me if he could borrow my Camaro, so he and one of the Orlando brothers could run over to Tampa. Now this car, even though it was just a car, was special to me. I bought it without an engine at a very good price and made it a restoration project. For years I had various pick-up trucks, vans, even a couple of nice Cadillacs and Lincolns, but they were all for their functionality. This Z 28 was the first cage I had taken any real interest in since I bought my Harley five years before. Its function was to be fun, and after dropping a beefed-up 350 in it, it fulfilled its purpose. Against my better judgment—and I was doing many things against my better judgment that trip—I let them borrow it. Termite had promised to be back the next afternoon and, sure enough, he was . . . only without my car. I was given some lame story about how they had a problem with it, but that I would get it back in a couple of days. I did, too, but not in the condition I lent it. Not that it had been wrecked, dented, or even scratched. It just was not that beautiful Chevy competition orange any more. It was not beautiful anything anymore—it was grey primer. In addition, when I got it back, the front license plate was in the trunk, and I was advised to back it into the driveway for a week or so and leave it there. I did not even ask. I did not want to know. I just did as was suggested. So much for having a nice-looking hot rod.

While I was staying down there with Hambone, I lost another possession in which I took pride and from which I got a lot of enjoyment. Hicks had acquired a pit bull somewhere along the way, and he kept this dog at the Crescent Raceway clubhouse. This dog was a ball to have around the place. He was short, almost as wide as he was tall, with a big head and rippling with muscles from stem to stern. His name was Bo Diddley, and he would hang on a chunk of motorcycle tire attached to a huge spring suspended from the A-frame I used to lower the motor into my Camaro. He could hang there for at least half an hour, and if you yelled, "Shake it up, Bo," he would growl and violently shake the whole frame. He was a neat dog, and when he got another of Hicks' pit bulls pregnant, I put my order in for a male puppy. Boy, did I ever get one! There were two males in the litter, and Kato got the other one. Both were the spitting image of their daddy in size, build, and temperament. Since we were Mongols at the time, I named my pup Genghis Khan.

I had a lot of fun with Khan, as I called him. He would run around the yard in the spring and trap bees in his cavernous mouth until they stung him, then he would shake his head and go find another. He was a terror on cats, and soon none of the ghetto felines would dare enter the clubhouse grounds—not while Khan was out anyway. He did not play well with other animals, and I will never forget the day one of the guard dogs from outside the perimeter got loose and into the yard. It was a Doberman/Chow mix and it attacked my year-old puppy. It did not take long for Khan's breeding to kick in, and he soon had that junkyard dog, which was twice his weight and three times his age, on its back with his jaws locked around its throat. I hollered at him to let go, but he just looked up at me apologetically, as if to say, "Sorry, this is what I do." One of the guys came out of the clubhouse with a pool cue, and I pried Khan's jaws apart to release the mutt he had on the brink of suffocation. I was never into dog fighting myself and did my best to keep Khan from such situations, but to be honest, I was proud of him that day. After all, he was the victim. He had been attacked. I did not feel the least bit remorseful that he won. Neither did he.

I was sad when the phone call came that he had died. The fellas at home knew he meant a lot to me, so they called to ask me what I wanted them to do with him. Usually dead dogs ended up down by the railroad tracks or in a dumpster somewhere. I did not want that for Genghis Khan. In a sentimental moment, I told them to keep him on ice until I found how much it would cost to get him stuffed; that way I could continue to enjoy him. Since it was the dead of winter in Ohio, preserving the old boy was easy. They put him in a plastic bag and laid him in an old bathtub in the yard. It was not long before he was encased in solid ice. My research revealed that I was not going to be able to afford to stuff Khan, so I decided that when I got home I would defrost him, cut his humongous head off and keep his skull. By the time I finally returned North, he had thawed and refrozen several times and was currently in a state of severe rigor mortis, not to mention, he stunk. In spite of all my best intentions to immortalize my little bull dog, I ended up burying him under my bedroom window at 38 North Hawley Street. Life goes on. There would be other dogs.

Chapter 10

Ride to Live, Live to Ride

*Ashes to ashes, dust to dust. If it wasn't for Outlaws,
the fast lane would rust.*

As important as brotherhood was—and as much fun as we had partying, fighting, and freaking people out with our outrageous behavior—the thing that brought us together in the first place was riding our motorcycles. I remember Taco and I leading a pack of well over one hundred bikes west on Interstate 40 between Nashville and Memphis, Tennessee, for a national run in 1984. When I looked back over my shoulder and saw Harley-Davidsons stretching back as far as I could see, it sent chills down my spine. I thought, *How could life get any better than this?* I'd been in long packs before, but they were usually funeral processions if they were this big, winding slowly and ceremoniously through whatever city we happened to be in, heading for another graveyard. This pack was on an interstate highway, averaging seventy miles per hour, and I was up front—Taco on the left, me on the right. It was exhilarating, to say the least.

Most people cannot comprehend the bond that can exist between man and machine. It doesn't necessarily have to be a motorcycle, but it was for me. For me, that love affair involved riding the machine that I had spent hours and hours designing, fabricating, and assembling, not to mention proving, testing, and trusting. One summer while in Tampa, I decided to put my rigid-frame Shovelhead to a test. It was the Fourth of July, and, as several of the fellows were discussing where we should go for the best party and fireworks, I began packing up my gear. In answer to their inquisitive gazes, I announced I was going home to Toledo. Immediately, a couple of brothers volunteered to ride along, but I told them I would be going alone. When they asked me why, my response was, "Just to do it." I wanted to get out there on the open highway with the machine I had built, and I did. I rode 460 miles the first day, experiencing some battery problems near Warner Robbins, Georgia, when I stopped to fuel. I got a jump-start, hit the road, and rolled in to the Atlanta clubhouse that evening in time to have a few drinks with Sidecar, the chapter boss.

Several of the brothers there thought I was nuts riding alone that far, colors flying, but Sidecar understood why I was doing it. He was a fellow Brother Bike Tramp (BBT), and probably the most dedicated rider I'd ever met. He rode a thousand miles, by himself, from Oklahoma City to Toledo for Ralph's funeral in December, with much of the trip in bone-chilling rain. Not only that, but he also was the only one who rode in from over 150 miles away. Everyone, except for the Detroit and Dayton chapters, understandably trucked their bikes in for the winter funeral. Sidecar was a true one-percenter in every sense of the word, and the epitome of a BBT. The next morning a Detroit Outlaw named Speed gave me forty dollars to buy a new battery, and I was on my way. I rode the remaining 670 miles to the Toledo clubhouse with no problems. Yes, there was a great sense of accomplishment.

On another occasion, Kato and I left the Orlando clubhouse together, headed for Atlanta. It was a beautiful day for a ride. Kato and I had ridden literally thousands of miles together. We were well accustomed to each other's riding habits. We crossed the Georgia state line, approaching Valdosta, when Kato revved his engine to get my attention. He pointed over to the east side of the highway to the KOA campground. It was the very campground where we rendezvoused for the Run to the Sun back in 1978—the run that eventually led to us meeting the Outlaws MC in the first place.

Just south of Tifton, Georgia, we passed a carload of college girls heading home from spring break. They waved and honked. We slowed a bit, downshifted and roared up the road. We were in our element: colors flying, wind in our hair, profiling to the max, and enjoying the attention. About an hour later, a sudden thunderstorm broke out, and before we could find an overpass to pull under to break out our leathers and bandanas, we were drenched to the bone. We weren't profiling down the road now, trying to impress anybody. The faster you go in the rain, the more it hurts, like needles on the face and arms. We were doing all we could to just to see the highway in front of us and to keep going. No point in pulling over and just standing along the side of the road in the rain; we needed an exit or an overpass. Don't you know that while we were hunkered down, hands over our faces, that same carload of girls caught up with us. I looked over at Kato and we both straightened up and tried to pretend the rain didn't bother us, but we must have been a sight—anything but macho. They weren't honking and waving now. They were laughing at us. I can't blame them.

No matter how long you've been riding, how experienced you are, or how sound your machine is, riding a motorcycle is dangerous. Potential hazards can come from any direction at any time. Loose gravel or sand on the road is generally no big deal in a car. It can be devastating on a scooter, however. Cage drivers give little consideration to the little black spots of oil at many stoplights, or in front of tollbooths, but they can spell havoc to a motorcycle rider. Caution is needed when letting the clutch out when those conditions exist. Rain takes on a completely new meaning on a bike. No rolling up the windows and turning on the wipers. Not only can it be painful but also hazardous because visibility is greatly hindered. Those oil spots I mentioned only get worse in the rain. Whereas cars experience fender benders, that's not so for bikes, where the riders' limbs are exposed and unprotected. As important as correct footwear and leathers are, they do little to prevent injury when it comes to a collision with a car or some other immovable object. I've seen injuries ranging from severe road rash and multiple broken bones to amputations and a severed spine in my years on the back of my beloved Harley. Things happen so quickly. Caution is always required. Attention is always necessary.

When Hicks went to prison and I became the Toledo boss, I made Jay my vice president. After all, he had held the office before he went to Arizona. Jay was a longtime friend, an excellent Harley mechanic, and an accomplished rider. He even taught his wife to ride. Lana weighed about ninety pounds and could handle a full dresser better than some men I've met. I'll never forget the night Jay got so drunk in the Waterville bar that he had to have her ride him home. We told him he had to take his colors off lest anyone see him being chauffeured by a female. This was back in the day when women rode on the back. Things have changed.

As potentially perilous as motorcycles can be on a good day, they are a thousand times more treacherous if the operator is under the influence. Sadly, this was the cause of far more tragedies, including deaths, than little old ladies pulling out in front of us. Jay turned out to be a perfect example. Late one night, roaring down Western Avenue heading toward the clubhouse, Jay had a terrible accident that literally changed his life forever. A Toledo street department crew had used a backhoe to cut a trench all the way across the road at the intersection of Spencer Street and Western Avenue. Since no city road crew ever finished any job they started in one day, they left a gaping hole in the street. In all fairness, they did place their backhoe across the entire street, boom extended.

That worked well enough for everyone except Jay Buck. On this particular morning, as in 3:00 a.m., Jay was just high enough, just drunk enough, and going just fast enough that he did not get stopped before slamming into the bucket of that back hoe. The road had been perfectly clear earlier in the day, and he took it for granted it would be clear that night, just as you or I would. Acknowledging that any problem on a motorcycle can be deadly, adding dope and liquor to the mix is insane, yet we still did it often. It's a wonder any of us survived for that aspect alone, let alone all the other potential dangers of "the life."

That backhoe did not give an inch when Jay broadsided it in an attempt to lay his bike down. He literally tore his right leg off just below the knee. Only skin and ligaments kept it attached to the rest of his body. It's a miracle he didn't bleed to death, and it's a miracle Lana wasn't on the back. She would surely have been killed. I marveled that the doctors even considered trying to save his leg.

They were experimenting with a new method called a Hoffmann Device. It consisted of a cage around his leg with pins going right in through the skin and screwed into the bones. It looked like an old-fashioned television antennae. It hurt me just to look at it. The contraption seemed so fragile, as if even the slightest bump would damage it, let alone send waves of intense pain to the wearer. After all, we did not lead a fragile existence.

As I said, this changed Jay's life forever. His rehabilitation went on for many months. His progress was severely hindered by his insistence on drinking constantly, though I'm sure it must have helped him with the pain. His drinking problem eventually cost him his wife, his position as vice president, and, finally, his membership in the club he loved so much. It was a sad finale for a man who loved his motorcycles, loved the brotherhood, and would give you the shirt off his back. Jay was one of the best brothers I ever knew. At the risk of getting preachy here, let me stress this point again. Motorcycles are dangerous on a good day, let alone when you add anything that will hinder your ability to be alert and on your toes. It's not worth it. Don't drink and operate a motorcycle. Don't get high and operate a motorcycle. If you had seen as much carnage as I have, if you had buried as many people as I have, you would understand my adamancy on this issue. Don't do it. It is *stupid* and *dangerous.*

In June 1982, an Ohio man was indicted for murdering Ralph. A *Toledo Blade* newspaper article said murdering an enemy of the club was part of his initiation into the Cleveland chapter of the Hells Angels Motorcycle Club. Whether that was true or not, I honestly could not tell you. I was never a member of the Hells Angels. I was an Outlaw. I can tell you this: murdering a Hells Angel member, or anybody else for that matter, was never part of any initiation rite to becoming a member of the Outlaws Motorcycle Club. To become an Outlaw, you had to prove your love for bikin' and brotherhood.

His trial was scheduled to take place in Toledo, and the weeks preceding it found Hells Angels coming into town to get ready for the high profile media event. One of our members answered the door at the clubhouse one day to find an officer of the court there to serve subpoenas on Kato and me. Since Kato and I found Ralph the night he was murdered, the prosecutor intended to use us as witnesses on the government's behalf. Neither of us had any intention of being used by anybody against another club for any reason. When the subpoenas came, Kato was in Florida, and I was on my way to Las Vegas. Neither of us was ever served and neither of us was anywhere near Toledo when that trial came down. When the trial was over, their guy was acquitted, and they left town.

Somewhere Hambone got the idea it would be fun to get married in Vegas, so he planned a four or five week trip out there and asked me to go with him.

He knew I would. Hambone was a riding fool. He had two scooters, so one was always ready to go. I think he originally intended to ride his swing-arm Shovelhead until I commented that of the five of us going, only I, the Toledo representative for this adventure, would be riding a rigid frame. He wasn't about to concede those kind of bragging rights to another chapter boss and chose to ride his rigid Shovel chopper too. Three other Dayton Outlaws made the trip with us. We left Dayton and headed south toward Nashville in order to get on Interstate 40. One of the Nashville brothers had recently suffered a tragic accident with some explosives, so we wanted to stop by the clubhouse there to see him. In spite of losing his hands and his vision, his spirit was incredible. We stayed and partied with him and the Nashville chapter for a few days, then set out, westward bound. On the way out of town, we were stopped by Nashville's Finest, motorcycle version. They were not very cordial, to say the least. They acted more like a gang than we did. After being detained (harassed) for over two hours, I began to wonder if we were even going to make it out of Davidson County that night.

We finally got going and had an uneventful two-hundred-mile ride to the Memphis clubhouse, where we partied a few more days. As you can see, we were not in much of a hurry. There was no better way to get to know your brothers than going to where they lived and hanging out for a while. Every chapter was always eager to show off their city, from the tourist attractions right down to the nightlife.

When it was time to head west from Memphis, we didn't have another clubhouse until we made it to Oklahoma City. We got an early start and put in a long day, arriving there after dark. They were anxious to show us a good time for several reasons. They were far off the beaten path, five hundred miles from the closest Outlaw chapter. Their clubhouse didn't get near as many visitors as Toledo, for example, which was situated at the crossroads of two main interstate highways. We had visitors from Chicago, Detroit, Youngstown, and Warren on a regular basis. Brothers from the South heading to Detroit would always spend some time with us. The Outlaw Nation had been courting the remnant of the Dirt and Grime MC in Sandusky, Ohio, and the Chosen Few MC in Buffalo, New York, so we were able to see those guys regularly as well.

Oklahoma City, on the other hand, was in the middle of nowhere as far as our Nation was concerned. They were on the outer edge of our territory, or perhaps better said, the leading edge of our westward expansion. Either way, they didn't get near as many brothers stopping through as most chapters did. They were gracious hosts and went out of their way to show us a good time. To me, this was what being an Outlaw was all about. Riding state to state, city to city, chapter to chapter, partying, and enjoying the camaraderie of others who loved the same things you did. You never had to worry about where to sleep, or where you were going to get your next meal. If your bike was broken down, someone always knew someone or some way to get it fixed. We took care of each other. We were brothers.

We hung out in OKC for a week, and then headed into uncharted territory—that is, beyond the boundaries of the Outlaw Nation. Taco was apprehensive about this trip for two reasons: We would be a long way from help if we needed it, but more importantly, we were heading deep into territory of some clubs that didn't like us at all. Hambone's heart was set on this adventure, and I was very excited about it too, so Taco did not object too much. He could have shut it down, but he knew that out of all his men, Hambone and I could take care of ourselves as good as any, and better than most. Besides, three other brothers accompanied us. There would be no backup truck, so we carried some basic tools, and the two of us who were not convicted felons carried several pistols apiece in case there was trouble.

It was the ride of a lifetime, and we thoroughly enjoyed every mile of it. Hambone had the smallest gas tank of the five of us and could only go about eighty-five miles before it was bone dry. When his scooter would begin to spit and sputter, he would lower his left passenger peg, and I'd drift over and put my right foot on it. He would reach out and grab my fork tube, and the two of us would motor down the highway as a single unit to the next gas station. It was called "pegging," and we were very good at it. We could maintain highway speeds of sixty-five or seventy miles per hour for as long as it took to find a gas station. It was an ingenious method invented for the sake of getting a stranded brother off the interstate and to a place considered safe, or at least defendable. As I said, there were people out there who didn't like us very much.

As we traveled, we would stop at each state line, smoke a cigarette, take a couple swigs of Jack Daniel's, and get our picture taken under the welcome sign. One of us was worried about an old traffic warrant in Arizona, so at that state line, he dug deep into his saddlebags to reveal a driver's license bearing a different name and social security number. Just prior to entering Sin City, we had to cross the Hoover Dam. It was quite a sight. One of our number, a brother named Harley, had lost his right leg at the pelvis in a motorcycle accident some years previous and rode a stripped-down Shovelhead dresser with a side-hack frame attached: no sidecar, just the frame. He had a piece of plywood bolted to it, and that made it sort of a flatbed three-wheeler. It came in handy on this particular trip because he carried extra tools, oil, and a few spare parts. It became particularly convenient when the only parking anywhere near the elevator going down to the bottom of the dam was a handicap spot right on top. He pulled into it and so did the rest of us. There was plenty of room for our motorcycles alongside Harley's scooter.

The Dam security people went ballistic and tried to make us move because we didn't have handicap placards. Hambone started talking to them and found out one was a Vietnam Vet like he was, and before it was all over, not only did they let us park there, but they also promised to keep an eye on our bikes while we all took the tour. Hoover Dam was an incredible sight to see, one that I would highly recommend.

Casinos soon came into view as we rode up Highway 93, heading toward Vegas. We stopped at the very first one we saw. One of the guys, Shorty Rat, won fifty dollars in dimes on a slot machine. We were ready for the Strip more than ever after that. Harley knew a guy in a local bike club there, so the plan was to party with them that first night in town and play it by ear from there. To be kind, let's just say they weren't very impressive. By the next morning, we couldn't wait to get out of there. I'll never forget stopping in at a local greasy spoon on the way downtown and seeing people playing slot machines at eight in the morning.

Hambone had an old friend known as Car Lot, and he was flying into Las Vegas that day for Hambone's wedding. We called him that because he dealt in expensive cars for a living. I drove my first Maseratti when he picked me up at the Orlando airport one time. He always had some fancy car to drive. We were to rendezvous with him at Caesar's Palace and spend the next four days enjoying ourselves, all expenses paid. We arrived at the world-famous casino at the same time he was dropped off by an airport limousine. As we rode up on our Harleys, I will never forget the look on the valet parking attendant's face. Security started to protest, but Car Lot intercepted them, brandishing our reservations for three rooms there at the hotel. In Vegas, money talks, and soon the bellhops were loading their luggage carts with saddlebags, bedrolls, leather jackets, chaps, and helmets.

There was no way we were going to let anyone valet park our bikes for us, so they allowed us to ride them into the guarded lot ourselves. Once they were secure, we were ready to enter the casino and head to our rooms. We were escorted through the heart of Caesar's Palace with our colors on while several bellhops pushed carts with our "luggage." I saw a section of slot machines with a million-dollar payout. People were gambling everywhere, all the while being waited on by women taking free drink orders. As long as you were spending money, it didn't cost you to drink. I had never seen anything like this place, or this town, before in my life. As preoccupied as all the patrons of the casino were with trying their luck, most stopped to observe the motley crew of bikers in their midst. It was fun to see the look of astonishment on their faces.

We stowed our gear in lavish, pagan-Rome décor suites and anticipated an evening out on the town. We had already been in Las Vegas long enough to acquire some party supplies: namely, cocaine, marijuana, and

Sour Mash Tennessee whiskey. Before heading out onto the Strip to see the bright lights, we kicked back to relax and to reflect on our accomplishment. We had been on the road for several weeks and had stopped at all the clubhouses along the way. We were eleven hundred miles past the outer limits of the Outlaw Nation, with no backup truck and just a few handguns between the five of us. We were staying in suites in Caesar's Palace and did not have a care in the world, at least for the moment. It was a good day to be an Outlaw.

While we were in Vegas, we saw Hank Williams Jr. perform as well as several other shows, and we gambled some. Shorty Rat and Pud fancied themselves to be poker players and spent most of their time and money trying to beat the odds. They didn't. Hambone, Harley, and I mainly just stuck to playing the slot machines, drinking, and enjoying the sights. There was plenty to look at. Neither Hambone nor I were big gamblers. We were bike riders. The reason Las Vegas was chosen as the destination for this adventure rather than somewhere else was that Hambone got it in his head he wanted to marry his old lady at one of the chapels on the Strip.

There were plenty of wedding chapels in Las Vegas, and Clark County made it very easy to get a marriage license. Twenty-five bucks and you were on your way. We found a chapel across the street from a casino called Circus Circus that agreed to let us park our scooters on its outside patio so the ceremony could take place between them. Like I said, in Vegas, money talks. With our friend Car Lot footing most of the bills, it was easy for us to have it our way. The wedding was unique, at least as far as the chapel's owner was concerned. Hambone and his bride-to-be had special vows prepared wherein she promised to keep his Harley clean, his oil changed, and to make sure he always had spending money in his pocket. It was very touching. Yeah, right. The wedding was simply an excuse to party, for people who needed no excuse.

Finally, the day came for Car Lot to go back to the airport and for us to start on our way home. We were once again escorted by security through Caesar's Palace, wearing our colors, followed by the boys pushing the carts loaded with our gear. I guarantee we weren't the only ones who'd had a memorable four days on the Strip. No doubt, they breathed a sigh of relief as they saw "Charlie" leave their property and disappear into traffic. It had been a good stay. There had been no problems whatsoever. We made a deal with them, "You treat us right, and we'll treat you right." We kept our word. It was that simple. The stress we seemed to routinely generate was largely because most people do not realize that bikers rarely look for trouble. They don't need to. It usually finds them.

As we looked at the map to plan the trip home, there was no way not to notice that the Grand Canyon was only fifty miles off Interstate 40. We knew we had to go by there on our way east. We might have stopped on the way to Vegas except for our reservations. Now we had no time constraints at all. No need to hurry home, since a phone call revealed that the trial was still going on in Ohio. Taco made sure Toledo had plenty of "help" while the Hells Angels MC was maintaining a high profile in support of their man. I wasn't needed for anything, and I still had no intention of participating in any trial.

The Grand Canyon was magnificent. We enjoyed looking at it for a while, and then we enjoyed getting drunk at the little tavern there in Tusayan. The ride home went much like the ride out. Hambone still ran out of gas between exits a couple of times, and we had no motorcycle problems we weren't able to deal with ourselves. Once we got back within the boundaries of our Nation, we stopped at all our clubhouses again and told the brothers what they had missed. This is what it was all about . . . the freedom of the open road, the sense of pride that went with riding a machine that you had designed and built yourself, and the idea of having like-minded brothers all over the country who would welcome you in and go out of their way to make sure you had a good time. Life was good.

Cowboy 1‰er, Outlaws Motorcycle Club, 1990

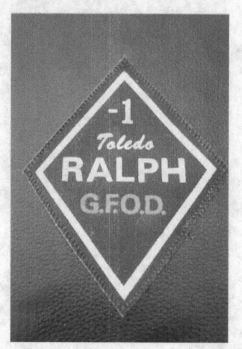

Ralph 1%er's memory patch,
Toledo Outlaws,
November 30, 1980

The official "God Forgives, Outlaws Don't" patch.
Another version included "July 4, 1999."

US Paratrooper, 1972. 19 years old.

The front end of my beloved Shovelhead. Notice the stepped lower legs.

My FXCH the day after I laid it down doing
about 85 miles per hour. April, 1975

My '75 Shovel with 1954 three-and-a-half-gallon Fat Bobs (my favorite)

The 1954 Pan chopper that led me to meet Jay Buck, May 1975

My first rigid: 1956 straight leg frame with 1960 Fat Bob tanks

Hobbit and me, Mongols MC, 1977

Taco 1%er with Mongols Porkchop and Hobbit, 1978

Arizona Run, 1978

Man Is Slain At Birthday Party

Stabbed During Fight With Motorcycle Gang

A Springfield Township man was stabbed fatally early Sunday in a fight that sheriff's deputies said erupted after about 20 members of a motorcycle gang were asked to leave the victim's birthday party.

Thomas Polaski, 26, of 7349 Hill Ave., died at 1:30 a.m. Sunday in Medical College Hospital of a stab wound that severed vital arteries in the right side of the neck, Dr. Harry Mignerey, county coroner, said. He ruled the death a homicide.

Lucas County sheriff's deputies have a warrant charging Wayne Hicks, 24, whose present address is unknown, with murder in connection with the stabbing. Hicks had not been located this morning, deputies said.

Robert Chromik, a Lucas County sheriff's detective, said that Mr. Polaski had been observing his birthday with a day-long party for about 140 neighbors and guests when members of a motorcycle gang showed up about midnight.

The uninvited gang members became unruly with some of the guests shortly after and were asked to leave, Mr. Chromik said.

One of the guests and a gang member got involved in a scuffle and Mr. Polaski was fighting with another man when he was stabbed, Mr. Chromik said.

Reprinted with permission of the *Blade* of Toledo, Ohio; July 1978

No Action Planned On Funeral Gunfire

Toledo police do not intend to act against members of a motorcycle gang who fired handguns into the air Saturday at graveside services in Forest Cemetery for a slain comrade.

The incident occurred during services for Ralph Tanner, 25, who was found shot to death Nov. 30 behind the clubhouse of the Toledo chapter of the Outlaws motorcycle gang in the unit block of North Hawley Street.

Discharging a firearm within the city constitutes a misdemeanor.

Deputy Police Chief Richard Kwiatkowski said Monday that no policemen were in the cemetery when the gang members fired the handguns.

He said that uniformed police crews who were in the vicinity of the cemetery as a precaution did not receive any complaints of unruly activity by the gang members, many of whom came from across the country to attend the service.

"Because their were no complaints from citizens, and we observed no illegal activity as far as we are concerned, the funeral was concluded without serious incident," the chief said.

Reprinted with permission of the *Blade* of Toledo, Ohio, December 1980

Reprinted with permission of the *Blade* of Toledo, Ohio, December 1980

Member Of Motorcycle Club Shot, Killed Near Group's Headquarters

A member of a Toledo motorcycle club was shot to death early Sunday while he was riding his motorcycle back to the group's clubhouse from a Western Avenue tavern.

Police said Ralph Tanner, 25, a member of the Outlaw motorcycle club, was riding about 2:45 a.m. in the alley behind the unit block of North Hawley Street, where the group's clubhouse is located.

Two other club members told police that they were following Mr. Tanner back from the tavern, and that he turned into the alley ahead of them. When they reached the alley they said that they found him lying on the ground, and signs that he had crashed into and been dragged along a fence. He was pronounced dead at the scene.

Dr. Harry Mignerey, county coroner, ruled the death homicide. He said Mr. Tanner has been shot twice, once in the right side of the back. There is some indication, Dr. Mignerey said, that the bullets may have been dipped in mercury to cause blood poisoning.

Mr. Tanner apparently was living in the group's clubhouse, 36 North Hawley St., a coroner's investigator said.

Motorcycle Gang Gives Slain Brother Special Rites

"God forgives. Outlaws don't!"

With that cry and a salute of handguns, members of the Outlaws motorcycle gang lowered one of their slain brothers into the ground Saturday morning.

More than 250 members of the nationwide gang came to Toledo to pay their respects to Ralph Tanner, 25, who was shot to death behind the Toledo chapter's clubhouse Nov. 30. The death has been ruled a homicide, but no one has been arrested.

The motorcyclists huddled outside on the steps and inside the lobby of the H.H. Birkenkamp Mortuary on Broadway during the short funeral service.

"What I've seen here today is something I've never experienced in my 23 years in the ministry — it's something I've only read about," the Rev. Frederick Matchinski said during the service.

"What I see is an expression of love and brotherhood and care," he said.

As Mr. Matchinski spoke, members of the gang and Mr. Tanner's family stared at the open coffin that was draped with a swastika-imprinted dark red flag. Surrounding the coffin were displays of carnations painted black. A leather hat hung from the coffin lid, and the club's skull insignia rested against the satin interior.

Brass knuckles, belt buckles, rings, and other mementoes left by fellow gang members — including an emblem one man tore from his leather vest after the service — were tucked around the body.

"You brothers in your way have given to your brother the token of things most important to you," Mr. Matchinski said. "What I am giving is the word of God."

Escort Of Motorcycles

Pallbearers dressed in the club's "colors" of blue jeans and leather vests or jackets carried the coffin to the waiting hearse, then climbed onto their motorcycles to escort the body and the family to Forest Cemetery in North Toledo.

A line of cars, trucks, vans, and 50 motorcycles snaked down the city streets. When the entourage reached the cemetery, gang members took control.

Two motorcyclists rôde up to the grave, supporting Mr. Tanner's riderless bike between them.

"There ain't much more you can say about Ralph that hasn't already been said," one said at the gravesite.

With that short speech, many of the cyclists drew handguns and fired them into the air.

Coffin Lowered Into Ground

The coffin was lowered into the ground after the spent shell casings were thrown into the grave, and a cemetery worker sealed the vault.

The gang members threw flowers atop the coffin and shoveled dirt into the grave until it was filled.

"They don't want to leave until they know he's all right," one family member whispered to another.

With the dirt packed onto the grave, gang members jumped onto their bikes and into their cars and roared out of the cemetery.

A lone man walked up to the grave, kickstarted a gray motorcycle parked nearby, and sped off. The bike was Mr. Tanner's.

Reprinted with permission of the *Blade* of Toledo, Ohio, December 1980

Vegas Crew: left to right, Harley 1‰er, Pud 1‰er,
Shorty Rat 1‰er, Me, Hambone 1‰er.

Hambone and me, Vegas Run, 1982

One sweet rigid Shovelhead, Las Vegas bound, 1982

Wally 1%er and I about to cross the Mackinaw Bridge
in the rain, Great Northern Nut Pack, 1983.

Loading up three blown-up Shovelheads,
Great Northern Nut Pack, 1983

AOA Louisville clubhouse, 1984

Taco 1%er arriving at Hawley Street clubhouse, 1984

Left to right: me, Taco 1%er (Detroit), Bear 1%er (Dayton)

Partyin' at the Louisville clubhouse, 1981. Left to right: Little Wolf 1%er (OKC), Samson 1%er (Dayton), Hambone 1%er (Dayton), Cowboy 1%er (Toledo), Kato 1%er (Toledo).

The "Big Five" bosses in the late '80s: Myself (East), Mikey 1%er (South), Taco 1%er (National President, Detroit), Wayne Hicks (Florida), Grease Lightning 1%er (Midwest).

My daughter Rachel (10 months old) and me
at Big Moe's funeral, Aug 1990

Ridin' high, 1990

Genghis Khan and me, Hawley Street clubhouse

Self-portrait at 45 miles-per-hour, Sturgis, 1990

1984 FXRS basket case I inherited when Hambone was murdered

NAME:	SPURGEON, David Charles
ALIASES:	PUGH, David E. SLINGER, Samuel G. SCHMIDT, Fred SPURLINGTON, Dan
STREET NAME:	COWBOY
ADDRESS:	1419 Broom Lane Dayton, Ohio
PHYSICAL DESCRIPTION:	Caucasian; male; DPOB: 02/10/53, Tennessee; 5'10"; 230 lbs; brown hair; blue eyes

COMMENTS:

Member of the Dayton, Ohio Chapter, OUTLAWS MOTORCYCLE CLUB.
SPURGEON is also a National Enforcer for the Club. He was
residing or may have been visiting the South Florida area in
early 1987 . He was acting as a bodyguard for National President
Harry BOWMAN at the Daytona Bike Week in March 1988. SPURGEON
was arrested on October 30, 1990 after 401 weapons and six ounces
of cocaine were seized from his residence. Also, $14,463 was
seized. Information obtained at the time indicated that SPURGEON
was the Northern Regional President of the OUTLAWS. SPURGEON
pleaded guilty to possession of a firearm during a drug
trafficking offense on January 9, 1991, sentencing was postponed
until November 1991 due to his wife being pregnant.

Self-explanatory

AO 93 (Rev. 5/85) Search Warrant ●

FILED
U.S. MAGISTRATE
OCT 29 1990
SOUTHERN DIST. OHI
WEST DIV. DAYTON

United States District Court

SOUTHERN _____ DISTRICT OF _____ OHIO

In the Matter of the Search of
(Name, address or brief description of person or property to be searched)

1419 BROOM LANE, DAYTON, OHIO
WHITE, 2 STORY, WOOD FRAME DUPLEX,
EAST SIDE OF DUPLEX, #1419 APPEAR ON
THE WALL ADJACENT TO THE DOOR

SEARCH WARRANT

CASE NUMBER: M-3-90-169

TO: S.A. Lary Clendinen, BATF _____ and any Authorized Officer of the United States

Affidavit(s) having been made before me by _____ S.A. LARY CLENDINEN, BATF _____ who has reason to
                                                              Affiant

believe that ☐ on the person of or ☒ on the premises known as (name, description and/or location)

   1419 BROOM LANE, DAYTON, OHIO. as more fully described above.

in the _____ Southern _____ District of _____ Ohio _____ there is now
concealed a certain person or property, namely (describe the person or property)

Marijuana, drug paraphanalia, scales, apparatus used for growing and
processing marijuana, U.S. currency, drug records and receipts, firearms, and any and all other contraband.

I am satisfied that the affidavit(s) and any recorded testimony establish probable cause to believe that the person
or property so described is now concealed on the person or premises above-described and establish grounds for
the issuance of this warrant.

YOU ARE HEREBY COMMANDED to search on or before _____ November 7, 1990 _____
                                                                          Date

(not to exceed 10 days) the person or place named above for the person or property specified, serving this warrant
and making the search (in the daytime — 6:00 A.M. to 10:00 P.M.) (at anytime in the day or night as I find reasonable cause has been established) and if the person or property be found there to seize same, leaving a copy
of this warrant and receipt for the person or property taken, and prepare a written inventory of the person or prop-
erty seized and promptly return this warrant to _____ Michael R. Mey _____
                                                                          U.S. Judge or Magistrate
as required by law.

2:14 P.M. on 10/29/90 _____   at _____ Dayton, Ohio _____
Date and Time Issued   City and State

Michael R. Mey U.S. Magistrate   Michael R. M
Name and Title of Judicial Officer   Signature of Judicial Officer

Copy & Recd 11-08-90 -hand delivered

Search warrant of my residence issued to the Bureau
of Alcohol, Tobacco, and Firearms, 1990

FILED

NOV 26 1990

KENNETH J. MURPHY, Clerk
DAYTON, OHIO

IN THE UNITED STATES DISTRICT COURT
FOR THE SOUTHERN DISTRICT OF OHIO
WESTERN DIVISION

UNITED STATES OF AMERICA   :   CASE NO. CR 3 90 102

        V.   :

DAVID CHARLES SPURGEON   :   I N F O R M A T I O N
                                     18 U.S.C. § 924(c)(1)
                                     21 U.S.C. § 841(a)(1)

THE UNITED STATES ATTORNEY CHARGES THAT:

COUNT 1

On or about October 30, 1990, in the Southern District of Ohio, DAVID CHARLES SPURGEON, the defendant, did knowingly, intentionally and unlawfully possess cocaine, a Schedule II Controlled Substance, with intent to distribute.

In violation of 21 U.S.C. § 841(a)(1).

COUNT II

On or about October 30, 1990, in the Southern District of Ohio, DAVID CHARLES SPURGEON, the defendant, knowingly, intentionally and unlawfully used a firearm, to wit: a Colt Model M1911A1, U.S. Army Caliber .45 ACP semi-automatic pistol, serial number 835237, during and in relation to a drug trafficking crime for which he may be prosecuted in a court of the United States, that is: possession of cocaine, a Schedule II Controlled

United States of America v. David Charles Spurgeon

Hambone 1%er, Dayton Outlaws, headstone

AOA Dayton, Ohio clubhouse

Big Moe 1%er, Dayton Outlaws, headstone

Fat Louie 1%er, Dayton Outlaws, headstone

Spittin' image of cell #2, E-3-N, Montgomery County Jail, Dayton, OH

Dave Spurgeon, March 2013, El Capitan State Beach,
25 miles west of Santa Barbara, CA

Chapter 11

Honorable Mention

In the course of my years in the fast lane, there were so many experiences and adventures that there is no way I could accurately remember them all, let alone write about them. That said, this literary effort does attempt to document some of them from a decade and a half of bikin' and brotherhood. The following accounts stick out in my mind as worthy of elaboration, hence the chapter title.

The most memorable fight I was ever in took place on the infield of Churchill Downs during the 108th running of the world's most famous horse race, the Kentucky Derby. In the spring of 1982, several large packs of Outlaws were heading north on Interstate 65 on our way home from a national run in Tennessee. It made perfect sense to us to begin each year in the sunny South after a long winter up North. As the group I was leading reached the junction of I-65 and I-264 just south of downtown Louisville, Kentucky, I could see the on-ramp lined with police cars. No doubt, they were waiting for us. Soon they had us surrounded, and I gave the signal to pull over. They exited their cars with their guns drawn, giving commands to dismount slowly—then don't dismount—then dismount slowly again. I don't know why they were so nervous. We were the ones looking down the business end of their service pistols. I came to learn their superiors would really get them psyched up prior to any confrontation with bike clubs. Truth be known, we were more used to this kind of thing than they were. "Step away from the vehicle. Put your hands in the air!" was commonly heard throughout the course of any Outlaw's career.

Having no desire to be shot by a nervous rookie, I assured the female officer that we wouldn't be giving them any problems. I told the fellas to cooperate and tried to calm the cops down. It had started to sprinkle and when a couple of guys went by on Goldwings wearing bright yellow rain suits, I attempted to insert a little levity into the situation. I told the officers near me they had just missed our "war wagon." In answer to their questioning looks, I said, "All our guns were in the tour packs of those big Japanese dressers." They knew I was making fun of them because they also knew no self-respecting Outlaw would ever ride a Honda, let alone wear a bright yellow rain suit. As the cops intently scrutinized our machines looking for reasons to write citations, I made another grand effort to diffuse the tension of our predicament. I asked a petite lady cop if she would like to go for a ride after she got off work. That did not go over very well. It was obvious these folks took themselves way too seriously. It was also obvious they took themselves a lot more seriously than we took them. That just made them angrier. Oh well. I tried.

When asked for my club name, instead of answering "Cowboy," I responded with, "Buffalo Bill, never worked and never will." By now, one of the local news channels had arrived, so they quoted me saying that in the paper the next day. In the subsequent search of our possessions, three of our guys were discovered to have loaded firearms in their saddlebags and were arrested. Imagine that. I personally knew of at least three other handguns they missed. As they handcuffed them, I laughed and told the reporter, "I'll have them out by sundown." He also included that in the article, and we all got a laugh out of it. Actually, it was Friday afternoon, and I couldn't get a bond posted for them until sundown the following Monday. It sounded good in the press, though.

When I got the rest of my pack to the Louisville clubhouse, there were fifteen or twenty other out-of-towners already there, including Taco. It was April 30, the day before the famous Kentucky Derby. The Louisville chapter had gone several times and found out that the party atmosphere in the infield attracted over a hundred thousand good ole boys and girls every year. This year, about twenty of us decided to join in on the festivities with the local chapter.

The actual Kentucky Derby was the seventh race of the day. I placed my bet and headed out into the great expanse of people to enjoy the afternoon. I was close friends with Wally, president of the chapter in Buffalo, New York, so we hung out together all day. People were partying everywhere—drinking, smoking dope, and more. We made our way from one end of the infield to the other, taking a swig here and a toke there. The weather was beautiful, and just about everyone seemed to have a good attitude. Eventually, we found Taco and Kraut in the middle of the backstretch, anticipating the seventh race. They had made friends with an old, black man who had brought in a portable, battery-operated television. He had it tuned to the channel that was broadcasting the famous event, and the camera focused on the starting gate.

At the ringing of the loud bell, the announcer shouted, "And they're off!" as the horses bolted from their gates. The 108 Kentucky Derby was underway as the horses and their jockeys went into the first turn. We anticipated seeing them dash by us as we each cheered for the horse on whom we had placed our money. It was just about then that some stranger came running up to us, saying that some Outlaws were involved in a big fight by the flagpole in the center of the infield. The four of us bid farewell to our host with his portable TV and immediately made our way there. When we arrived, it was hard to tell there was a fight going on. What we did find was a bunch of rednecks kicking at something lying on the ground. A pair of feet shod with engineer boots stuck out of the melee, and we determined they must be connected to one of our guys. We waded into the mass and began pulling them off, punching them as we went. Sure enough, those boots had Outlaw feet in them. Actually, there were two of our men at the bottom of the pile, with ten or twelve guys all trying to put a boot to them while they were down. The tables turned quickly when the cavalry arrived.

During the course of that fight, the pack of horses had passed the backstretch where we had been and were racing toward the homestretch. It was as if all the people on the back fence decided to run across the infield toward the finish line, many passing right by the big fight at the flagpole. It didn't take very long for things to get way out of hand. I began to wonder if every jerk who had ever been whipped by a biker, or had his girlfriend stolen by one, took the opportunity to throw a punch at us as he ran by. I was pulled off my feet by my hair twice. Surrounded by men intent on trying to kick my brains out, I realized why some people hated bikers so much. Bike clubs have been known to gang up on their enemies much like what was happening to us this day. This was not a fun position in which to be. I was kicked in the face several times and still have a dent in my forehead from that day. I grabbed the work boot that had landed a solid blow to my right eye and gave it a hard twist with all my might. I could hear the cartilage ripping as its owner let out a bloodcurdling cry of pain I will never forget. Neither will he, I'll wager. His scream distracted his buddies just long enough for me to get up onto my feet and make everyone I could get my hands on regret he had come to the Derby that day.

I grabbed a guy by the shirt and was about to hammer him when he screamed, "Wait, I'm on your side." I yelled back, "Find my glasses," and pushed him away. I devoted my attention to those who wanted to try their luck with the bikers while they thought the odds might be in their favor. That guy returned with a pair of glasses, but they were Taco's, not mine. I stuffed them down my shirt and said, "These aren't mine. Keep looking."

I was beginning to wonder, *Where are all those cops we saw coming in?* This was turning out to be the longest fight of my life, and it wasn't letting up. At one point, my right knee went out, and I went down for a third time. When I got up, the pain from an old paratrooper injury was much worse than a couple of boots to the head. I glanced over at Taco. I will never forget the look in his eye. He was the fiercest fighter I'd ever seen, and I was glad he and I were on the same side.

I eventually got my glasses back and put them on just in time to see the Kentucky State Police surrounding us. They were dressed in riot-control helmets and carrying walnut walking sticks reminiscent of Sheriff Buford Pusser of *Walking Tall* fame. We were easy to identify as our opponents blended back into crowd, the ones who could walk, anyway. When things started to look really bad, out of nowhere people began telling the cops the fight wasn't our fault. It all started when a group of rednecks felt comfortable enough with the odds to give two of our guys a hard time, no doubt trying to impress their girlfriends. These idiots had no idea that two Outlaws would not back down just because the odds were six to one. To us, it would be better to lose a fight than to lose your honor. I was glad the police were listening to these folks, so I could catch my breath should there be a round two with them. I could hardly believe my ears when the KSP told us to leave the property immediately. They got no argument from us.

By now, the race was over. (My horse lost, by the way.) I gave Taco his glasses, and we began the long walk from the infield out to the parking lot, which included going through the tunnel that went under the racetrack. I was lagging behind to the extent that by the time we got into the tunnel, I could no longer even see Taco, Kraut, or Wally. I'm generally not a paranoid person. However, the combination of being surrounded by these people who looked exactly like the ones we'd just been fighting, being separated from my brothers, and being in extreme pain due to my knee, began to make me a little nervous. I knew if the fight started again in that tunnel, I would have no choice but to pull my knife in order to defend myself. I knew if that happened, this day would not finish well for me or whoever I tangled with.

I cannot express how glad I was to see Outlaw colors when I came out of the tunnel. Several Dayton brothers who weren't in the fight were diligently looking for stragglers. They found one. Me. They told me the word was someone had been cut pretty badly, and we needed to get out of there before the cops changed their minds. My right eye was swollen shut and had turned black and blue, so I had to borrow a pair of sunglasses to conceal my injury.

We left Churchill Downs that Saturday with me hobbling a bit, but I made sure I wasn't left behind again. We had been dropped off at the racetrack and had planned to call for a ride back, but that plan was scrapped. Everyone was on his own as we went into escape-and-evade mode. We walked several blocks down some side streets until we found a tavern, and by this time, I was ready for a double shot of Jack. One of the locals, noticing our colors, said he had just witnessed a big fight between a half dozen of our members and a whole bunch of others in the infield. I said, "Really? How did they do?" He said the Outlaws were clobbering them when the state police broke it up. With my eye throbbing and my knee aching, I couldn't help but swell up with pride when he said that. It turned out to be the most memorable fight of my life.

When I found out he had a pickup truck, I asked him if he'd like to give us a ride to the Outlaw clubhouse. His eyes lit up as he said he would be honored. We took our colors off and climbed into the back of his truck. As we drove past the track, I saw several ambulances there with lights flashing. Although I personally had no knowledge of anyone being stabbed, it didn't surprise me when it was confirmed. It got crazy in there very fast, and it was a miracle that more people were not hurt more seriously than they were.

When we got back to the clubhouse, we saw that some had not made it back yet. We waited, wondering if anyone had been arrested. Finally, Taco and Kraut showed up. They were the last two. We had all gotten away from Churchill Downs, making it safely back to the clubhouse. That did not mean the cops couldn't (or wouldn't) come there, but it would be harder to pick out the participants of the fight from among a hundred of us. There was a problem, though. Taco had been stabbed in the side with a broken bottle. Evidently, it had just happened when I spotted him earlier with that wild look in his eye. He had just knocked out the punk who had cut him. The wound was bleeding badly, and it looked horrible. He could not go to a hospital, though. We didn't know what all might have happened on the infield and couldn't risk being connected to a serious crime. As it turned out, nineteen of them were hospitalized for injuries ranging from dislocated knees to broken ribs to a broken jaw. Allegedly, one man was stuck by an Outlaw. He initially wanted to press charges, but later decided against it. Smart boy. By the way, none of us went to the hospital, injured or not.

I always carried a first-aid kit containing a sealed packet of surgical catgut. I had never sewed anyone up before, and I was not thrilled that Taco would be my first patient. With a bottle of Jack Daniel's as anesthesia, I proceeded to stitch up the jagged gash in his side. True to the traditional Old West manner, I poured whiskey on the injury, took a swig myself, and handed the bottle to the patient. By the time I was done, neither of us felt any pain. The wound actually looked worse than before, but at least it wasn't bleeding, and it never did get infected. Oh well; of such scars are war stories born. This scar was nothing compared to the one Taco received many years earlier when another punk nearly gutted him. I've been in many great fights, but the Derby of '82, no doubt, stands out above the rest.

As memorable as the Vegas Run was, I would have to say that the ride that sticks out in my mind the most was the one that earned the nickname "The Great Northern Nut Pack." Hobbit and I had helped move my parents back to Tennessee when dad retired in 1983. When we had unloaded their household goods at their new address and returned the truck and trailer to the local U-Haul dealer, he and I rode the 175 picturesque miles east to the Chattanooga clubhouse. There was a mandatory national run just a week away in Oshkosh, Wisconsin, so we hooked up with a couple of brothers heading up there. We stopped at the clubhouses in Nashville, Louisville, Indianapolis, and Chicago on the way, and at almost every chapter, someone would join us. By the time we arrived in Oshkosh, there were fifteen of us.

Although the National turned out to be a great success, it began with tragedy. I will never forget that July afternoon. We were returning to the club's party site. Bones was the last in a group of twelve of us, and an automobile crossed the center line just enough to push his left foot into the compensating sprocket. It never made sense to me to run an open primary; this is the reason why. If Bones would have had a primary cover on his '65 Pan, his foot no doubt would have been badly broken, probably crushed. That would have been bad enough, but the result of it coming into contact with the primary chain rotating at 1,500 rpm was comparable to putting it into a high-speed meat grinder. His foot was violently amputated before his bike even went down. His life was changed forever because the driver of a cage took her eyes off the road for just a moment. Bones was not doing anything wrong that day. It was a beautiful July afternoon. We were not speeding or riding foolishly. None of us were buzzed up. We were simply enjoying a beautiful afternoon ride. That was what bikin' and brotherhood was all about.

Here's how it is. Cars have fender benders, but not so with motorcycles. Although I have seen people survive unbelievable accidents with little or no injuries just as I did when I laid my Super Glide down back in 1975, I also know of a brother who died simply from hitting his head wrong in a low-speed incident. No one could believe it. A North Carolina brother once severed his spine when a wheelie he was attempting went bad. In any confrontation between a motorcycle and a car, the car always comes out on the better end of the deal. No matter how good a rider you are, it is always dangerous to ride in traffic, with people not paying attention, not able to see you, or talking on a cell phone. That is why, to this day, I always say "Be careful" to bikers anywhere I see them. If you are reading this and you are a motorcycle rider, *be careful*! You can be right in terms of who did what on the road but still come out the big loser.

Bones was carted off to a hospital in Oshkosh where the emergency room pumped him so full of pain medication that he was laughing when I showed up. He was so high he couldn't have cared less about having his foot chewed off. Before all the surgeries were over, he ended up with a stump below his knee just big enough to attach a "wooden leg," as I called it. The subsequent bout with pain medication and the problems they created were almost as bad as the damage the accident itself had caused. He survived, though. He got himself a fake leg, a pair of crutches, a side hack frame for his bike and continued to live life in the fast lane.

After the National was over, about thirty of us rode 135 miles north to the Menominee Indian Reservation. There the annual four-day Mole Lake Bluegrass Festival was going on. Some of our Milwaukee brothers had been up there in the past and said it was a great party. Since it was on an Indian reservation, it was a lot looser than a regular concert would be cop-wise. The Indians had their own police force, and from what I personally observed, it didn't look like they cared much about what you did, as long as you spent money. They even had slot machines at the little restaurants on the reservation. It was an ideal, tailor-made environment for a bunch of Outlaws. We made friends with some of the Indians, and a few of us left the festival grounds with them to get some insight into how federally subsidized reservation life really operated. These folks had learned to play the system for everything it was worth and were laughing all the way to the bank. This was 1983. I can only imagine how it is now for the many tribes cashing in on the white man by way of the casinos. The joke is on them, though. The abundance of wealth has enhanced the already severe drug and alcohol problem that exists on most reservations today.

The Bluegrass Festival attracted several thousand people who were all there to have a good time. For most, that meant getting drunk, getting high, and getting to know someone of the opposite sex. As with almost every run, my responsibility as a boss prevented me from getting too out of hand myself. At times, my affection for cocaine and Jack Daniel's did cause me to make horrendous judgment errors. Looking back, I am appalled at much of my own conduct while under the influence, and am amazed I am still alive.

Someone once said, "Necessity is the mother of invention." I've seen that come to pass on more than a few occasions. Once, when an Outlaw I knew extremely well needed some quick cash to make an eleven-hundred-mile trip north from Orlando, Florida, he went into a 7-Eleven convenience store, where he shoplifted a bottle of Tabasco sauce. He waited outside the side door of a popular club for a prime candidate to help him get the money he needed for the trip. Finally, a lone drunk stumbled out and got the neck of the hot sauce bottle stuck in his ribs. The next thing he heard was, "Ring, wallet, and watch. Nothing personal, but if you turn around, I'll kill ya." The drunk gave up all three and the brother made his trip home, laughing as he retold the incident.

One of the most hilarious scams I saw, though, was here at Mole Lake. We were hundreds of miles from any large city. People's stashes of dope never lasted as long as they hoped at events like this. The Indians made sure the beer and liquor kept flowing, at an exorbitant black market rate. By Saturday, the market for party supplies opened up and American ingenuity stepped in to address it. A couple of our men rode into the little town of Crandon, Wisconsin, and purchased several bottles of saccharin tablets and two washable magic markers. On Saturday afternoon, they took the yellow marker, colored a bottle full of the tablets yellow and placed them in a baggy. They went out among the crowd in front of the stage while Bill Monroe and other famous bluegrass greats were singing and playing, and they sold "acid" for three dollars a hit. What struck me as so comical was that their fingertips had also turned yellow from holding the little white pills while the ink soaked in to them. It didn't seem to matter to their customers a bit. They sold everything they had in the course of the evening. Early Sunday morning they were back at work, coloring the next batch blue. Same result, including blue fingertips this time. They sold almost all they had again, mostly to repeat customers from the night before! I personally heard a guy say it was the best acid he had ever had. I believed him too. He had a watermelon rind hollowed out and was wearing it on his head. He even had holes cut out for his ears. He looked like a cone head, stumbling around the place and trippin' his brains out on artificial sweetener and magic-marker ink.

As we were packing up to leave Monday morning, another guy came by and asked if there was any acid left for the road. The entrepreneur had about twenty "hits" left in a baggy he was just about to throw away, and he made the chump a deal. He would let them go for a dollar apiece if he bought them all. The dummy couldn't believe his good luck and he jumped on it.

The entire Outlaw Nation lay south of Wisconsin, and law enforcement was taking advantage of all our National traffic being funneled through Milwaukee and/or Chicago. Someone in our group had called the Milwaukee clubhouse and was told police were stopping groups of Outlaws at the city limits and down at the state line, doing the usual warrant checks and registration verifications. I suggested we head north to avoid the hassle and for the adventure of going somewhere new. To some, that sounded like a ridiculous suggestion. They were already farther north than they ever wanted to be, and had no intention of going any farther. They headed south from Mole Lake and got jacked up, just like they had been told they were going to be. Two were arrested on old warrants, one for carrying a concealed weapon. That never did make any sense to me. Some of us were a little short on imagination, I guess. To my way of thinking, that made it too easy for the police. Many in the law enforcement community actually liked the challenge of earning their salary, and I was all for letting them.

As I looked at the map, it appeared we could ride east to Iron Mountain, Michigan, into the Upper Peninsula, cross the Mackinaw Bridge, and drop down into Detroit from the north. By going this route, we would miss Milwaukee, the state line, and Chicago all at the same time. Personally, I was not worried about the police. I didn't have any warrants. My motivation for this plan was simple: it looked like a fun ride. I had no idea how interesting it would be until I realized eighteen of the guys wanted to go along. That did not even include the two Indians with whom we had made friends. One was a Sioux who had been hiding out in Wisconsin because of a federal warrant pertaining to the Wounded Knee protest of 1973 in South Dakota. The other was his buddy, a Menominee, and they both wanted to go along with us! They had an old van, so I told them as long as they acted right, they could tag along.

There was a Detroit Outlaw named Baby John doing triple life in the state correctional facility in Marquette, Michigan. Being locked up five hundred miles north of Detroit prevented him from getting many visitors. He had been up there a long time, and none of us from the Toledo chapter had ever met him. Kraut, the Detroit Outlaw who had rescued Hicks and me in Daytona five years before, suggested we try to get in to visit him. It was only fifty or sixty miles out of our way, so I said, "Why not?"

We had been on the road, sleeping on the ground, for several weeks by this time. On our best day, we ran a great risk of rejection for any prison visit, let alone how we looked now. We realized if we were even going to have a chance at getting in to see this brother, we were going to need a shower. We found a small motel that desperately needed some business and rented us most of their rooms. The saccharin money sure came in handy there. I had forgotten what a mattress felt like. The next morning we looked like a different crew, rested up, and spiffed up as much as possible. Even our Indian friends were willing to try to make the visit. Corry Two-Crows, our Sioux friend, had an ID that he felt would get him cleared, and he was willing to risk it. It did.

I have to hand it to the prison. They must have been sympathetic to the fact that most of their prisoners were far, far from home and received very few visits. They approved all twenty-one of us to visit with Baby John, including the Indians. He spent all day in the visitation room, and the guards let us in two and three at a time. Only Kraut actually knew him, but he was glad to see all of us, and we were glad to see him. It definitely gave them something to talk about for a while: the day nineteen Outlaws and two Indians came to visit.

Since we were all the way up in Marquette, it didn't seem right not to make the effort to see Lake Superior. It was not hard to find. It stretched out in front of us like an ocean. To commemorate this momentous occasion, we all lined up along the shore and urinated into the Great Lake. *So much for that. Time to hit the road.* Our Indian friends needed to head back to Wisconsin, so we bid them farewell and went our separate ways, never to hear of either of them again. That's the way life was: here today, gone tomorrow.

From Marquette, we headed southeast toward the bridge that would take us toward the Lower Peninsula and to Detroit. The Upper Peninsula is a desolate place in

August; I can't imagine what it was like in the winter. As we made our way down the two-lane roads through the vast forests, I thought of all the environmentalists who whine about cutting down trees. I can tell you from personal experience, there is no tree shortage in America . . . just a brain shortage. Places to eat were few and far between. We finally came to the little town of Manistique, which had a restaurant and a bar—just what the doctor ordered. It was quite a bit fancier (read: more expensive) than we were looking for, but it was the only game in town, and it was the only town for a long way. After riding the great expanse on top of Lake Michigan, some of the Southern brothers with us developed a craving for seafood. At the restaurant, they ordered shrimp, scallops, and the like, but were disappointed and complained that their ocean fare wasn't as fresh as they thought it would be, considering we were right on the water. I tried to explain to them that Lake Michigan was one of the Great Lakes, and that it was fresh water, not an ocean. I don't think they ever did get it.

Later that night, our Great Northern Nut Pack pulled in at a KOA campground just north of the Mackinaw Bridge. You can imagine the look on the faces of the vacationers when nineteen Harley-Davidsons rolled in, disrupting the tranquility of the otherwise perfect August evening. When I went into the office to arrange for us to sleep there, the apprehensive proprietor noticed the Toledo bottom rocker of my colors. He had graduated from the University of Toledo, so that broke the ice. I promised him if he could give us a primitive camping spot off to ourselves, none of my people would bother any of his campers. He agreed and even gave us a discounted rate. I made it very clear to our group that I had given my word we would be cool, and we were. We enjoyed the peace and quiet of a low-key campfire and a good night's sleep. Truth be known, we probably had a better night's sleep than anyone else in that campground.

The next morning we rode over the world famous Mackinaw Bridge in the pouring rain. We were three hundred miles from the Detroit clubhouse and very much looking forward to being back in familiar territory. The Great Northern Nut Pack, so called because everyone thought we were nuts to head north from Wisconsin, was supposed to disperse after arriving in Detroit. It had gone eight hundred miles together since the national gathering at Oshkosh, and some of us had been together since Chattanooga, almost three weeks before. However, it did not disperse in Detroit after all. When we arrived there, we got word that TJ, a Tampa brother, had died. He had some sort of stomach cancer for a while, and it finally killed him. He was a nice guy and a much-loved brother. We saddled up again the next day and headed to Gainesville, Florida, where the funeral would be later that week. We stopped at the clubhouses in Toledo, Dayton, Knoxville, and Atlanta on the way down.

The Great Northern Nut Pack should have broken up a second time after TJ's funeral, but it didn't there either. It seems an important meeting had been set up with the Devils Disciples MC in Birmingham, Alabama. At the funeral, the Southern region's boss asked for anyone who could make it to follow his crew up there. The GNNP decided to stay together and lend our support to that meeting. The Iron Cross MC in Columbus, Georgia, had been partying with our Atlanta and Jacksonville chapters during the course of the summer, so the entire group also stopped there on the way to Birmingham. Both of those clubs treated us like royalty. The Great Northern Nut Pack finally broke up in Alabama, with everyone going their own way in smaller groups. We rode 2,300 miles together in two and a half weeks. Hobbit and I had begun this ride in Lawrenceburg, Tennessee, and ended it there before having to load both our bikes due to major engine problems. For us, this adventure consisted of 3,400 miles in three and a half weeks. These were the glory days. This was riding—bikin' and brotherhood at its best.

Since we are talking memorable things in this chapter, in all fairness to man's best friend, I had better take the time to mention something about dogs. Bikers love dogs. I do not seem to be able to recall any who loved cats, except for big cats, like the African lion cub one of my friends had or the Bengal tiger one of the Dayton Outlaws kept in a pen behind his house. Those were the exceptions. I knew some who had snakes. That never made any sense to me. Many, on the other hand, owned and loved dogs. I'm not talking about little sissy dogs. I'm talking about cool dogs.

There is always an exception, and in this case it was a brother in the Warren, Ohio, chapter who had a poodle. He claimed it was his wife's, but who knows? During a meeting at his house one time, that poodle constantly ran from one window to the next, barking his fool head off at any and every activity going on outside. As much as I did not like that kind of dog, I took note that only an idiot would attempt to break in a house with a dog like that. The poodle couldn't do much, but the man it might wake up could have a shotgun. I kept that observation to myself, though, lest someone get the impression I liked poodles. Not hardly.

I had many dogs in my life, and most of them were worthless, but I had three that are worth mentioning. The first of the three was an incredible dog, the pit bull named Genghis Khan described in detail in chapter 9. During the summer after Khan died, I was able to acquire an incredible full-blooded, male German Shepherd to take his place. This three-year-old beauty was attack and obedience trained before I ever met him. He had been hired to provide security at a local massage parlor to protect the "ladies" should any of the late-night clients get out of hand. His name was Fritz, which was appropriate because this German dog only took commands in German. The problem for me was I did not speak German. Nevertheless, this magnificent animal fascinated me, and the wheels began to turn as to how to make him mine.

I made a point to befriend Fritz and helped the girls rehearse what to tell the owner and the police about how he had run away one night while being walked. On the morning I loaded him into the back of my Z 28, I was acutely aware that I had no real idea about how this 120-pound animal was going to act toward me outside of the massage parlor. I was leery of taking him to the clubhouse right away and exposing him to the variety of people who would all want to see him. I didn't want him to hurt anyone. In other words, I did not want to have to kill him if he did.

My parents lived out in the country, so I decided to take Fritz out to their place to let my dad work with him for a week or two. Dad grew up on a farm, and was good with animals. He had no problem with that. My mom, on the other hand, did not trust Fritz one bit. "You better take a pistol when you go out there, Joe," she would tell him. He never did. He wasn't afraid of any dog. He was not afraid of anything, as far as I recall.

I went out to my folks' place about a week later to check on Fritz. He was chained up in the back yard, just lying around looking pretty content. As I figured, Dad had no problem with him at all. As he went out and worked with him every night after work, he was very impressed with the animal's intelligence. He never asked me where I got him or what I paid for him. My parents were careful not to ask questions to which they might not want to know the answers. I always appreciated that about them. They loved me and made sure I knew it, even though they did not condone the lifestyle I chose to live.

I loaded Fritz back up in the Camaro and headed to the clubhouse. He fit right in. I chained him to a tree right outside the front door of 38 North Hawley Street, and he was a terrific guard dog for the next five years. He was a very protective and intimidating canine. One time I was summoned to Maggie Valley, North Carolina, for a gathering that required me to take a cage rather than my scooter. I had a beautiful 1968 Cadillac El Dorado at the time, and I took Fritz with me. At a gas station in Tennessee, a police officer began to get curious and started toward the car to check me out. As the officer got closer, I began to roll the window down and whispered, "Watch him, Fritz." He growled and lunged for the opening. The expression on that cop's face was priceless. I guarantee he had to change his BVDs before his wife let him in the house that night.

Fritz didn't just terrorize police officers and citizens; many brothers were afraid of him. Once in North Carolina, I parked along a dirt lane where we were partying, and I stretched out in the spacious trunk of my ghetto cruiser. Fritz was tied to the bumper and he would just lie there perfectly still, watching every one that walked by. A couple of brothers who'd had plenty to drink decided it would be funny to shut the lid on me. Bad decision. As soon as one of them touched that car, Fritz chomped down on his leg without so much as a bark. The scream from that Outlaw woke me up, and the expression on his face was unforgettable. Fritz let go when I told him to, and that brother limped away—threatening to kill my dog—while I laughed and laughed. Fritz was the coolest dog I had ever been around, let alone owned, and that's why he got mentioned in this book.

King was Fritz's replacement. He was a 130-pound rottweiler-shepherd mix that the Buffalo chapter was training to be one of their security dogs. At a party there the spring after Fritz died, I spotted this beauty on a chain out back. He was huge. He was built like a giant German Shepherd, with a thick coat, long tail, and ears that stood straight up. The similarities ended there, though. He was black as midnight, with a thick neck, and a rounded snout like a rott. When I met King, he was about sixteen months old and already weighed 110 pounds. He had a deep bark and was very aggressive. I fell in love with him immediately and spent a good part of the afternoon playing with him. His chain was attached to a cable, so there was a lot of room for him to run. I would taunt him to where he would lunge at me and then I would pull back, just out of his range. One time, I teased him so mercilessly, when he lunged, he stretched the cable about two feet farther than he had before. I needed to move farther to get out of his way, but I couldn't because of a table in my way. As I abruptly backed into it, the half pint of Jack Daniel's in my back pocket broke, cutting me there. To add insult to injury, King nailed me on the upper leg. I had successfully worked him up and when he finally got me, he drew blood. I was bleeding from both sides at once. The brothers standing around thought it was hilarious, and so did I. This was one cool dog, and I let it be known that I really liked him.

Later that year, the police raided the Buffalo clubhouse. This was not the normal knock-on-the-door-we-have-a-search-warrant type of raid. It was a tear-gas-through-the-windows-smash-the-door-down kind of raid. We were used to that stuff, but the landlord wasn't. When it was over, he wanted us out. Can't really blame him. The Feds messed it up pretty good. When Wally informed me of the eviction notice, he asked me if I wanted King. They no longer had a place for him and no one paid more attention to him than I did. I assured him King would have a welcome place with me. Wally showed up one Saturday night shortly thereafter at about 3:00 a.m. He asked me to come outside; he had something to show me. In the bed of his pickup truck was a very large doghouse. It was so big the opening of its doorway was about three inches higher than the tailgate. As I looked in, I could see two eyes looking back out at me. King never made a sound. He just stared at me. I remember thinking this dog was not nearly this big the last time I saw him.

Wally and I went in to have a few drinks while he caught me up on what was going on in Buffalo. I knew the time had come to reintroduce myself to this enormous canine, whose last memory of me was the taste of my blood. I went out alone and stood at the back of the truck to have a talk with King. I told him I respected him and would take good care of him. I promised him I would not break his spirit, but he needed to understand that I was going to be his master. If he could live with that, he would have a good home. If he decided to attack me when I opened that tailgate, I promised him I would kill him on the spot. With that being said, I dropped the tailgate and prepared for whatever might come out of that doghouse. He actually had to duck a little to come out the hole, and I could see he had filled out considerably since our last encounter. As he took a step towards the edge of the tailgate, I approached him, eye to eye. He knew I was not afraid of him, and he knew I was no threat to him. He just looked at me, and then he licked me on the face. He was a great dog for many years to come.

Chapter 12

Change of Command

In the forties, George Orwell wrote a science fiction novel titled *1984*. It described an unimaginable future world where totalitarianism really was total. It went into extravagant detail as to how many things would radically change by that date, which at the time, seemed to be in the very distant future. Although most of those things did not come to pass, looking back, I see that many did. Regardless, 1984 was a year of great change for the Outlaws Motorcycle Club and for me.

It began routinely enough with a national run in the South for New Year's Eve and the anticipation of the annual Daytona Beach Bike Week. It occurred the first week of March every year and coincided with the world famous Daytona 500 motorcycle race. I went to Bike Week more times than I can count but have yet to see the inside of the track. That just isn't why we went. Bike Week for us, and for many others, had nothing to do with the motorcycle races, and it wouldn't have mattered one bit if they weren't going on at all.

I was usually among the handful of brothers that didn't go home between the two nationals. We went south in late December, prepared to spend the rest of the winter in the Sunshine State. We left the New Year's Eve party in Atlanta this particular year and went on down to visit the Florida chapters. Tampa, Jacksonville, and Fort Lauderdale were in the height of their best riding seasons at that time of year. Our intention was to enjoy the beautiful weather before converging on Orlando in mid-February to get ready for Daytona.

Bike Week usually came and went without a lot of controversy. There was always the nickel-and-dime police harassment. The Daytona Beach Police Department knew Speed Week, Bike Week, and spring break created a large percentage of their city's annual budget. They really did not like the multitudes of people these events attracted, but they loved the millions of dollars their presence generated. The cops seemed to do a better job tolerating everyone else than they did us. It was painfully obvious there was no love between the Outlaws Motorcycle Club and Daytona's Finest.

There were always the fistfights that erupted when some of the wannabe bikers got a little too much liquor in them, or their girlfriends paid a little too much attention to one of the big, bad one-percenters. It happened all the time. Girls were fascinated by our mystique, but most had no business around us at all. We didn't play well with others. They were better off with their weekend-warrior boyfriends. Committed one-percenter old ladies were a tough crowd. They had to be. This life wasn't a hobby, a fad, or a game. It was life *and* death.

Daytona's Bike Week drew thousands of beautiful motorcycles from all over the country each year. Harley-Davidson would bring antique bikes down from the museum in York, Pennsylvania, and set up a beautiful display at the Holiday Inn. Storefront businesses that normally plied their trade as bakeries, bikini boutiques, and beach-accessory joints would vacate their properties, charging an exorbitant amount of money to rent their establishments out for the weeklong festivities. I watched coffee shops become temporary tattoo parlors and souvenir shops transform into motorcycle-accessory retail outlets overnight. If you didn't know better, you'd think Daytona Beach, Florida, was biker paradise—and for one week a year, it was.

Very early on in the course of the Ohio Mongols partying with the Outlaws, we were visited by an extremely prominent Outlaw who went by the name of Stairway Harry. He was a Chicago Outlaw and the National President of the entire organization. I marveled that he found the time, or had the interest, to stop by our little club in Toledo. What I was unable to conceive at the time was the importance of the location of Toledo, Ohio, not only because of its strategic position at the intersection of several major interstate highways, but also due to its optimal proximity to the rest of the Outlaw Nation. I later wondered if that wasn't more important to the "politicos" of the club than picking up a handful of new brothers. I'm glad I didn't know anything about the political aspect of national clubs back then. Then again, had I known, perhaps I would have been spared a lot of misery in the years to come.

Stairway had been the National boss for some time when he and I met in 1978, and he was still the boss in March 1984. We didn't have campaigns or elections. We didn't claim to be a democracy. If you had a job, you did it as long as you could do it better than anyone else could. Obviously, if you were indicted or went on the run, you couldn't do your job. If you became a victim of the drugs or liquor that flowed so freely among us, and weren't able to keep the best interests of the club as your top priority, you couldn't do your job. Someone else was always more than ready to step up to the plate.

By the spring of '84, it became apparent that Stairway's health was beginning to interfere with his ability to run the organization, so discussion began at the national level about a change of command. The obvious candidates from whom a successor would come were the men who were already national vice presidents. There were four in the United States. Sidecar of Atlanta was the regional boss of the Southern states. He definitely had the experience and the reputation required for the job. He was highly respected, and his love of bikin' and brotherhood was never doubted, but he didn't have a political bone in his body. He became regional boss solely because of his unquestionable dedication to the club. He could be trusted because the good of the organization, and his willingness to help a brother, was his only agenda.

The regional boss of Florida was a former Airborne Ranger who had served in Vietnam named Wild Bill. Florida was a region all to itself, consisting of only four chapters at the time. They generally were larger in number than the average-sized chapter in the rest of the Outlaw Nation because many brothers from the North moved down there for the extended riding season and the opportunities to make money. Florida was the gate through which a large percentage of illegal drugs entered this country, and there were plenty of ambitious entrepreneurs willing to try their hand at the business. Wild Bill was a good brother but, like Sidecar, had no political aspirations whatsoever. His brothers, his bike, and his freedom were the most important things to him.

Grease Lightning, on the other hand, would have loved to become national boss. He had been a loyal Outlaw for years and got his name because he was a motorcycle drag racer who had actually competed successfully on the national circuit. He was as fast as greased lightning on the strip, and I saw him race many times. He ran the region that included Illinois, Indiana, and Wisconsin and was the boss of the mother chapter. Chicago had been the home chapter for every national president for as long as anyone could remember. Grease Lightning figured that would give him an edge in the candidacy to take Stairway Harry's place at the helm of one of the world's largest motorcycle clubs.

Last, but certainly not least, was my boss. When I met Taco he had just come out of prison and was the vice president of the Detroit Outlaws. He became the Detroit boss when Lenny went on the run over a RICO indictment in the early '80s. That made him the leader of the largest and most powerful region of the Outlaw Nation. His responsibility included Michigan, Ohio, Kentucky, Pennsylvania, and New York, consisting of nine chapters. Since he was the boss of the region in which I was a member, he was my choice, without a doubt. Others may have been able to do a good job, but I felt Taco was the best choice. He was dedicated, proven, and virtually fearless. He was an outstanding regional boss, and many of us felt he was a natural for national leader.

This, of course, presented a bit of a problem. He wasn't a Chicago Outlaw. Tradition was strong in this area, and some were concerned division would result if any attempt was made to move the National Headquarters from the Windy City to the Motor City. When all was said and done, though, Taco was unanimously agreed upon to best lead the American Outlaw Association. The suggestion that he move his membership to Chicago was immediately rejected. Though Taco was completely comfortable in Chi-town and spent much time there, his heart was in Detroit. Taco officially became the National president in June 1984.

Taco recommended a Detroit Outlaw by the name of Gypsy to take his place as president of the Detroit chapter, and the brothers there agreed. His former position as regional boss now needed to be filled. The presidents who were considered qualified for the position included Hambone of Dayton, Max of Youngstown, and me. None of the three of us had any political aspirations either, so there was no competition for the office. What was best for the club was what all of us wanted. Though I was the youngest of the three, both in physical age and time in the club, the job fell to me. Personally, I always felt Hambone was undoubtedly the most qualified, but he wanted no part of it. He was interested in riding and having a good time and did not want the extra headaches that the position afforded. Looking back, I understand that better now than I did then. I considered it a great honor to be chosen, though I was somewhat overwhelmed by the responsibility. I had just turned thirty-one years old, having been a member and chapter boss for only four and a half years. Many of the men who had taught me the ropes had been in the club for at least ten years longer than I had, and now I was to be their boss.

I recommended Kato take my place as Toledo chapter president. The chapter unanimously agreed. It wouldn't have been unanimous had Wayne Hicks still been a member there, for two reasons. First, Kato was his kid brother. Having his little brother in charge would not have been acceptable to him. The real reason Hicks would have protested fervently was he wanted to be the boss himself. Toledo had become an Outlaw chapter while he was prison for murdering Tom Polaski. He had been the charter president of the Mongols, so I knew he intended to take over again when he got out. I made it very clear to him and the rest of the chapter that I would never be under his authority again. Don't get me wrong. I didn't feel like I had to be in charge, but Wayne Hicks was never going to be my boss again. Period. Once he knew he would never get past me in his quest for power, he began to look for a place to go where he could work his way into a leadership position again.

When he finished his parole, he got permission from Taco to move his membership to Fort Lauderdale. I was more than happy to see him go. Because of the RICO heat from the Racketeer Influenced and Corrupt Organization Act bearing down heavily on the Florida boys, it didn't take him long to con his way into becoming the boss of the South Florida chapter. He had leadership experience from the Mongols, and he was highly motivated. He was a smooth talker, to be sure. Problem was, brotherhood was never his main agenda. To him, brotherhood was simply a means to an end. Wayne Hicks was always his main agenda.

Taco had already been my boss for several years, so our relationship didn't really change much when he became national president, and I became one of his VPs. We were already accustomed to working together, whether tending to club business or just enjoying the open road together. Soon after this historical change of command, we got an invitation from a mutual friend to spend Fourth of July week with him at a resort in Kentucky. Car Lot brought his boat up from Florida to Lake Cumberland for the holiday. He put it in the water at the Connelly Bottom Marina and parked his motor home in the adjoining campground. He fit right in with the normal clientele of this vacation oasis, but that wasn't the case for Taco and me. You should have seen the looks on the faces of the high-class campers when we rolled in on our very loud choppers. It was a riot. In the midst of the expensive, recreational vehicles, we bungee-corded my army poncho between our scooters and unrolled our sleeping bags underneath. Talk about lowering the value of the neighborhood. Their disdain was apparent as they watched the tattooed bikers heading down to the marina where they docked all their fancy boats.

One boat stuck out like a sore thumb among all the others. It wasn't a pontoon boat, or a bass boat, or even a swanky, decked-out house boat. It was a long, low, offshore ocean racer known as a cigarette boat. She was twenty-eight feet long and powered by a huge Chevrolet V8. The best thing about this boat was that it was ours for the week. Car Lot had towed it up from Miami, and we looked forward to taking advantage of it. For some reason, the attitude of the snooty crowd changed toward us when they saw us climb aboard. It couldn't have had anything to do with the fact that this Pantera was the most expensive boat at the marina, could it?

We definitely had everyone's attention when she fired up. As that built 454 engine came to life, flames shot out from the headers. The deep rumble echoed throughout the cove. It wasn't a Harley, but it sure sounded good. I idled her out of the no-wake zone, anticipating letting her loose. As I gave it full throttle, the front end lifted up so high that I had to stand up just to see where I was going. When she planed out, we were flat-out moving. We flew up and down the entire coastline of Lake Cumberland exploring coves and taking turns behind the wheel. Taco came up with the bright idea to water ski behind this powerful boat. Car Lot was all for it, and he had everything necessary. He and Taco both knew how to water ski. On the other hand, I did not. I was a biker. I had been a paratrooper. I was raised in Northern Ohio's farm country by a carpenter. When would I have ever been around boats, or water, for that matter? When I was a kid, Lake Erie was so polluted you didn't dare go in it to swim. The game fish were gone. Once famous for walleye and perch, it had become the home of nothing but carp, garbage, and bacteria. The standing joke was this: "How many square feet are there in Lake Erie?" The answer was, "Always room for two more," referring to the greatest value the polluted body of water had: disposing of the dead bodies of disgruntled mafia associates, via cement shoes.

I didn't mind the idea of them water skiing. It obviously made me the designated driver, and this boat was fun to drive. Taco was snatched up out the water effortlessly, skiing like a pro. I tried to figure out when he'd learned to do that, growing up in Detroit. Anyway, he sure made it look easy, as did Car Lot when it was his turn. Although I was more than happy to be the boat captain with no desire to water ski, they talked me into trying it. As I said, they made it look easy. It turned out that it wasn't easy for me.

I got into position as they told me to and then gave Taco the signal to accelerate. As he did, slowly at first, I'd just about thought I was actually going to get up on those skis before having my arms almost ripped off. Sounds like fun, doesn't it? Here I was, this longhaired, bearded, tattooed biker being dragged around this lake on his face. After I finally let go, they circled me as I floated there in the life vest, Taco offering me a hand to get back in the boat. I wouldn't take it, of course. I couldn't accept the fact that I could not do something as simple as water ski. After twenty-one failed attempts, I finally made it up! No one, including me at that point, could believe it. People on other boats cheered as Taco steered our vessel out of the cove into the open water of Lake Cumberland. It was a blast once I finally got the hang of it.

It turned out to be a very relaxing week, far from the fast lane we normally lived in. From there, as Taco and I rode south, the road took us to a place called Ruskin Cave, about eleven miles northwest of Dickson, Tennessee. The property that included the historic cave was then the home of David Allen Coe, the country music songwriter and singer. David was once a member of the Nashville Outlaw chapter, so all the old-timers like Taco knew him before he was a big star.

David had recently bought Ruskin Cave and the beautiful surrounding Tennessee countryside. There was an old farmhouse on the property, but the main attraction was a fabulous rock house David had built for himself, though he was rarely ever there. Also under construction were apartments intended for use by David's future harem. He was going through a Mormon kick at the time, intending to get himself about ten young wives to all live there peacefully together while he was on the road performing and looking for more young wives. Yeah, right. I've found out through the years that you can talk yourself into just about anything if you want it bad enough, regardless of common sense. I don't know how any of that panned out. The last time I stopped by Ruskin Cave, the apartments were still empty.

The caretaker of the property was a good guy named Roger. One day Roger and Taco took a trip into Dickson, but I stayed back to ride Roger's Honda three-wheeler around on the surrounding trails. David always had extra guys hanging around, and when I came out of the woods this particular afternoon, one of them challenged me to a moonshine drinking contest. The premise was this: he was a Southerner and I was a Yankee, and everybody knows no Yankee can keep up with a Southerner when it comes to drinking white lightning. Everybody knows that, right?

This particular batch wasn't like the moonshine I'd had before. It was kind of yellowish and didn't taste as smooth, but it didn't matter. We weren't drinking for enjoyment. If we had, I would have been drinking Jack Daniels Tennessee Sour Mash Whiskey. This was a contest, North versus South. We sat facing each other on the front porch of the old structure they called the "band house." A gallon jug sat between us on a small wire spool table. The rules were simple: we would each take a swig until one of us passed out. People have drunk themselves to death doing this kind of thing, but neither of us was thinking about that at the time. I won the toss to go first, so I took a pull and then passed the jug to him. This went on and on, and we were both starting to get pretty tipsy. After an hour or so, he confessed, in his best Southern drawl, that he was actually from Galion, Ohio. Soon after that, he turned aside and started puking his guts out right on the porch. I gave him a minute and then asked him,

"Are ya done?" "No way, Yank" was his reply as he got back on his stool, wiping vomit from his beard.

We went on awhile longer, and he went to puking again. I asked him, "Are ya done yet?" His response was unintelligible this time, but he made way his back to the table one more time. Not for long, though. As his eyes started to roll back in his head, I knew he was done, whether he knew it or not. I said, "There's something you need to know before you pass out. It may say Toledo on my colors, but I was born in Lawrenceburg, Tennessee, you Yankee." With that, he fell off his chair into his own puke. That's where he was when Taco and Roger came home hours later. Me? I was sitting in David Allen Coe's personal rocking chair on the front porch of the rock house with what was left of that jug of moonshine in my hand, just smiling away.

David maintained a decent relationship with the club. He even had a Louisville Outlaw travel with him for many years as security. Several other big-name country stars had motorcycle club members as bodyguards as well. Waylon Jennings and Willie Nelson were known to employ Hells Angels MC members for this purpose. Such was the case when Willie did a concert with Coe in Dayton's Hara Arena in the mid-'80s. About twenty of us from various Ohio chapters were in Dayton for a party at the time, and we all went to the concert. The standing rule was that Outlaws and their old ladies got in backstage at David's concerts for free. At this particular concert with Willie Nelson, that meant that a full-patch Hells Angel would also be backstage. There was never a lack of tension between the two clubs, and this created the potential for a problem here. How big a problem would depend on how we handled it. I put the word out that we needed to remember that our Louisville brother would also be in the reverse situation in Angel towns. I also made it clear that we weren't going to party with the Angel, but we weren't going to interfere with him doing his job either. That all looks good on paper, but when you add whiskey and dope to any equation, you never really know for sure if things are going to work out the way you planned or not.

Fortunately, this time things did, and I was glad. We were celebrating our new Sandusky chapter getting their charter just weeks before in Milwaukee. I had sponsored them and spent a lot of time working with the former Dirt and Grime MC chapter, so I was especially proud of them. Their president, Pearl, a 450-pound gentle giant, was a very good friend of mine, and I was looking forward to introducing him to David Allen Coe personally.

David had been Willie Nelson's opening act that night and, after Willie finished his set, they were going to do a medley together for the grand finale. David was sitting in the right corner of the platform while Willie played his last number. As I approached the bottom of the stairs with Pearl, Willie's bodyguard stepped in front of the gate to prevent us from coming up. That was his job while Willie was up there. I understood that. I looked at him, as my brothers looked on to see what I was going to do, and I pointed to David Allen Coe. The Angel knew my reason for wanting on stage had nothing to do with Willie, so he stepped aside. I nodded to him as we made our way over to David so I could introduce Pearl. We had our backs to the audience in the dimly lit corner when suddenly I could feel the warmth of the main spotlight on us as it turned from Willie to where we were standing. Pearl's brand new shiny black and white Outlaw patch glistened brightly for the crowd to see. I glanced over at Willie, and I'll never forget the scowl of disgust on his face because we'd stolen his spotlight. These guys are unbelievably vain. I smiled and flipped him the traditional sign language to signify how sorry I was.

The last stop on our vacation road trip was my parents' home. They had known Taco for several years, and we would occasionally stop if we were passing through Lawrenceburg. My cousin was a dispatcher for the Tennessee State Highway Patrol, so on this particular occasion, when the call came in about two Outlaws with Ohio and Michigan license plates, she got on the microphone and announced, "That's my cousin David, and he's just coming home to see his momma. He's not here to cause any trouble."

Upon arriving at my folks' house, we learned that my ninety-seven-year-old grandmother was to undergo surgery at the end of the week. There was a possibility she wouldn't make it, so I told Taco I wanted to hang out there until after her operation and I'd catch up with him later. After we visited her in the nursing home, he told me he would be happy to stay too.

It was a busy week for my parents, so Taco and I tried to help as much as we could. One afternoon when Mom, Dad, and I came home from the hospital, Taco was on the deck with an apron on, cooking pork chops for my family. *If only all the people who feared him could see him now*, I thought. There was a side to him few ever knew, but I did. He was always very respectful and friendly to all my relatives. After Grandma came through her surgery with flying colors, Taco reserved box seats on the bull line at the local rodeo so my folks could enjoy a night away from the stress of all the medical issues. I'm not saying Taco was a saint or someone who didn't deserved to be feared, but I am saying he was a lot more human than some people tried to make him out to be.

After spending another week together in Alabama, Taco and I parted company. He was heading south, and I needed to deal with some things back up North. The club had developed an elaborate "Support Your Local Outlaws" campaign to aid in raising funds for our mounting legal bills. We emblazoned the slogan on T-shirts, ball caps, and rubber beer can coolers. Anything that would sell, we would make. Someone came up with the brainstorm of having the motto imprinted on butane lighters. That was a great idea because lighters don't last as long as T-shirts, and as they ran out of fuel, the need for a new one was created. Ingenious, right?

It turned out the most cost-effective place to have the lighters made was in Ontario, Canada. The cheaper we got them, the more profit for the club. The problem came when the first batch got taxed at the border before bringing them into the country. The duty tariff drove the price up to more than they would cost to be made here. Bad move. To make matters worse, we had twenty thousand of them already paid for, sitting in a brother's garage in Windsor.

It seemed obvious enough what needed to be done. The Detroit River is only about two thousand feet wide between downtown Detroit and Windsor, Ontario. With four thousand lighters per box, it wouldn't require a huge boat to bring them across, bypassing customs entirely. With all the smuggling of drugs and weapons that continually went on between the US and Canada, this seemed like a minor endeavor. The Detroit chapter had a friend who had access to a twin screw, twenty-eight-foot Wellcraft speedboat with a cuddy cabin. It was determined it would be large enough to transport the five boxes of lighters into Michigan. The Weather Channel was consulted, and a beautiful day was chosen. This friend, Tom, and an Outlaw headed down the Detroit River to the predetermined rendezvous point on the Windsor side. Our Canadian brother picked a fancy floating restaurant and met them there with a van full of Support Your Local Outlaws cigarette lighters.

It was necessary to disguise this clandestine endeavor by pretending to be meeting for lunch. The brother who went along couldn't even pronounce half the stuff on the menu, let alone know what the items were. That's how he got tricked into trying escargot the first time. After enjoying about three of them, he was informed he was eating snails. To be honest, he said they weren't too bad. It seems the right amount of Jack Daniels can make just about anything palatable. After the high dollar dining experience, they loaded the boxes into the small cabin of the boat to head back up the river.

Tom definitely knew what he was doing. He went by all the buoys on the correct side, yielding courteously to other vessels when it was appropriate. From what I was told, getting to the pick-up point was actually fun. When they began this adventure, the sky was blue and sunny, but as they headed back north past the Saint Clair Light, it became menacingly dark.

When the rain began, it wasn't too bad. After all, if you're going to freak out about getting a little wet, you shouldn't be on a boat in the first place. As it began to rain harder, it must have been similar to getting caught in rain on the interstate on a motorcycle. At seventy miles per hour, the water droplets feel like needles on your forehead and bare arms. So it did on this boat ride, though they weren't moving nearly that fast. It began to rain very, very hard. Slowing down lessened the discomfort a bit, but on the interstate you could eventually find an overpass to pull under to wait it out. Not so out there. The rain was coming down like cats and dogs, and the water was getting extremely rough.

Suddenly, a bolt of lightning struck the water about seventy-five yards off their starboard bow. That was neat to see and to hear, but it also alerted them to the fact that they were in a potentially very hazardous situation. They weren't worried about the boat sinking. It was just a boat, and it wasn't theirs anyway. They had life preservers. They knew they could float around long enough to be rescued. The part that made it dangerous was the fact that they were carrying twenty thousand butane cigarette lighters, and about sixty gallons of gasoline. If they were hit by lightning, they would explode like a Fourth of July fireworks celebration. As I was told this story, I pictured the twin 350 Chevy motors sinking to the bottom of Anchor Bay, while little pieces of plastic with Support Your Local Outlaws on them eventually littered the eastern shoreline. Tom did a good job of letting her drive until the storm subsided. On their way in, they saw a couple of boats whose captains hadn't done so well, and their vessels were being towed. Both had capsized in the waves. It's a good thing our crew stayed afloat and made it safely to shore. Twenty thousand cigarette lighters would have been difficult to explain to the Coast Guard.

Chapter 13

Adventures in Paradise

The 1983 RICO trial had successfully crippled the leadership structure of the club in the Florida region. Though relatively new to the Fort Lauderdale chapter, Hicks made it clear that he would be willing to take over. After all, he had started a club in Ohio that eventually became an Outlaw chapter, no thanks to him by the way. He convinced them his leadership experience might be just the ticket to help the famous chapter survive. What a crock. He was the most self-serving "brother" I ever met. He had his sights on the president's job there before he ever left Toledo. In fact, I don't doubt the unstable situation there helped him to choose to move to South Florida instead of somewhere else. Being the con artist that he was, it wasn't long before he was voted in as local chapter president. He thrived in South Florida. Fort Lauderdale, Pompano Beach, and West Palm Beach were full of go-go bars and dancing girls. He probably thought he had died and gone to heaven. Drugs were also plentiful, as was the money that accompanied them. He soon learned to take advantage of the girls and the dope dealers.

I came to Florida every year to help orchestrate the Bike Week Run. I had to be on my toes the entire time, always prepared to deal with the unexpected, so it wasn't a party for me like it was for most of the brothers. When it ended, I was ready to relax, do some partying, and some serious riding. It just made sense to stay down in Florida and wait out the month of March before going home. It was usually still pretty cold in Ohio in the early spring. My region's annual update was April 1st, and my presence wasn't required until our mandatory regional shakedown run the following weekend.

South Florida produced a new breed of characters during the mid-'80s that Hicks also learned to use to his advantage. Upon arrival at the clubhouse one afternoon after Bike Week, I saw the parking area had become home to some new "toys" that were not there when I had visited last. There was a beautiful Ranger bass boat, a shiny Ford F-150 pickup truck, and, most interesting to me, an airboat. "Where'd all this stuff come from?" I asked the brother who opened the gate for me. "Rock monsters" was his reply. Rock monsters? I had never heard of such a thing.

Florida was full of average nine-to-five citizens who worked hard all week, so they could collect fancy toys like these, then spend the weekends at the bars bragging about their success. Outlaws learned early on how to swindle these types out of their money, either by selling them dope or pretending to be their friends. Their kind existed everywhere, but Florida always seemed to have more than its share of just about everything, including fools.

Once these people discovered crack cocaine, things got out of control for them very quickly. Outlaws themselves were not allowed to do crack. It had fallen under the national bylaw against smoking cocaine, a statute instituted after some brothers got so successful at being drug dealers that they literally destroyed themselves freebasing. Did that completely stop it from happening? Of course not; we were Outlaws. Our very nature was to do the opposite of what we were told. However, the new ruling did have a major, positive impact on most of us, including me. Because of it, I never freebased coke, and I never even saw crack. I am glad. I did not need any more bad habits.

These rock monsters were prone to spend their hard-earned money quicker than normal once they were introduced to crack. By Saturday night, with their paychecks quickly running out, many of them suddenly became willing to part with some of their toys at incredibly low prices, oftentimes for little more than just enough to finish the weekend partying. If a brother had several thousand dollars on hand at the right time, he could literally make out like a bandit. Hicks had several dancing girls turning over their money to him, so he was able to jump on several such good deals as they came along. That is how he got the airboat. It was not a very fancy one, to be sure, but he got it for next to nothing. It had a V8, water-cooled, automobile motor rather than an air-cooled aircraft engine, which made it kind of cheesy, but who cared? We were bikers, not boaters. It was just for fun anyway, not for serious Everglade exploration.

I had never even seen an airboat up close before, let alone been on one, so I was eager to check it out. Hicks and I left early one morning to put it in the water at the Everglades Holiday Park, west of Lauderdale. He assured me that he had been out here before, so he knew what he was doing. I must admit, I was looking forward to this new adventure. I had my Colt .45 with me at all times back in those days, so I wasn't worried about running into any unsavory characters out there, man or beast. I did take note concerning a bit of advice an old Outlaw by the name of Wild Bill gave me. He said, "Don't get in the water for any reason. The moccasins are breeding this time of year, and you can't tell where the nests are." He knew of someone who found a nest the hard way: by being bitten several dozen times by baby cottonmouths. Needless to say, that person did not make it out of the swamp alive.

Hicks and I headed west on the Miami Canal before branching off into some areas with which he claimed to be familiar. I jumped at the chance to take the driver's perch high above the deck and navigate this strange contraption through the water trails amid the tall saw grass. I must say, it was a blast. There were several shacks built way out in the swamp that served as fishing cabins or fish camps. We stopped at one to give the boat, and us, a rest. It was incredibly quiet and peaceful out there once we turned off the deafening airboat. I could see why men liked to come out to this tranquil place, far from the rat race of everyday life.

It was at this camp that I noticed antifreeze leaking from the radiator. We let the motor cool down before topping it off with swamp water. We also decided to head back to civilization rather than risk getting stuck way out there in the middle of nowhere. This was before cell phones. We were fifty miles out in the Everglades and had not seen another human being for hours. I was relatively sure my AAA card was not going to be of any value whatsoever out there, so I was more than ready for us to start making our way back to solid, dry land. We went several miles before it became obvious that we were starting to lose power as the engine began to heat up. We shut her down to drift a while, allowing the engine to cool again, while at the same time pouring water on the radiator with an old antifreeze jug Hicks had on board the boat. It was going to take a long time to get home at this rate.

Once we got going again, Hicks decided to take a shortcut. Rather than follow the water trails, he cut directly across the saw grass with the motor wide open. His thinking was to save some time. It would not have been a bad idea had we been able to operate under full power. It wasn't long before we were stuck high on top of the thick, razor grass, almost completely out of the water. We were not able to move an inch, no matter what we did to shift the weight around, or gun the ailing motor. We needed a tow truck, or towboat, and it was obvious that neither would ever come.

Hicks said one of us was going to have to get off the boat and try to lift it up off the mound that held us captive. *One of us?* I thought. I knew I could drive the boat, but was he strong enough to lift it up enough to make any difference? We both knew he wasn't. I absolutely did not want to get into that water, especially after Wild Bill's warning, but I had no choice. Hicks let it cool down again so he could get the most power possible out of it. I eased over the side as he fired it up. The water was only about three feet deep, but then I sunk another foot in the muck at the bottom. I was able to lift that airboat up enough that it started moving off the grass, as Hicks gunned the motor. Then it hit me like a ton of bricks: once I freed the airboat, he wouldn't be able to come back for me. Looking back, and knowing what I know now, he wouldn't have even tried. As the boat began to pick up speed, I held on to the side, hoping I would not be dragged through a poisonous snake nest. I finally was able to throw my leg up onto the deck to pull myself aboard. If my name wouldn't have been Cowboy already, it deserved to be after that.

Hopefully heading back toward the Miami Canal, we were at least still several miles out. As it started to get dark, I noticed things were beginning to change, from the sound of the birds to the movement of the gators. The ones we had seen earlier in the day were sunning themselves on the banks, looking more like statues than predators. Gradually, as evening settled in and the sun made its way below the treetops, they became quite active. The whole day out in the swamp, we had seen maybe ten. Now I counted thirty alligators in the water in as many minutes. We were moving so slow we did not even bother them. They looked at us the way one looks at a menu at a steakhouse.

Occasionally, we would see a small plane overhead, and Hicks explained that drug dealers liked to drop their loads into the water to waiting airboats. I knew if we ran across any of them, there was going to be a shootout because we could not outrun anybody. He also told me the Drug Enforcement Agency patrolled by air to spot them. I would have gladly welcomed the assistance of a Fed cop boat about this time. I noticed Hicks had a citizen's band antennae clamped to the railing, so I asked him where the radio was. He kept it in a compartment under the deck, wrapped in plastic. It was for emergency use. As I looked at the gators watching us, I suggested we might be having one sooner than later. I carefully got the CB radio out, connected it to the battery, and hooked up the antennae. I was never successful in communicating with anyone, though, because I don't speak Spanish. Every single channel with any traffic at all was in Spanish. I accused Hicks of being such a cheapskate that he bought a Latin CB. I could not even pick up a Department of Natural Resources plane that flew over the canal several times.

To keep water in the radiator faster than it was leaking out, I would hold a gallon antifreeze jug off the side of the airboat, filling it with swamp water. Every time the engine sputtered and acted like it was going to stall, it seemed like more alligators would make their way into the canal. I knew exactly what they were thinking, *Look at these fools. Don't they know that when that boat stops, they are sitting ducks?* Yes, in fact I did know it. I was contemplating where to best place a .45-caliber ACP round to kill one of those things, knowing my two magazines were not going to be enough. I envisioned the next morning's headlines in the *Miami Herald,* "Two Men from Toledo, Ohio, Disappear in the Everglades." I thought to myself, *Is this the way it's going to end?" After three years in the army and ten in motorcycle clubs, am I going to be eaten alive by a lizard?* I knew exactly what everyone was going to say, "What in the world were they doing out there in the first place?" At least that's the question I was asking myself at the time.

The sun sank in the trees behind us as we headed east. As it got darker, the sounds of the 'Glades became more ominous. I heard a panther cry out in the distance once and could even hear monkeys chatter, though I never saw any. I realized the swamp was like the city. Things changed radically when the day turned into night. The peaceful gave way to the predator. In the city at night, we were at the top of the food chain, but not out here. We were helpless, possibly soon-to-be victims, like so many on the streets. I did not like the feeling at all.

Suddenly, I heard the unmistakable sound of a very powerful motor in the distance. My heart leaped within my chest! There was human life ahead! I did not care who they were. At this point, I would rather deal with Cuban dope dealers or federal agents than alligators. As we rounded a slight turn in the canal, there was a bass boat! The owner was gunning its huge Merc to get it up onto its trailer. We had made it back to a boat ramp. Beyond that, we could see Hicks' truck and trailer. I was never so glad to get my feet onto dry land as I was that day. I also never went back out there with Hicks again. Don't get me wrong; it was a blast until we had problems. Kind of like life. But I have always tried to learn from my mistakes. There was no way I would go back out there with an inexperienced operator, trusting my life to a piece of junk some rock monster had hocked to get enough money to buy more crack. I have come to find out people like that do not take very good care of their stuff. What am I saying? Simply this: When something looks too good to be true, it probably is.

Besides Bike Week and great riding weather, another highlight of heading to South Florida was going all the way down to Key West on Highway 1. It is as far south as you can go in the United States, and the ride through the Keys is beautiful. There are breathtaking stretches where the Atlantic Ocean is highly visible on your left, while the blue-green waters of the Gulf of Mexico are clearly seen to your right. The little towns along the way provided many opportunities to relax, fuel, eat, and of course, bar hop. Folks were generally very friendly, being acclimated to the tourist influx every year anyway.

A couple of ex-Florida Outlaws lived near Key West, so finding a place to roll out our sleeping bags was never a problem once we got down there. Duval Street provided plenty of nightlife, and one of my favorite hangouts was the famous Sloppy Joe's Bar on the corner of Greene and Duval. It attracted many visitors from across the country, as well as the rest of the world. Many folks were as fascinated to see a real Outlaw as they were any other aspect of the island paradise. That, of course, opened the door for us to allow them to buy us drinks. It didn't cost much to get there, it didn't cost anything to stay there, and it cost very little to party there. All in all, it was right up our alley, especially compared to the alternative of sitting around the clubhouse in Toledo, waiting for the snow to melt.

The problem with any island, though, is that after a week or so it starts to get a little claustrophobic. Key West was a nice place to visit, but eventually the need for wind in the hair dominated the enjoyment found under the bright lights of the quaint little village at the end of the highway. I enjoyed getting on the road to leave as much as I had enjoyed getting there.

The real thrill was the ride. The greatest excitement wasn't sitting in a bar with a motorcycle outside backed up to the curb. This life was about the exhilaration that comes from straddling five-hundred-plus pounds of lean, mean, motorcycle machine, then accelerating it out onto the open road. It was about feeling the warmth of the sun or the coolness of an ocean breeze on your face. It was about listening to the sound of those forty-inch drag pipes bellowing out their infamous *pa-tay-ta, pa-tay-ta, pa-tay-ta* as opposed to relaxing in comfort to the surround sound of an expensive automobile stereo system. It was about being out there in traffic, amid the cages, semis, and little old ladies, without the protection of four-thousand-plus pounds of steel, plastic, and glass wrapped around you to keep you safe. It was a place where there were no fender benders. Minor accidents that dented cars tore legs off motorcycle riders. Safety had to do with skill rather than a seat belt or an air bag. This life was about freedom, or that was the idea anyway. Looking back, what started out as pure enjoyment sure got complicated before it was over.

Upon arriving back at the SW 40th Avenue clubhouse from Key West, I was informed of an upcoming biker event in the Tampa Bay area called the Easyrider's Rodeo. It was sponsored by the famous biker magazine, *Easyriders*. The periodical had risen from almost cult status in the mid-'70s to become a household word in the biker world in a few short years. What started with beautiful motorcycle photos and remarkable artwork by Dave Mann quickly turned into a commercial enterprise putting more emphasis on half-naked women laying all over bikes, rather than in-depth features about the motorcycles themselves or the lifestyle the love of the machine generated. Now they were cashing in on the energy of the biker community, thus sponsoring weekend events around the country that attracted thousands of enthusiasts. Our Tampa Bay chapter felt obligated to attend just to make sure none of the clubs with whom we weren't friendly decided to make an appearance. Their habit at events like this was to send in a few members incognito, then, if there were no Outlaws present, they would don their colors and make a showing.

Tampa Bay had put out the invitation to the other Florida chapters to come, so the day after arriving from the Keys, I headed up there. I left at night and rode up Highway 27 through the endless acres of fields that dominated the terrain of South Florida. Sugarcane and swamps were all the soft light the three-quarter moon revealed. The night was clear and cool. Many of the highways in Florida are straight and smooth, not filled with the mass of potholes you find in the highways up North. The lack of overloaded eighteen-wheelers, coupled with the absence of the expansion and contraction of the asphalt common to the northern states during winter, make for smooth sailing. I made great time as I headed for a little bar in Sebring, Florida, called the Wild Turkey Tavern, 150 miles from the clubhouse in Hollywood. I intended to be there by midnight to have a few before going on.

As I entered the city limits, my front end started to wobble, and I realized the tire had gone flat. I had been doing eighty-plus miles per hour since I had last fueled. Somewhere in those sixty miles, the air from my front tire decided to go AWOL. Now you might think that would have created a fatal situation at that speed, but the truth of the matter is, I did not even realize it had gone soft. Centrifugal force is a beautiful thing. That tire stayed centered on the rim just fine going that fast. It's when I started to slow down that it became obvious there was a problem. Thankfully, I was no rookie, and the Wild Turkey was a lot closer to the edge of town than it is now. I nursed my scooter to the tavern and went in to throw down a few drinks while trying to figure what to do next. One thing was for sure: I was not going any farther that night. I drank until the bar shut down, then pushed my bike behind it and unrolled my sleeping bag, hoping no gators or moccasins were on the prowl back there that night. The next morning, after lifting my bike up onto

273

an old-fashioned metal milk crate, with my front wheel in hand, I walked into a Yamaha dealer up the road and, sure enough, they had a nineteen-inch tube. In no time, I had the front wheel back on and I was again heading to Tampa.

The Easyriders Rodeo was at the fairgrounds and did indeed attract many local bikers, as it intended. There were quite a few Outlaws there, possibly as many as thirty. I wasn't the only one who had enough sense to hang around Florida for a few extra weeks before going north. At first, everything went as it usually does at these types of events. Inevitably, some citizen biker always ended up getting cocky and getting himself punched in the teeth for it. It never failed. One of us would usually make a comment to some guy's girlfriend that would put him in a catch-22 situation. For example, "Hey, sweetheart, why don't you ditch your little brother, and I'll take you for a ride on a real motorcycle?" It was a win-win situation for us: if she goes for a ride, great; if her boyfriend sticks up for her, then you have a fight. Either outcome was more exciting than spending your life in front of the boob tube. At gatherings like this, someone usually ran across a local who owed them money or a tattoo artist with a design too similar to "Charlie." There was never a shortage for potential excitement. We knew how to make things happen.

This time was no different. It was actually somewhat boring, until one of the Tampa Bay brothers came to the bleachers where I was sitting, announcing a rival club had shown up. He also reported that they outnumbered us considerably. To us, their guest appearance was out-and-out arrogance on their part. They had sent in their spies, knew how many of us were there, and then decided the odds were in their favor. The difference between them and us was this: we didn't care about the odds; we cared about honor. This was a concept most people knew very little about.

We met them near the entrance, and the fight was on. There was no talking, no handshaking, no Mexican standoff. We went in slugging. Some of them stood their ground, putting up a good fight. I respected that. Some of them had been so convinced we would not attack, that when we did, they headed for the hills. I felt sorry for the ones who stood for having "brothers" like that. Overall, it was a good fight. We won, of course. We always won. We had to. We were one-percenters. The authorities finally arrived to break it up, so we headed back to the bleachers. Some of our guys had been hurt, although nothing very serious. I had been tagged pretty hard several times, but that's par for the course. If you are close enough to connect, you are close enough to be hit. Thankfully, I always could take a punch well and throw one even better. Ambidextrous, no less. That speed bag in the basement at 36 North Hawley Street had served its purpose well.

I was surprised as an ambulance arrived, sirens wailing. We did a quick survey of our crew. We didn't have anyone missing, but those paramedics were loading up somebody. Our wonderment ended when the law enforcement officers, including the arrival of their backup force, became focused solely on us. They surrounded, detained, and subjected us to the identification process once again. Drivers' licenses were scrutinized; photographs were taken. Finally, we found out what it was all about, one of the members of the other team had gotten himself stabbed. The cops wanted to make sure they knew which Outlaws were there in case he died. By the time they finished the gestapo process, word came back that he had. I started getting flashbacks to Big Boy's murder years before up in Ohio. Whatever happened to the old-fashioned gang-fight, without knives, or guns, or killing? I missed the good old days back at the Longbranch Saloon when things were simple. The cops did not arrest anyone that day because no witnesses volunteered to identify which one of us stuck the guy, if anyone even knew. To my knowledge, no one ever confessed to doing it. They never would. We learned a long time ago that it is easier to tell the truth than to lie. The truth was, if you did not have an absolute need to know something, you did not want to know.

The Tampa Bay Buccaneers NFL team had a famous defensive line in the '80s called the Tampa Bay Crunch Bunch, and our Tampa chapter liked that. They had quite a reputation themselves as fist fighters, so they had Tampa Bay Crunch Bunch patches made for their colors, with Charlie in the center. The Crunch Brunch was a prestigious clique, like the Indianapolis Horsepower Junkies, known for incredibly fast Harleys. Very few members of other chapters ever were awarded the Crunch Bunch patch. I was an exception, though, due to my very active participation in the Easyriders Rodeo confrontation. I always did like a good fight. Although I was proud to have earned the patch, I never did sew it on my colors because of the fatal stabbing. I had an aversion to senseless killing. I still do.

To end this chapter on a bit lighter note, maybe I should say here that we were not all work and no play. In other words, we did do other things besides ride and fight. Some of the guys, like Pearl, charter president of the Sandusky chapter, liked to hunt. On December 1, 1986, Ohio opened its first handgun season for whitetail deer. Pearl was excited about it and relentlessly tried to talk me into going with him opening day. I had never been deer hunting, nor did I have any desire to start. The kinds of weapons I was into were not considered sporting equipment. Pearl said he had a pistol I could borrow, promising me there were so many bucks out there that we could sit in his van and shoot them as they ran by. Finally, I agreed to go with him. Pearl loaned me a Ruger New Model Super Blackhawk .44 magnum. It wasn't quite as easy as he promised, but before the morning was over, I shot a nine-point buck that weighed in at well over 230 pounds. That deer's head hangs over my fireplace to this day.

Wally from Buffalo, on the other hand, was an angler. He was my right hand man and a great "road dog" when club affairs took me across the Outlaw Nation. He and I spent many hours traveling together from chapter to chapter. Oftentimes, the time on the road was spent smoking big, fat, exotic joints while he explained the finer aspects of fishing to me. I mean he *loved* to fish. He had a boat and all kinds of rods, reels, lures, and techniques. He knew what different fish liked and didn't like. He knew what they were thinking as they watched the action of certain lures in the water, whether they were realistic or not. It was a hilarious to hear him talk about what was going on in a fish's head.

Our annual New Year's Eve national run was somewhere in the South, often somewhere between Atlanta and Orlando. It was a great way for the Northern brothers, who'd been cooped up in the snow country for a couple of months, to get away. Most would show up in cars while some would truck or trailer their bikes to get in on some riding. Daytona Beach Bike Week was only two months away, which was also often a mandatory national run. I got to the point where I would go to the New Year's Eve party and just stay South until our region's update in April. I had two Harleys most of the time, sometimes three, so I always had one up and running while customizing another.

The Outlaws would keep an eye on Daytona for several weeks prior to Bike Week, checking to see if any of the other big clubs were setting up for an appearance. That would include finding temporary dancing jobs for their old ladies, or lining up motel or campground accommodations. Proprietors of most businesses had no idea of the rivalries that existed between bike clubs, so they would even sometimes brag about how they had space reserved for some other large gathering. Being the selfless volunteer that I was, I made a point of spearheading this recon operation many times throughout the '80s. It was hard to be in central Florida during the months of January and February every year while the homeboys were shoveling snow, but somebody had to do it. Wally was one of the faithful that made the sacrifice with me on more than a few occasions, even though I know he must have missed Buffalo in January. Anything for the club, right?

Wally loved to take advantage of the nice weather to go fishing whenever he could. While I was trying to figure out how to motivate more Outlaws to come to Florida early to help me with the influx of bikers from all over the country, Wally suggested we have a bass tournament. I thought he was out of his mind, or at least just messing with mine, but he was serious. He thought it would be a good reason for many brothers to come to Florida early. Of course, he thought most everyone would jump on the opportunity to do some serious fishing, especially if you made a contest out of it. The idea had some merit. It would make a good excuse to congregate in the Orlando area during the weeks prior to Bike Week. Interest was high when we kicked the idea around with the other regional bosses. More brothers liked to fish than I thought. The first thing Taco did, after approving the endeavor, was to have T-shirts made advertising the First Annual Outlaws MC Bass Tournament. Those shirts should be worth some money today. There never was a Second Annual Outlaws MC Bass Tournament.

Clear Lake, in Orange County, was chosen mostly because the Orlando clubhouse property bordered a canal that lead out into it. Wally did all the fish measuring and documentation for the tournament. First prize was $1,000, with the contest being open to other clubs, as a public relations gesture. Many came, fished, rode their scooters, and enjoyed being in the sunny South because of the fishing tournament. The Orlando chapter took full advantage of all the out-of-towners, flaunting the high profile it afforded them. They were good hosts, taking brothers to the many go-go bars along the infamous Orange Blossom Trail. Many went to some of the famous tourist attractions in the region. There was nothing like a bunch of smoked-up Outlaws on the Pirates of the Caribbean ride at Disney World or cheering for Shamu at SeaWorld while sipping on Mai Tais.

Wally was in angler's heaven. He talked about fishing every day to lots of the brothers. He definitely knew more about it than anyone else. He also went out on Clear Lake himself every day for a month. The downside was he often talked me into going with him. We were partners, only this partner was not much of a fisherman. To make matters worse, in spite of all the great training I was getting from Wally, and all this top-of-the-line equipment I was accumulating, I still wasn't catching any fish. Wally, on the other hand, was catching fish every day while having the time of his life.

The end of the tournament finally arrived as Bike Week approached, so the grand-prize winner had to be determined. As the records were examined, it was determined to allow a member of another club be the winner. One of the Scorpions from Dallas was chosen. It was a political decision. I was against it, but it didn't matter. I was a biker, not a politician. It seems the days of just being a biker were slipping away. Who really caught the biggest bass in the First (and only) Annual Outlaws MC Bass Tournament? Wally, of course!

With the Bass Tournament over, those of us in Orlando headed over to Daytona. Many brothers were on the road, so our job was to secure lodging, making sure everything would go smoothly for them as they arrived for Bike Week '88. We rented an entire floor of the hotel that sat on the seaside of Atlantic and Volusia Avenues. There was a restaurant and bar on the property that went by the name of Checkers Café, so the heat made it their gathering place to keep an eye on us. That did not prevent us from going in there, though. Our theory was that we could make them feel as uncomfortable as they were trying to make us feel. Did it work? Probably not, but it was a good theory.

Our arrangement with the hotel was that we promised to pay for any damage our people caused and for them not to worry about it. We didn't need the law called every time someone smashed a lamp or a window. They were happy with our agreement. The hotel owners told us they would much rather have bikers there than the spring break crowd. The college kids broke things, stole items, and then snuck out of town. The motorcyclists had a much better reputation for owning up to whatever damage they did. At the end of the week, the hotel did inventory on our rooms and we kept our promise, paying the bill. Of course, I then went to individual bosses to pass the bill on to those responsible for whatever damage their members did.

Checker's Café became the gathering spot for about a dozen of us each morning during Bike Week. Usually there were plenty of hangovers being nursed with very few adhering to the "hair of the dog that bit you" philosophy of countering a throbbing head with more of what gave it to you. We had plenty of people like that, but they were not seated around the circular bar at Checker's Cafe. This group consisted of men responsible for everything going according to plan. Remember, there were always at least half a dozen law enforcement officers sitting at their table, so this was not any kind of confidential gathering; more like a regrouping from the night before. It was time to give damage reports: who was in jail, who needed a lawyer, who got into a wreck, or who went to the hospital. Oh yeah, and on whom and where the nickel-dime police harassment was being focused.

Midweek, one of the brothers, having a great time amid the bright lights, loud motorcycles, and all the biker women, asked me, "Cowboy, how's it going?" My response was, "I'll let you know when it's over." What I meant was there was simply too much responsibility for me to risk getting much of a buzz that week. We bosses would party later, when hundreds of brothers' safety was not depending on us making the right decisions. On about the third day, as we sat there sipping banana daiquiris for breakfast, I started laughing out loud at the formidable sight before me. Some of the toughest, most serious bikers in America were sipping fruit drinks, piled high with whipped cream, topped with a cherry. It was hilarious to see the white cream in the mustaches and beards of this rowdy bunch. I remarked, "I hope no Angels come in here right now and see us like this." Everyone laughed, including the cops.

When Bike Week was over, Wally and I headed to Fort Lauderdale to wait out the winter. Moose had a Ranger bass boat he had acquired from one of those rock monsters, and somehow Wally talked me into going fishing again, this time out in the saw grass of the Everglades. I had been out there before, but this time it would be on top-notch equipment and with brothers who knew what they were doing. The gators were still there, larger than ever it seemed, but we were able to maneuver circles around them. A twelve-footer lay basking on top of the grass one afternoon as we fished nearby. Earlier that morning I had caught a good-sized Oscar, so I decided to use him to have some fun with this gator. I hooked the Oscar onto my line and cast him inches in front this gator's nose. He never flinched. I reeled in and cast again, this time over the gator, with the fishing line lying just behind his head. I slowly reeled the Oscar in again, still with no reaction from my harassment victim. When the little fish became snagged on one of the massive ridges on his back, I gave my line a hearty jerk, which sent this huge alligator into contortions. I was amazed this huge reptile could move so fast as it entered the water to get away from us. I was acutely aware at that moment that these animals were not to be taken lightly. We were in their domain. That gator could have swamped our boat had he taken a notion to, and a pistol would have been no match for him in the water.

I didn't mess with the gators anymore, but after several more days, I finally landed a six-and-a-half pound largemouth bass that made all of the previous months of vain efforts worthwhile. I know much bigger ones have been caught out there, but to me, this was a keeper. Those are great memories of a few of good times I had with Wally and Pearl, two of the finest one-percenter brothers that ever walked the earth.

Chapter 14

Harsh Reality

Life in the fast lane had a price. In the mid-'80s, Hambone went through a series of events that really boggled the mind. Some of the local hillbilly mafia boys in Dayton began to harass a local massage parlor where some of the Dayton chapter's old ladies worked. The result was that it began to affect their income. When Hambone got wind of it, he immediately went to the source of the problem to get the situation worked out, but it worked itself out of control instead. These two-bit gangsters were so intimidated by Hambone that when their chief hood came into the room where 'Bone was sitting, he pulled his Saturday night special and shot him in the abdomen. Hambone had a fierce reputation on the street, but the situation in no way warranted this kind of response. Cowards.

Hambone was taken to Good Samaritan Hospital on Dayton's west side. They saved his life but said they couldn't remove the bullet due to its proximity to his spine. If they tried, the hospital determined he would certainly risk permanent paralysis. He was eventually released, but the wound simply would not heal. His body raged with infection in the months that followed, and all the doctors did was increase his dosage of pain killers. He lost almost thirty pounds, being unable even to walk to the bathroom unassisted. There was no way he could think about riding. Hambone was a hard partier for sure, but more than anything else he was a one-percenter brother and a motorcycle rider. Not being able to get out on the road on his bright-red Shovelhead with its chrome frame was even worse on him than the constant pain. The Dayton brothers had brought his motorcycle into the living room where he was wasting away, eyes often glazed over from the buzz caused by the prescription drugs. If he couldn't ride it, at least he could look at it.

By this time, I'd been to many funerals and buried some very close brothers, as well as some whom I didn't know very well. It was an accepted fact that this life demanded a hefty toll, be it through violence or substance abuse, but watching this very strong and virile Vietnam combat veteran and friend deteriorate before my very eyes was rough. I visited him often in the North Dayton apartment, which had become his prison. Considering our affection for drugs, some brothers were highly tempted by Hambone's abundant supply of Percodans. He was always very generous with whatever he had, and this didn't stop after he'd been shot. He ate them like candy and offered some to anyone who visited him. More than a few times, I'd show up and he would have several visitors, all almost as high as he was from his medication. That bothered me. Not because I thought I was better than anyone else was; I liked Percs as much as the next guy. Let's face it: feeling good feels good, but this was different. These pills kept Hambone from the horrible pain that was racking his body because of the acute infection the medical geniuses couldn't prevent or even explain. Not only would I not take any, but I also seriously tried to guilt trip anyone else from taking them too. Some heeded, some didn't—like always.

One morning I got a frantic call from Hambone's old lady. He had been taken to the hospital, temperature soaring. She said he had all the nurses freaking out; he was yelling, cussing, and threatening to commit suicide. His mom and stepdad had driven up from Lexington, Kentucky, the night before, and all this was hard on his mom. No one knew what to do with him, not the doctors or the local brothers. Hambone was one of the nicest guys I had ever met but, like most of the Outlaws, he could be extremely scary when he was angry. And he was very angry.

I left for the hospital within a half hour of the call and averaged just over ninety miles an hour from Toledo to Dayton. I was changing lanes and running the white line between semis the whole way, wanting to get there before someone did something stupid and caused

Hambone to hurt them. I knew the situation was serious. We weren't known for having pity parties for ourselves, or for threatening to commit suicide.

Once before, I got a call that a brother, distraught over the death of another brother, was threateningly waving a pistol around in the clubhouse. He was intent on revenge, and if he couldn't have it, he said he was going to blow his own brains out. He wouldn't listen to reason from anyone there and wouldn't put the pistol away either. This brother was an old-timer who'd done prison time for shooting rival club members before. He was capable of anything. I went over to the clubhouse and told him to give me the pistol. He did. I asked him what the problem was, and then I let him blow off steam for a while. When he was through, I tossed the pistol back to him and said, "If you're going kill yourself, go out in the woods somewhere and get it over with. Don't you dare do anything that's going to bring unnecessary heat on the club, and quit stressing out all your brothers." That may sound insensitive, but it wasn't really. We didn't play games with each other. He was seriously bummed out over some events that had transpired, as we all were. The thing was, he had been there and had seen his brother gunned down. He needed to get it out, so I let him. He also needed to know his actions affected the other brothers. He understood. He got a grip.

As I rode toward Dayton, I didn't believe that Hambone's threat to kill himself was serious for a second, although I also knew that months and months on pain pills can mess up your mind. When I got to the hospital, I saw his mom crying, and his old lady was in a state of near panic. Hambone had just thrown a tray at a doctor and security was on its way. The nurses looked like they had seen a ghost. A couple of the local members just shrugged their shoulders, not sure what to do. Hambone didn't want to talk to anyone but me, so in I went. He had a wild, crazy-man look in his eye until I shut the door behind me.

I went over to the bed, shook his hand, and gave him a brotherly embrace. After we greeted one another, I pulled up a chair and said, "You're driving these people nuts, 'Bone. What's going on?" Just as calmly as ever, he told me that he had requested that they remove the bullet, in spite of the risk. They refused. Too dangerous, they said. It would probably paralyze him or kill him. Hambone told them he didn't care what the risks were. Nothing could be worse than the way he'd been existing these last several months. When they refused again, he got irate, and that's putting it mildly. The threats were to get their attention, and they worked. He had their attention, all right. Now he needed a voice. He had that too. Mine.

When I stepped out of the room amid the apprehensive gazes of all involved in this tragic drama, I motioned to the doctor to come over to the door. I calmly told him that it was Hambone's sincere desire that he remove the bullet that was obviously causing the persistent pain, not to mention the merciless infection. When the doctor began to object, I opened the door and escorted him to the bedside of a now calm patient. Hambone told the doctor, "I'm paralyzed already. I'm dead already. Anything would be better than this, Doc."

They scheduled Hambone for surgery that afternoon. A tiny piece of fabric was found attached to the bullet. The surgeon felt the operation had been a total success. His spinal column wasn't damaged at all. After this long, dreadful ordeal was over, Hambone was finally on the road to recovery. He was thirty pounds underweight, had a colostomy bag, and was addicted to Percodans, but one thing at a time. At least the source of the infection was finally gone from his body.

Hambone's love of riding his motorcycle yielded him monumental progress in his battle to overcome his body's dependency on the painkillers. We were all very pleased with his ability to wean himself from them. As soon as he did, he began to put on weight and strength. He was an incredibly strong man, so it was good to see him walk, think straight, and take command of the Dayton Outlaws again. The brother who filled his position did a good job keeping the ship on course, but it was good to have 'Bone back at the helm.

Hambone was my number one drinking buddy. He's the one who taught me to enjoy Jack Daniel's. The first occasion of him going out in public to party after all his medical problems was important enough to me to be there. It was not because I was worried about anything happening to him. The Dayton Outlaws had always had a reputation of being able to handle themselves very well. I just wanted to be there to celebrate the victory of him coming back from the dead. We went to one of his favorite bars on Salem Avenue and proceeded to have a good time. We weren't looking for trouble, especially in light of the fact that Hambone still had a colostomy bag attached to his side. In the fast lane, you never have to look for trouble, though; it looks for you. After a couple of hours of us drinking and sneaking out back to smoke a joint every once in a while, in walked the president of another local bike club with whom the Dayton Outlaws did not get along. His name was Phil. How's that for an intimidating street name?

He was alone, except for his old lady. None of us could believe they just walked in like that. I think we figured out later it had something to do with him "zinging and binging" on THC. When he saw us, he knew he'd made a big mistake and immediately said, "I want to speak to whoever's in charge." Hambone and I made our way across the bar toward him, with 'Bone motioning everyone else to back off. This dummy said something like, "We need to talk before somebody gets hurt." Just about that time, Hambone busted him upside the head with a fist that had been idle for months. I could see 'Bone enjoyed getting back into the swing of things, literally. No one piled on. No one else got involved at all.

Hambone didn't need any help. He punched Phil several more times, then told him to get out and never come back in there again. As far as I know, he never did.

In spite of how dumb this Phil was, his old lady showed a lot of class that night. As soon as her old man got punched the first time, she reached into her purse and pulled a Charter Arms .44 Bulldog. She never said a word. She didn't run her mouth, like most women do. The look in her eye left no doubt she was prepared to use it. She was either very brave or extremely stupid. Personally, I think she was very dedicated. I was impressed. Of course, she didn't get the chance to use it. By the time she had that revolver half way out, Ranger One had her arm pinned behind her back, relieving her of it. We were always watching for that sort of thing because we had all seen women get liquored up and pull knives or Saturday night specials before. It's never taken lightly. A one-hundred-ten-pound girl can kill you just as dead as a two hundred-pound man can. Because of her courage and dedication to her man, I made sure nothing happened to her, except the permanent confiscation of her pistol. I remember thinking, *What is a good-looking gal with this much heart doing with such a jerk?* I also thought to myself, *She would have made a good Outlaw ole' lady.*

Hambone designated several of his men to be on high alert just in case some of Phil's buddies decided to exact some kind of revenge. Sure enough, within an hour, a car sped down Salem Avenue, firing several shots toward the bar and our bikes. That took a lot of guts, didn't it? That kind of thing happened all the time, though. I've seen bikes shot at or knocked over on numerous occasions. One time, I was standing next to a Sportster when a stray bullet penetrated the tank and gasoline started to pour out of the hole at my feet. Another time up in Toledo, a guy who'd been spurned by a dancer at the Exotic Lounge pushed Jay Buck's Shovelhead over and lit it on fire. What a mess that made. When the tires caught fire, the intense heat they generated did a lot of damage. Thankfully, steel and aluminum don't burn. Once Jay stripped all the burnt wire and rubber away, his Harley Davidson was still underneath. Several motorcycles were "confiscated" in the next week or so to help supply the parts he needed to restore it. People really should take more caution when it comes to securing their bikes.

That was all that ever came out of that confrontation between Hambone and Phil, but before the night was over, we had another incident. At about 11:30, the door opened and seven men walked in together. They weren't bikers, and they didn't look like cops. The barmaid had never seen them before, so we kept an eye on them, as we do everyone else. They ordered drinks and headed toward the pool table. The bar wasn't crowded, especially in light of the drive-by shooting, and soon it basically was just us and them in there. An argument started over who was up next on the pool table, and it became obvious these boys weren't in there to play pool or to drink. Turns out, they were a local karate class who had pumped themselves up enough to take their martial arts skills to the real world and try them out. We loved these kind of guys. Although some truly are skilled and quite deadly, most have a vital ingredient missing in their training: experiencing intense personal pain. You can be fast and have all the kung fu moves you want, but you had better know how to take a punch. I'm not talking about in the chest, or abdomen, or thigh. I'm talking about dead in the face. A split second's hesitation after a blow to the nose or temple will turn the tide in a fight that has no rules, no referee, and no consideration for anything except being the one standing when it's over. Fighting wasn't a sport or hobby to us. It was serious business.

These martial arts guys were no different than others we'd seen in the past. Though the two instructors were extremely proficient, the students were not. I guess they weren't taught what to do when their nose was splattered all over their face. It's amazing how much blood a man can lose through his nose without being seriously injured. These guys should have stayed in their dojos, watching *Kung Fu* reruns. I have to admit, the instructors were pretty tough. One got the better of Hambone because of his weakened condition, so I grabbed him by the hair and stuck my Colt .45 in his face. Bone had his shirt off and it was rather obvious he was wearing a colostomy bag. "Bruce Lee" said that wasn't fair, like it was fair for him to unleash his black belt experience on a guy just out of major surgery. Enough was enough. Black belt, meet pistol belt.

That brought that little skirmish to an end, or so I thought. The karate boys vowed retribution as they limped out. We were so intimidated we ordered another round. It wasn't long, though, before one of our guys came in shouting, "The cops are here." Those of us that were packing immediately stashed our pistols in the trash can behind the bar, knowing we were going to be searched. Hambone laughed, removed his almost full colostomy bag, and emptied the contents into the trashcan, all over the pistols, my Colt included. Seconds later, the front door burst open, the Kung Fu kid leading the way with Dayton's Finest following. I was by the door when it opened and the guy yelled, "That's him! That's the one with the gun." I didn't mind that so much, but he felt the need to include some unacceptable adjectives in his description of me. That caused me to feel the need to punch him in the teeth, even with a policeman at each side. He fell back through the door into the arms of the other cops; I never did see him again. One of the officers looked at me and said, "That was stupid of him." He thought my reaction was reasonable. After all, this was Salem Avenue, not Oakwood. The officer in charge said hello to Hambone, then told him they needed to look for a weapon. Hambone replied, "Go ahead."

I'll never forget the look on the officer's face when he gingerly pulled my Colt .45 from the trash can, covered in the contents of Hambone's colostomy bag. It stunk to high heaven, but it was still hilarious. They got another brother's .44 out of there too, and I asked them if they were going to dust them for prints. Everyone, including the cops, laughed. They knew us. They could see what happened with the karate boys, and why it happened. They were just glad they didn't have to write any reports of serious injuries or arrests. Hambone's first night out had proven to be an eventful one. That was par for the course of life in the fast lane. I was glad I didn't miss it, even though I did lose a very nice pistol that night. Oh, well. There was always another pistol.

The next big event worthy of mention also involved Hambone in a major way. As I said, he was a dedicated one-percenter brother, extremely active, and almost fearless. If there was an assignment that needed a man of his experience, he'd volunteer. Such was the case in Louisville in the summer of '88. Several high-ranking members of the Hells Angels Motorcycle Club were indicted on federal conspiracy charges to blow up our clubhouse there and to specifically kill one of our members. All this stemmed from the death of one of theirs who had come to Kentucky to visit relatives. He had been a member of the Louisville Outlaws many years prior and still had family in the area. The way I got the story was he had to leave Kentucky because of trouble with the law, so he went out West. He found some like-minded folks— the Hells Angels MC—and joined up. This, of course, took place years before the tension between the Angels and the Outlaws escalated to the status of what the law enforcement community calls "war."

There were few Louisville Outlaws still around who would have even remembered, let alone recognized this guy, but as luck would have it, he ran into an old-timer who did. An argument became a shootout and when the smoke cleared, the former Outlaw was dead. According to an Alaskan Angel boss turned informant, that did not sit too well with the big wigs in the Hells Angel aristocracy in California. I can't say as I blame them. We didn't like it when similar misfortunes befell our guys in the course of pursuing life in the fast lane either.

The story has it that some of the Hells Angels conspired to exact revenge and the plan was all recorded for the Feds, thanks to the snitch. The Federal conspiracy trial was to be in Louisville, deep in the heart of Outlaw territory. Our little chapter there came under much scrutiny by law enforcement during this time, as the Hells Angels prepared to make a grand showing in support of their brothers in trouble. It was obvious we needed a more experienced man on the scene to deal with the situation, so Hambone volunteered for the job. When more and more Angels made their presence visible in and around the courthouse, Hambone asked for men to come so that our presence could be more prevalent than ever in the bars and on the streets.

I asked for volunteers and in no time had thirty in Louisville, ready to stay as long as needed. Wally and I partnered up again and spent almost a month there trying to keep an eye on things. Tensions were very high with the Angels in our city, and the potential for one of our guys to do something unwise was tremendous. Feds were everywhere, watching them, watching us, not caring who did what. They intended to pick up the pieces and get as many of us off the street as they could. That was their job. We understood that. We also understood this was no time for us to be stupid. Whatever beef the Angels had with us or we had with them was between us. The Hells Angel leadership knew that too. Because of this, an unprecedented meeting was set up between their top ranking members and ours to agree that we wouldn't be settling any of our disputes in public, in front of the cops or the press.

For this historic meeting, Sonny Barger and Irish O'Farrell represented the Hells Angels. Both were indicted and on trial for conspiracy. I had the privilege of accompanying Taco to represent the Outlaws. The meeting took place in our attorney's conference room. As far as I know, it was the only time Taco and Sonny ever met face to face. That would make it historical in and of itself. It was the only time I ever personally spoke with Barger. As tense as you might think a meeting like that would be, it was conducted professionally, and even cordially. All the tough guy bravado was left behind. No one in this room had to prove anything to anyone. Both sides knew what was at stake here. If any of the guys, either theirs or ours, got out of hand, the only winner would be the cops. They were anxiously waiting for an opportunity to take down everyone they could from either side. Taco and Sonny agreed that day that there would be plenty of time to settle personal differences after the legal matters were in the past.

At the close of that meeting, we had a limousine standing by to take Barger and O'Farrell back to their downtown hotel. They had rented a large portion of the Best Western not far from the courthouse. No doubt, the Feds occupied a substantial part of the rest of it. Patch-wearing Hells Angels dominated the outside of the building, nervously awaiting the safe return of their leaders. And safely returned they were, just like we promised. To prove we weren't setting them up, I even rode in the backseat of the limo between Sonny and Irish. You should have seen the look on the faces of their guys when we got out together and made a point to shake hands as we bid each other farewell, to the disappointment of the Feds and the news media alike.

We had no problems on the street during the course of the trial. Everyone kept his word. When the trial was over, the Hells Angels left town, and things quickly got back to normal. The proceedings resulted in Sonny and Irish getting some prison time out of the deal. I found out later that Irish O'Farrell was killed in an altercation in an Oakland bar prior to beginning his sentence. I thanked my crew and sent them home. I returned to Toledo myself, and Hambone, who had spent close to a year in Louisville for the club, moved back to Dayton. Life goes on.

Chapter 15

Clermont County Catastrophe

Early Saturday afternoon on January 21, 1989, an event occurred that changed the course of my life. A Dayton Outlaw named Bear called to inform me of a tragedy of monumental proportion, even by our standards. I was at home at the clubhouse in Toledo, and he told me to sit down because he had some very bad news. He wasn't exaggerating. I'll never forget that conversation. Three Dayton Outlaws had been shot, and another brother was in jail. While he was suggesting I come down there immediately, I was already preparing to do just that. I could hardly believe what I was hearing as Bear told me about a shootout at a rural Clermont County bar called Vic's Brew and Cue. I had never even heard of Clermont County, let alone this little dive, but Vic's Brew and Cue made Outlaw history that day. In my opinion, one of our organization's worst catastrophes happened there.

Earlier in the month, Hambone and some of the Dayton brothers were partying with a small bike club on Cincinnati's Northwest side. They were celebrating a birthday at a local go-go bar. That didn't sit very well with a rival bike club in the Queen City, so several days later they rolled into the same bar with guns and ball bats, doling out a sound thrashing to the Outlaw sympathizers.

Hambone was enraged when he heard about it. When he was informed of a meeting of small Southwest Ohio clubs that was going to take place at Vic's Brew and Cue, he vowed to attend and support those who'd been hospitable to us. Hambone assembled a formidable crew to go that day, including some faithful friends of the club, but he didn't inform anyone else. He could have had two dozen more brothers with him just by making one phone call, but he had no reason to think his crew could not handle whatever situation might arise.

Probably the biggest thing Hambone underestimated was how intimidating he was. His reputation for more than twenty years in the club was that he would not back down. He was a fighter. He would fight for fun. He would fight for his brothers, and he would fight to defend anyone who had ever shown kindness to an Outlaw. The Dayton Outlaws in general had a fierce reputation as being relentless warriors, not afraid to risk their lives for the club or a friend of the club.

This club in Cincinnati was notorious for pushing locals and go-go girls around, but they knew a face-to-face confrontation with our Dayton chapter was more than they could handle. We learned later that they made distress calls to every chapter they had, even as far away as upstate New York. Their members were instructed that this meeting was a mandatory function for them, and they would lose their patch if they didn't show up. They did show up, in full force. It was estimated that well over a hundred were there, armed to the teeth. I'm sure they felt confident that their numbers would be enough to give them the upper hand, and I suppose it did. What they lost that day was nothing compared to what we lost.

As Bear explained it to me on the phone, most of the enemy was there incognito. They were intermingled with all the citizen bikers and small groups who had no clue what was going on that day. (Let me make a point here to say that I have not mentioned the name of this rival club on purpose. They don't deserve the respect I'd be showing them if I put their name in this book.) A small group of them were wearing colors when Hambone and his crew arrived, so Hambone cut to the chase as always. No handshake. No buying a drink. No sitting down at a table to talk. None of that garbage. Hambone told their boss that ganging up on guys and pushing girls around was a punk stunt and if they had a problem with Outlaws being in Cincinnati, they should take it up with Outlaws. In response to Hambone's comment, "citizens" all around the bar began to remove their winter coats to reveal their colors. Now the odds had shifted to seventy or eighty

305

to twelve, with another thirty or forty of them outside. This development emboldened their boss to demand the Outlaws remove and surrender their colors, the ultimate disgrace for a patch holder. They underestimated Hambone and the Outlaws once again. It wasn't going to happen, even at gunpoint. Hambone issued a very easy-to-understand, two-word response and followed it with a left hook that knocked their boss to the floor. Their enforcer then shot Hambone in the back the first time. From what Bear told me, an Outlaw blew that guy's brains out and the full-scale shootout was on. Hambone was hit several more times that day at Vic's Brew and Cue. Two other Dayton Outlaws were shot multiple times, as well as some members of the rival club. I heard later over two hundred rounds had been discharged in the bar that afternoon. It's a miracle more weren't killed.

When Bear called me, he had just escaped the melee himself. Brothers fought their way out in spite of the odds and the gunfire as law enforcement began to arrive. Bear didn't know what the extent of the damage was at that point, but he knew several of our guys were down, including Hambone. I immediately advised him and any others he could contact to head for Indianapolis. The rule of thumb was to get a state line between you and any possible warrants that may be coming out. That gives your lawyer more time as he fights extradition on your behalf. In this day and age of RICO and much greater cooperation between law enforcement agencies, that probably wouldn't help as much as it used to, but that was the rule of thumb at the time.

My next move was to make three phone calls. The first one, of course, was to my boss. I didn't have many details, but I assured him I was on it. The second was to Wally in Buffalo, New York, and the third to Pearl in Sandusky, Ohio. I told them we had a situation in Dayton, and to meet me there as soon as possible. They knew to bring one man with them and to be armed. At this point, my thoughts were on protection of our people should there be further aggression. The second was to gather information, and the third was to exact revenge if the opportunity presented itself. I called men who were willing to look, very hard if necessary, for the opportunity to present itself. I grabbed my paratrooper beret, which I only wore on Veteran's Day, and headed to Dayton, Ohio. I was the first to arrive, so I rented two rooms at the old Econo Lodge in North Dayton. That would be our base of operations until we knew into what kind of snake pit we were going.

When Wally and Pearl got there, we stashed most of our weapons and proceeded to go on a fact-finding mission. From some trusted friends who were actually at the shootout, we learned how the gruesome event had unfolded. One of the "friendlies" was dealing dope with the enemy. Hambone and the Dayton chapter had been sold out for the wholesale value of marijuana. Two of our guys were in intensive care units with multiple gunshot wounds, checked in under aliases due to the violent nature of the incident. The police were afraid someone might come to try to finish the job, so our guys were heavily guarded. Big Moe was the only Outlaw arrested, and it was for some minor charge. This thing got so crazy so fast that the Clermont County Sheriff deputies were a bit overwhelmed.

What I learned next nearly broke my heart. My greatest fear was realized when an eyewitness and longtime friend of the club told me Hambone had been killed. He also told me our guys did valiantly, considering the odds, but that was little compensation for losing Hambone. I should have never become regional boss. The office rightfully should have been his. He was my senior in every way and was a better brother and leader than I could ever be, but he didn't want the job. He didn't want the power or the pressure. He just wanted to be free to be a good brother. He wasn't the only one we had like that. Sidecar, from Atlanta, was like that. I should have stayed more like them.

I bailed Big Moe out of jail at 4:00 a.m. He filled us in on more details of the betrayal and ensuing gun battle. He said when their enforcer shot Hambone in the back, he pulled his .45 and shot the punk in the face, killing him instantly. We had no way of knowing how many of them were hurt, and I didn't particularly care. I was concerned about our men. Through relatives of our two hospitalized brothers, I obtained their locations and aliases and, by morning, I was at the bedside of each. They were a mess. Tubes and hoses and machines were everywhere. They didn't know Hambone was dead. At first, I didn't think it was a good time to tell them. Then I decided the news might anger them enough to make them fight for their own lives, if for no other reason, so that Hambone's death wouldn't have been in vain.

It was one of the saddest days of my life. I'd seen plenty of death. I'd been to many funerals. I'd lost other brothers, like Ralph, who were almost as close to me as Hambone. We knew what time it was. We knew it was a violent and dangerous lifestyle. We knew this was not only possible, but also inevitable. Seeing these two brothers in this condition, and having to tell Taco about Hambone's death, was a bit much. I'm glad Wally and Pearl were there with me. It was always good to have faithful brothers around, but especially during the rough times. And this was an extremely rough time.

I notified Taco of what I'd learned, and he put the word out. The mode went from defense, and/or offense, to funeral. The Outlaw Nation would converge in Dayton, Ohio to honor Hambone. Revenge would have to wait. Brothers began to arrive later that same day. Men from my region were the first to get there. By the next afternoon, all of my bosses were in Dayton. When I refer to these men as "my" bosses, what I mean is they were the individual chapters' presidents of the region for which I was responsible. They didn't work for me; they worked with me for the good of the club. We weren't gangsters—we were brothers. There is a big difference. These men were from Detroit, Michigan, as well as Toledo, Warren, and Youngstown, Ohio. One was from Western Pennsylvania and another from Louisville, Kentucky. Buffalo and Sandusky had been with me from that first night when we met up at the motel on the North side of Dayton. By the time these men assembled, the coroner had released Hambone's body. He was down at the funeral home in West Carrolton that the Dayton chapter always used. They had come to know us well over the years.

I took several of them to see Hambone's body. Not after he was "fixed up" and prepared for a viewing. We went there before they'd even cleaned the blood off from the autopsy, the incisions livid and the bullet holes obvious and ominous. As we stood there gazing down at our brother and our friend, I recalled the night eight years before when I stood in a similar room, looking down onto a stainless steel table where the lifeless body of a fallen comrade lay. I looked into the eyes of my men to see whether the predominant emotion was fear or hate. I was satisfied with what I saw, just as Taco had been those years before when he took Kato and me to see Ralph's body.

Hambone was a much-loved and longtime member of the Outlaws Motorcycle Club. He was instrumental in the formation of the Oklahoma City chapter, as well as the Toledo chapter. He served the club as the Dayton boss for well over ten years, and he answered the club's call to move to Louisville during the Hells Angels conspiracy trial. He was one of the truest examples of a one-percenter brother I have ever known. He was a Brother Bike Tramp in every sense of the word, and he was a great example to the rest of us. He had served honorably in combat in Vietnam, he lived as a true one-percenter Outlaw brother, and he died as one on January 21, 1989. It was a sad day for the Outlaw Nation. He was the best of the best. He wasn't a gangster. He wasn't a businessman. He wasn't a politician. He was old school. Bikin' and brotherhood was his life. Hambone was my friend. As the lid was being closed on his coffin, out of respect, I took my coveted paratrooper beret off my head and put it in the casket with him.

Within forty-eight hours, hundreds of Outlaws had made their way to Southern Ohio. We were able to put formidable groups in many of the bars on the nights before and after the funeral to assure the city that the Outlaws were not done in Dayton, despite rumors to the contrary. It became apparent we were going to have to maintain a reinforced presence there for some time. With Hambone dead, and his two right-hand men in intensive care, this chapter was in need of leadership as well as additional manpower.

My club career had begun in Toledo with the Mongols in 1975. In 1979, I became the charter president of the Outlaws Motorcycle Club chapter there. In 1984, I became the regional president of the "Blue" region, and thereby one of four national vice presidents. Though my duties in those capacities required me to travel much around the country, I was still a Toledo Outlaw. Specifically, that meant I wore a Toledo bottom rocker on my colors. That was about to change. It was obvious I was going to have to move to Dayton to ramrod the recovery of that chapter. Being best friends with Hambone for many years allowed me to learn the city and get to know many of the people there, both friends and enemies of the club alike. I had earned a considerable amount of respect there in my own right. The Dayton chapter was instrumental in the formation of the Toledo chapter, as was Detroit. Any sacrifice I could make to ensure that Hambone's dedication to the Dayton Outlaws would not be for naught would be a small sacrifice indeed.

Since this circumstance was generated by a conflict with another club, and one in which both sides had proven they weren't afraid to bring firepower into play, I had to carefully consider where I was going to "pitch my tent" in Dayton. I decided that rather than find some secure hideaway where I would be safe, I would reside on the club property in Drexel, a poor, white community west of downtown. To prove that I refused to live in fear and paranoia of future attacks by our enemies, I elected to place a small travel trailer in the middle of the yard at the clubhouse to live in. You could have shot an arrow through it, let alone a bullet. What was my reasoning for taking this risk? It was to instill confidence in the men. If the boss is scared, wouldn't that cause the men to be scared too?

Each of my chapters sent two men to hang out in Dayton for a month at a time. We easily kept an extra twelve to fourteen men around that way. That relieved a lot of pressure off the Dayton Outlaws who were left. We were determined to maintain a strong presence in the neighborhood and on the street. Many were waiting to see what would happen. Local gangsters and rival motorcycle clubs alike anticipated a rise in their own influence due to the possible decrease in the effectiveness of the Outlaws to maintain a firm hand. My crew and I shattered any myths floating around that there would be any power shift in Dayton. In fact, our concerted effort afforded the chapter a higher profile than it had previously experienced.

One night in a bar on North Main Street, a friend pointed out the president of a rival club who was in there with his old lady. This is precisely what happens in times like these. People try the waters to see if the rules have changed. We weren't wearing our colors due to it being February, and we were out and about in a car that night. Outlaws don't ride around in cages with their colors on. We weren't car punks. This rival boss was incognito as well. Too bad for him he didn't have someone to point me out to him. I approached him, asked his name, and before he got it all the way out of his mouth, I nailed him with a left hook. I followed through with a right that put him on the floor.

Tensions were very high at the time, and I could see that several of our guys were more than ready to put the boots to this poor sap. I stopped that from happening. That's not the reputation I wanted. I told him, "My name is Cowboy. I'm a Dayton Outlaw. Hambone told you never to come in here, and now I'm telling you. Don't ever let me hear of one of you in this place again unless you come to finish this." With that said, I let him up, and I let him go. I didn't try to make a punk out of him. I learned a long time ago that you earn far more respect on the street by allowing a man to maintain a semblance of his manhood. He was in the wrong place at the wrong time, and he needed to be taught a lesson. I also needed to send a message home with him. That confrontation went a long way toward letting people know that just because Hambone was dead, the rules had not changed. It was still an Outlaw town.

In the course of sorting out some of Hambone's stuff, the Dayton brothers had to decide what to do with a 1985 FXRS basket case Hambone had recently acquired and intended to build. It came from a debt owed to him and had been confiscated from its previous owner. The Dayton chapter agreed that this motorcycle be given to me for my long-term friendship with Hambone and the chapter for which he gave his life.

Most of the parts were supposed to be there, but one very important item was not included—the Ohio Department of Motor Vehicles title. With our high interstate profile, that presented a problem. Many of our motorcycles had been confiscated over the years because of questionable paperwork. There was no way I was going to invest time or money into building a machine that was probably going to produce more headaches than pleasure. Besides, I didn't even like the FXR. It had a hideous box-neck, café-style frame. The engine jiggled around in there like it was going to jump out due to its rubber mounting. It didn't help matters any that it had an Evolution motor. We called them Blockheads back then. After all, I have "Shovelhead Forever" tattooed on my left forearm. Perhaps what I detested most of all was the belt drive. It bothered me to think of trusting a rubber band over a steel chain. I built and rode stroked choppers. I rode them hard. There was no way a belt could stand up to the abuse through which I could put it. Or so I thought.

My opinions on the design of the FXR aside, the big issue at hand was trying to track down the previous owner so we could get a duplicate title made. It took some doing and some creative notary work by some friends, but eventually I was able to obtain an Ohio DMV-issued title. With that accomplished, I began thinking about building this bike. Since it was already in pieces, the first thing was to get the frame sandblasted and painted. The ugly frame actually cleaned up nicely with some finger molding over the unattractive welds. I took the engine down to West Carrollton, Ohio, to a Vietnam Vet named Larry Ring. He had been a friend to Hambone down through the years, and I trusted him with the rebuild of this newfangled motor. When Ring Racing got done with it, it was somewhere around ninety-four cubic inches. He promised me I'd be pleased. He had never lied to me before, and he didn't this time either.

When I put that scooter together and fired it up, I knew it was going to be powerful. It was. It turned out to be the fastest Harley I ever owned, by far. And that rubber band? I tried to break it, and I tried to stretch it. It never did either. It was amazing. It didn't loosen up or eat away at the underside of the electric starter housing like the chain on my shovel did. It was smooth. So was the rubber-mounted engine-transmission combination. Although I was set in my ways, after riding that thing just a little while, I had to admit Harley-Davidson was on to something. And it just kept getting better and better.

By the spring of 1989, just three months after Hambone's murder, many things had changed for me, including the rocker on my back and the motorcycle I was riding. I was thirty-six years old and had been a patch holder for fourteen years. I was now living in Dayton. I was short one more old friend. I had fought a lot, ridden a lot, partied a lot, and had been to a lot of funerals. I had buried thirty-some brothers. All had died of the natural causes that were part of the lifestyle of the one-percenter. In reality, life in the fast lane often resembled life in the death lane as I followed behind so many hearses that snaked their way through inner-city neighborhoods and out into the countryside, headed for yet another graveyard.

Chapter 16

The Dark Years

When I became associated with the Outlaws MC in 1978, I was informed there was what they called a Needle Law. It pertained to intravenous drug use. In the late '60s and early '70s, the club learned the hard way about the dangers of having its members shooting dope. The mentality at the time was this: An Outlaw can do anything he wants to do so long as it didn't violate the 1%er Creed. The Outlaws found out that a brother cannot maintain the type of loyalty the club demanded when enslaved by a drug addiction, despite his best intentions.

It didn't mean a brother couldn't sell needle drugs. What a man did on his own time was his own business. The club never demanded anyone, at least not while I rode with them, to sell dope or to be involved in any criminal activity for that matter. Don't get me wrong: we were often involved in a variety of illegal pursuits, which was the nature of life outside the laws and ethics of normal society. It's important to restate that the club did not require its members to sling dope and give percentages to the treasury, as I've heard said. Many folks, including a large number in the law enforcement community, seem to have that impression. Perhaps that's because it is true of some motorcycle clubs. It wasn't true of either of the two of which I was a member. I admit there was much illegal activity going on, but it was always solely between members or citizens, and again, what members did on their own time was their own business. Drug sales were never mandatory. It was never a topic of conversation at any meeting I was ever in, whether on the chapter, regional, or national level.

The premise for the statute prohibiting mainlining was based on this saying: "No man can serve two masters." Loyalty and dedication to the organization was the very essence of being a one-percenter. Drug addiction, even more than greed or jealousy, is the mortal enemy of brotherhood. I had no clue that the phrase "No man can serve two masters" was coined by a man nearly two thousand years before the Outlaws adopted it as a creed. I came to find out those words were first spoken by Jesus Christ. I wonder if any of us knew that. Here's what we did know: after too many occasions of brothers ripping each other off in order to get enough money to maintain their addiction, the Outlaws learned those words were true. Not to mention, the last thing you need in a high-speed pack of motorcycles is a member "jonesing" for a fix instead of paying attention, or on guard duty at the clubhouse, or covering your back in a brawl. Hence, the Needle Law.

As drug use evolved, so did the problems associated with the different aspects of it. In the late '70s, another drug gained the notoriety of being more dangerous than it was fun. That drug was called THC or T, for short. I've also heard it called "cocaine number 2" and "rubber medicine." No doubt, there were many other names for the powdered substance containing an intense dose of the potent chemical of the cannabis sativa plant. A snort the size of the end of a wooden matchstick was often enough to rob a person of their equilibrium and their common sense. It gives its users almost superhuman strength and resistance to pain. I remember busting a metal barstool over a T-head's skull when he became impossible to knock out conventionally. He shrugged it off. I've seen men endure unbelievable beatings while high on it and walk away. I have even heard of men breaking handcuffs and putting cops in the hospital who attempted to subdue them while under its influence. I won't even mention the effect it had on many females, causing them to do things they've regretted for the rest of their lives.

T use was allowed, until a beloved brother from one of our Southern chapters had a little too much and blew his beautiful girlfriend's brains out while sitting in a truck stop parking lot one night. When the sun came up and people began to notice the shattered, blood-splattered passenger window of their car, they summoned the authorities. The brother told them she was a Nazi Gestapo agent and had to be eliminated for the good of the cause. He didn't resist arrest, or even realize at the time he had done anything wrong. THC had robbed him of his mind temporarily and the love of his life permanently. It also had robbed him of the freedom we valued so highly, yet so often risked with foolish, dangerous, and illegal behavior. He got life in prison without the possibility of parole for her murder. What an unnecessary waste of two lives.

This particular brother was so well respected and loved that it caused those in charge at the time to take a serious look into this growing problem of unrestricted abuse of THC. There had been other problems: court cases, injuries, and violations of the code of honor by which we had sworn to live. Those in power determined it was again time to regulate. It was time for the Outlaws to have another drug law. No more T in any way, shape, or form. Members were not allowed to snort it, smoke it, or ingest it in any other creative fashion. They could still sell it; they just couldn't use it. Destroying other people's lives for money wasn't a major concern to us. The problem was, if you could still sell it, you would still have it around, and many brothers, as well as their old ladies, liked it and continued to use it.

Its use eventually faded out under the threat of club discipline. Standard methods of discipline might include a black eye, a fine, or, for extremely serious offences, even the temporary loss of one's colors. A chapter enforcer usually administered a black eye. It wasn't so much the pain as it was the fact that everyone else could see you'd gotten in trouble, including citizens that knew some of our ways. It was humiliating to have to stand there and take a punch in the face without dodging or blocking. That is flat out contrary to human nature, especially ours. That was the point, plus having the reminder "in (*on*) your face" when you looked in the mirror for the next couple of days. A brother wasn't supposed to be seriously hurt, though, just taught a lesson. If discipline was due, it was dealt with and done with. Once an issue had been addressed, it was over. Therefore, the smartest way to move on after you messed up was to take what you had coming like a man.

If the boss was mad enough, or the infraction serious enough, he would administer the black eye himself. When I was the Toledo boss, I almost always doled out the black eyes personally. A black eye wasn't supposed to be a bloody nose or a cracked jaw. I had enforcers who had plenty of enthusiasm, but often lacked the skill to land their fist in the right place with the appropriate amount of force. Working out with the speed bag I put up in the basement of the Hawley Street clubhouse afforded me the ability to do both.

Some members got so used to black eyes that it didn't bother them enough to provoke them to go by the rules. Then club discipline would require a fine instead. Back in the '70s and '80s, most of us were not high-rolling businessmen, no matter what anyone says, and a hundred bucks was still a lot of money. For example, discharging a firearm in the clubhouse was a hundred dollar fine, per bullet. Every Outlaw clubhouse I was ever in had holes in the ceiling where you could see the light of day shining through. Many had more than one.

Early one morning during a party, I was upstairs in my room at 38 North Hawley, high on cocaine and drunk on Jack Daniel's. I was mad about something a brother had done, and for emphasis, I picked up my trusty Colt 1911 Government Model and fired a round up through the ceiling. It had the desired effect on my subject and I liked that, so I fired it again. Brothers downstairs at number 36 were wondering what was going on as I continued firing. I emptied the magazine and loaded another. I discharged the second magazine, then pulled the SAA .45 Long Colt I got from Jac Coe from a drawer and emptied it as well. I was having fun and the brothers knew better than to interfere. I ended up firing every weapon I had.

When the smoke cleared, there were over forty holes in my bedroom ceiling. Personally, I thought it was hilarious, but no one else did. Even though we lived at the end of the alley in the worst part of Toledo's ghetto, it was still a miracle the police never came. It was a good thing for me they didn't, though, when it came time to face the music with my brothers. That would have made it much worse. I was glad I was the boss when it came time for punishment. I determined there would be no fine since I didn't have that kind of money. I asked anyone who wanted to volunteer for the job of giving me a black eye to step forward, but no one did; not that everyone there didn't think I deserved it, because I did. I threw my own case out of court and then commanded our new probationary member to get on the roof and fix all the holes. They did make me give my word not to do that anymore. I promised I would be a good boy, and that was that. Doesn't sound very fair, does it? That's the way it was at the chapter level. The higher up the ladder you went, the more hypocritical it often got, just like in every other area of life.

The most serious demonstration of club discipline was the revocation of a member's patch and return to probationary status. Though we all struggled with rules, whether society's or our own, our pride and joy were our beloved colors. They weren't easy to get and were worth doing anything to keep, including changing our ways accordingly. The most unthinkable consequence would be to have to become a probate again, waiting on the brothers hand and foot, keeping the bar stocked, and especially not being allowed to sit in on "church." Some members had treated other probates so badly that the very thought of being subject to them, now that they were members, was unthinkable. It didn't happen often or easily, but if a brother refused to get with the program, be it in his personal life or his public conduct as a patch holder, he could lose his colors.

Our drug laws got another supplement in the '80s with the addition of a law against smoking cocaine. Some Florida brothers became so affluent in the cocaine business they could afford to freebase. I was offered the opportunity to try it numerous times, but I refused. I was at the lowest level of cocaine abuse, which often involved snorting ridiculous amounts over a period of several days. Freebasing could send an ounce of the very pure, very expensive white powder literally up in smoke in a matter of hours. I didn't need any more bad habits, especially one that expensive. My personal drug abuse was already interfering with my first loves of riding and wrenching. I certainly didn't need to develop an affection for anything as costly and addictive as this new fad. The price tag of freebasing was not what brought legislative action against it. However, the damage it did to the minds, loyalty, and brotherhood of some very dedicated brothers did. Jesus said, "No man can serve two masters." We proved him right over and over again. Too bad we didn't listen to him.

One unforeseen benefit of the ban on smoking coke was it inadvertently pertained to crack. Although crack made its appearance on the street in the late '80s, I never tried it. I never knew anyone who sold it, and personally never even saw it. I am glad I didn't. By the end of that decade, I had enough problems with cocaine in the powdered form. Although I did a lot of different drugs through the years, nothing got a hold of me like the white "booger sugar." I drank Tennessee whiskey almost daily for over ten years, and it never captivated me like "devil's dandruff." When coke was scarce, I had no problem doing without it. When someone I knew would get a shipment in, it became readily available to me. When it was around, it became all I wanted to do. To my shame, it caused me to let my brothers down seriously on more than a few occasions. Had it not been for my longstanding and impeccable record of loyalty, self-control, and sound judgment, I surely would have been the subject of severe club discipline for drug abuse. By 1990, I was on a collision course with self-destruction.

Because of the drug trade, many members of the club were learning to become businessmen rather than bike riders. I found myself unable to make the conversion, though the opportunity was presented to me on many occasions. My heart was in the brotherhood, the motorcycle, and the open road. My feeble attempts to peddle dope resulted in my becoming strung out myself and always playing catch up with the bills. I had buried so many of my hard-riding, hard-fighting, hard-partying brothers, I really didn't care anymore. I ended up wasting many of my days and nights high on coke, drunk on whiskey, surrounded by guns, and waiting for the final gun battle with whoever caught up with me in the wrong mood.

Toward the end of my career as a patch-holding one-percenter, I made some decisions that went against things I believed, due to being under the influence of cocaine. Once I attended a meeting that required my utmost attention, wrung out after a binge. I could barely maintain my train of thought, let alone make the best choices for my beloved brothers. I led packs when I was so wasted that no one should have followed me ten feet, let alone down an interstate highway at eighty-plus miles per hour. We would say things like, "Drugs are a sign of weakness in a man." In truth, for some of us, drugs became more important than the motorcycle or the brotherhood. I'm ashamed to admit it, but for a time, that group would have included me. Looking back, I am amazed I survived.

I wasn't the only one corrupted by the ready access of dangerous drugs. A good example would be the account of the near murder of a dear friend of mine in a Miamisburg, Ohio, motel room in the early '80s. He'd come up from Florida to bring Christmas presents to his children. His marriage had become a casualty of drug abuse, even though he was a very successful businessman. Several of us went to his motel to see him while he was in town and, of course, to get high with him. He always had plenty of dope and plenty of money. A Detroit brother and I spent the day with him while others stopped in during the course of his stay there. A few hours after we left, two gunmen attempted to rob him in his room. He was shot multiple times.

When I got the call, he was on life support in a Cincinnati, Ohio, hospital, not expected to live. I remember thinking, *I was in that room all day and my fingerprints were all over the place. If he dies, I'll be a prime suspect.* I went down to the hospital to see him and possibly find out who did this to him while he was still alive. I was shocked to find out that it was two men he knew well. That explained how they got in the room without a struggle. They were trusted. They were friends. In an attempt to get some fast cash, and hopefully make off with a large stash of cocaine, they were willing to murder a friend. To make matters worse, had he died, I most likely would have been the one charged for it. Thank God he didn't die, and he had enough class, with some persuading, not to press charges. By the way, the two robbers, not to mention would-be killers, didn't even get the dope that day. It was wrapped up like a Christmas present with his kid's name on it. As a matter of fact, the cops didn't get it either.

The above incident is one of several that were too common during the "dark years." Not everyone, of course, was corrupted by the drugs. Some became subject to the power of something even more treacherous— money. For many, the prospect of making large amounts of cash completely changed their priorities. The emphasis went from bikin' and brotherhood to big bucks. I don't know which was worse: drug addiction or greed. I do know this: our world was changing rapidly, and not for the better.

The Feds were successfully taking advantage of our new focus, greed, and inexperience. While it is true we had some street-savvy operators, well equipped with the smarts and *cojones* to exploit the many opportunities that came along, most joined the club just to ride and party. Those of us in that category became easy prey for the well-funded war on organized crime the government was waging on us. They convicted some of our members of racketeering who weren't organized enough to remember where their own stash was.

In the mid-'80s, another RICO indictment came down against our club in Florida. The brothers who were rounded up this time were detained at the Miami Correctional Institution. The club hired a big-shot Miami lawyer to ramrod their defense team, and the membership contributed to pay his enormous retainer fee. Where to store the cash collected became an issue. We needed someone of impeccable character who would not be tempted by having $200,000 cash in his possession. Impeccable character? People like that were in short supply in the world we lived in. Finally, I was approached with regards to my father. "Would he be willing to sit on the defense fund as it accumulated until such time as it was ready to be transported to the attorney?" I was asked. "I'll find out," was all I could say. My dad was as honest as the day is long. I explained to him that every member was asked to donate, and we needed someone who could be trusted to secure it until it all came in. He had been a combat infantryman during WWII, so I wasn't worried about him getting robbed. I had given him a beautiful nickel-plated Colt 1911A1 Government Model for his birthday one year, and he knew how to use it. With two fingers missing from a construction accident, he could still handle a .45 better than most men I knew.

As the media began to publish and broadcast details of the "big Outlaw bust," we had the normal inquiries from the local television news teams requesting interviews. Our policy was to not talk to the press, except on rare occasions. We had learned that they really aren't interested in the truth at all. Generally, all they were after was another story. It was about this time I received a call from the South Florida boss. Two limousines had pulled into the driveway of the Southwest Fortieth Avenue clubhouse. They were detected immediately by closed-circuit cameras, which caused the brothers to "batten the hatches," as they were unsure of what was going on. As the gate to the backyard was being closed, Hicks stepped out onto the front porch, as Geraldo Rivera was getting out of the front limo. A camera man began to exit the second car, but was abruptly told that if he didn't turn the camera off, it would be put "where the sun doesn't shine." Geraldo motioned for the video cam to be put away. In response to Hick's inquiry, "What do you want?" Rivera responded, "I'd like an interview concerning the current RICO indictment against members of your organization. I think the American people would be interested in hearing your side of the story." Hicks told him he did not have that kind of authority, but said, "Give me a phone number. I'll have someone call you."

I got on a plane for Miami the next morning. I had purchased an old Dodge Fury cop car so I would have wheels at the Lauderdale clubhouse when flying to south Florida was necessary. I also kept a Model 19 S&W .357 there for the same reason. Collecting both car and pistol, I headed to the attorney's Biscayne Boulevard office. His advice was not to give anybody any interviews without him being present. I called Geraldo that afternoon, introduced myself, and informed him I did have the authority to speak with him, and that I would be willing to do so at our attorney's office the next afternoon. His response was as expected. He would not agree to meet with me there. "That's what I thought," I said, as I proceeded to give him my opinion about what I thought of people like him, whose only interest was to capitalize on any opportunity that would advance their own career. If telling our side of the story had really been his goal, why would he refuse to speak to me in front of credible witnesses? We both knew why. He wouldn't be able to spin the interview for his own purpose, like he would if it was just my word against his.

Since there would be no interview and I had some time to kill before flying home, I made a call to a Canadian acquaintance in the area. He happened to be flying over to Nassau the next day and asked me if I'd like to go along for the ride. I said, "Sure, why not? I've never been to the Bahamas." We took off on a Chalk's seaplane from the Fort Lauderdale airport but landed in the water just off Paradise Island. That was an experience. I'd jumped out of airplanes, but I had never landed on the water in one. I had also never seen the ocean as blue as it was around those islands. Magnificent! We were picked up by a Bahamian man in a Cadillac and driven across the bridge to Nassau. Our driver then took us under the bridge where vendors were selling vegetables, seafood, and the like. We stopped at a stand where a merchant pulled a live conch out of the huge shell, diced it up on the table before him, and then dropped the pieces into three baggies containing fresh lettuce, tomato, and onions. After mixing the ingredients thoroughly, he handed each of us a baggie. I couldn't imagine what for, until my companions dipped their fingers into theirs and began to eat. Not to be outdone, I followed suit. How was it? I'll just say this. It didn't taste like chicken.

After that introduction to island life, I was given the fifty-cent tour before being told the real purpose of the trip. This was a collection endeavor, and I had been asked to come along in case some muscle was needed. Here was I, attempting to appear incognito, wearing a polo shirt and my hair in a ponytail. It was too warm even to pretend to conceal my heavily tattooed arms with long sleeves. That would have looked even more out of place than I did already. In other words, I did not look like your average, run-of-the-mill tourist—not by a long shot. As we approached what I was told to be a very rough ghetto, I spotted a huge sign that read "Ronald Reagan for President… Forever." I was cautioned not to make eye contact with any of the locals. "Why not?" I asked. I was told, "Very simple. You are the wrong color." Our driver disappeared into a shack surrounded by dreadlock-wearing men who were blatantly smoking huge "chillums" of who knows exactly what. As they got higher, it wasn't long before our very presence there irritated them. They began to circle our vehicle, making comments I could not interpret, but I could definitely understand. I had been told people had disappeared here, never to be seen again, and I remember thinking, *I wish I had a pistol.* My friend said, "Don't look at them. Maybe they will move on." I was already working on a plan to burst out of the car and at least die fighting when our driver came out and smoothed everything over. I remember thinking to myself, *What am I doing on an island in the Atlantic Ocean, surrounded by drug-crazed natives, so far from my beloved Harley-Davidson?* What did all this have to do with bikin' and brotherhood? Absolutely nothing. Too many areas of my life now had nothing to do with bikin' and brotherhood. Where would it end? I had no idea.

By late 1989 and throughout 1990, my life was spiraling out of control at a rapid pace. Hambone was dead. Ralph was dead. A few of the brothers left the club. Some of my closest brothers became so successful in illegal pursuits that their love of bikin' and brotherhood began to give way to "business." Their primary focus shifted to taking advantage of the Outlaws vast and elaborate interstate network of brothers who had absolutely no particular moral convictions about breaking the law to make money.

After all, we were Outlaws. Legal employment was actually frowned upon in some of our chapters. If you couldn't live off of the fat of the land in America, what kind of Outlaw would you be? The mentality existed that even if a brother were a lame businessman, he ought to be able to find some working girl willing to support him, if for no other reason than just the thrill of being an Outlaw old lady.

For the ones who became successful at making money, a problem presented itself that I wouldn't have foreseen back in the Longbranch Saloon days of the mid-'70s. For money to become spendable on something besides party supplies and lawyer fees, it needed to be legitimized. Bike shops, used car lots, bars, and other enterprises began to spring up for the purpose of laundering profits from illegal endeavors. One such business was a Main Street bar I frequented in Dayton. The owners approached me about keeping an eye on the place for them when I was in town. In others words, I was asked to be the bouncer.

I hung out there anyway, so getting a title made it seem like I actually had a reason to be there, other than just destroying my life with Jack Daniel's and cocaine.

I had an easy chair brought in and placed at the high end of the bar. From there I could survey every corner of the place, as well as have my own back in such a position that no one could get behind me. Directly to my rear was a small room equipped with a mirror, razor blade, and a straw. Certain few were permitted entrance, and the "fee" was always a line for me. I would open a fifth of JD nightly, and from my elevated perch the patronage could gauge my tolerance for foolishness by how much whiskey was left in the bottle; the lower the amount, the shorter my fuse. I took my job seriously. To me, it meant nobody was allowed to fight in the bar, except me. When two men would have a disagreement, I would immediately insert myself into their altercation. If I could quell the situation, fine. If they ceased to back down, the fight was on, with me sometimes against them both.

One night, a huge guy came through the door cussing and shoving regular customers out of the way, threatening people with every breath. I was sizing him up, confident he wasn't going to take any kind of hint to cool his jets when he made an unacceptable comment to the barmaid. As experienced as she was, I could see she was visibly rattled by his presence, so I called out to her, "Debbie, call an ambulance." That's when he noticed me staring directly at him as I spoke to her. He looked around as if to see who was needing an ambulance. When he looked at me again, I told him it was for him. I said, "You can walk out of here, or you can go out on a gurney, but you're leaving my bar." As I began to stand, he opted to leave. Smart man. Do I think I could have whipped him? I don't know. I carried a Colt Combat Commander that could have, though.

I didn't fight every night because I thought I couldn't be whipped; I fought because I just didn't care what happened anymore. Between the federal heat, the transition within the club, and my own substance-abuse problems, I just did not care. I was sick and tired of peeking out of my window every time I heard a car in the alley, wondering if it was cops or a rival club. I signed up for freedom, and the life I was living now was anything but free.

Chapter 17

Sturgis 1990

Although Daytona was our biggest run of the year, it was decided in fall 1989 that we needed to go back to the Black Hills Classic in South Dakota the following year. The event was attracting hundreds of thousands of bikers every year, as well as getting an immense amount of exposure in all the biker magazines. The other big clubs had been cashing in on it, so we determined we needed to as well.

In January 1990, a scouting party was sent to Sturgis to make arrangements to accommodate several hundred of us. Taco (Detroit), Dan (Milwaukee), and I flew into Rapid City, rented a car, and headed west to the obscure, yet famous, town of Sturgis. I had never been there before, though the club had made an appearance there in 1978. Several members wore a Cattle Rustler patch on their colors after getting busted shooting a couple of cows in order to help feed the massive gathering of

Outlaws. Shooting a cow was no problem; however, dragging its dead carcass up into a U-Haul trailer was. My suggestion after the fact was, "Wouldn't it have been easier to have the cow walk into the trailer and then shoot it?" Hindsight is always 20/20, isn't it? That incident, as well as some other issues, worked together to do anything but endear us to the rural Western community. It was decided that the Outlaws would concentrate their energy and resources closer to home. Sturgis was in Bandido territory anyway.

The tiny town was anything but impressive to me when the three of us rolled in incognito. It was a dreary, overcast, and cold January day. The town consisted of about two blocks of Main Street, complete with what you'd expect in a Western community this size: a general store with groceries, a livestock feed store, and a clothing store or two. It was hard to picture this place hosting two hundred thousand bikers or to imagine why anyone would even want to come here.

We located the local distributors we were going to need for beer, ice, and meat. We decided to buy it this time, rather than forage for it. That stuff was easy. What we really needed to have nailed down by the end of this recon trip was a place to stay. We needed a place large enough for a national run, affordable, but most importantly, securable. We inquired at some motels and found out where the Hells Angels had made reservations. We checked out several campgrounds and were enlightened as to where some other large and unfriendly clubs were going to be staying. I'll never forget proprietors of two campgrounds opening their reservation books to us, showing us what sections other clubs had reserved, oblivious to the fact that they might be revealing important confidential information.

We finally found a large hill on the South side of town with only one access road and about five acres of usable area on top. We determined it would be perfect for us and rented it for the August Bike Week, as well as the week prior. With the logistical tasks complete, Taco, Dan, and I headed down to Deadwood, which had recently legalized gambling. The once-quiet town was now teeming with activity as tour buses brought people to try their luck. These weren't Vegas-style casinos by any means, but a blackjack table is a blackjack table. Taco and I both did pretty well, leaving with more money than we had when we went in. We, of course, were attracted to Saloon No. 10, where Wild Bill Hickok had been shot in the back and killed. They even had the chair he was sitting in at the time he was bushwhacked mounted over the door.

In the preparations to take the American Outlaw Association to the Black Hills, there were still a few important details that needed attention. South Dakota was technically a Bandido state. In fact, they had a chapter in Rapid City, which was only thirty miles southwest of Sturgis. Since they were also a one-percenter club, the respectful thing to do was to notify them of our intention to bring a large number of Outlaws through their territory. This presented no problem at all. Taco had known their national president, Ronnie Hodges, for years.

The next challenge was going to be much more interesting. It had to do with the fact that the Hells Angels would also be there. There had been tension, to put it mildly, between the Outlaws and the Angels dating back to before most members of either organization could remember. We both knew the law-enforcement community loved the fact that we didn't get along and looked forward to picking up the pieces after any confrontation. We resented the fact that the Feds often instigated problems between the clubs. They would be the real winners if anything got out of hand in Sturgis. The problem was, neither of us trusted the other enough to be able to agree on a meeting place to discuss keeping our personal differences personal.

The solution to the meeting location problem was solved through the Terre Haute Federal Penitentiary Jaycee Chapter. It was made up predominantly of members of the Outlaws and the Angels; there at least, the two clubs got along. They began to petition the warden for permission to have a prison bike show that would allow visitors into the yard for the event. It had been done before in other prisons and proved to be a good public-relations move, as well as a morale booster to the inmates involved.

It was determined that if the Outlaws and the Hells Angels could each get a high-ranking representative behind the ominous walls of this federal pen, perhaps groundwork could begin for a truce at the upcoming Sturgis Rally. Sonny Barger was currently serving time over the Louisville deal. The highest ranking Angel at the time of the May 1990 bike show was George Christy, president of the Ventura, California, Hells Angels chapter. He got cleared to go in and meet with the Outlaws spokesman, which was me.

George flew in to Indianapolis while I led a small pack west to Terre Haute from Dayton, Ohio. A half dozen of us were cleared to take our bikes in for entry in the show. Upon arrival, we were escorted into a sally port for careful inspection. We had already drained all but enough fuel to get us back to a gas station, so all that needed to be addressed was making sure the scooters wouldn't start. Taking the spark plugs out took care of that. Once inside the walls, we pushed the bikes into the yard where the judging would take place. Some other bikers showed up as well, and they had to go through the same process. Eventually, we had about fourteen bikes lined up, waiting for the prisoners to be released for participation in the event.

When the incarcerated brothers first appeared, I recognized several from before they went to prison. It was good to see them again. They were accompanied by some men I didn't know. One of them was an infamous Outlaw

343

who'd been locked up since before I'd come around. His name was Big Jim. He had been the Florida boss before getting into big trouble for numerous reasons. "Free Big Jim" T-shirts were frequently seen at Outlaw events back in the '70s, implying he'd been the target of some unfair effort to eliminate the club. If everyone behind bars who claimed to be innocent actually was, that would mean there must be an awful lot of very dangerous criminals on the loose. On second thought, there are.

I was introduced as the AOA officer-in-charge not only to the Outlaws, but also to the Hells Angels members of the prison Jaycee organization. We were all on the same page. Whatever different ideologies we had on the street, behind the walls of a penitentiary, we had more in common than not. If for no other reason than we were both white. That alone put us in a minority, and minorities stick together. Actually, we had much more in common than that. We were one-percenters, and our lives were dedicated to the principles of bikin' and brotherhood. That's no small thing.

It wasn't long before another Hells Angel made his way to the area designated for this bike show. He wasn't an inmate, though. George Christy and I introduced ourselves to each other, shook hands for all to see (especially the prison officials), and commenced to talk with our individual members for a while. As the prisoners gathered around to look at the bikes and the Jaycees assessed the motorcycles with their clipboards,

George and I stepped back to discuss the subject that had brought us to this place. We both knew there would be a multitude of law-enforcement personnel from every conceivable agency at Sturgis.

They'd be there with their expensive cameras and zoom lenses, recording the faces of as many members as possible. They'd be there looking for fugitives, like they did at all our events, including funerals. We knew we were going to make their job really easy for them by gathering together in one public place. In some ways, they would be looking forward to Sturgis more than we would. The Feds knew it would be all but impossible for us to avoid some kind of conflict. It was in our very nature. They didn't really care who did what to whom; they hated us all. They shouldn't have. We provided the means for their very handsome federal budget. Let's face it. Who's going to be easier to do surveillance on? A highly organized and secretive mafioso or a bunch of bearded, high-profile, colors-wearing bikers? Go figure. Without us, they would have had to work much harder for their salaries.

This historic meeting, built on the foundation of the one in Louisville, was for much the same purpose, only this time the subject was a national motorcycle event instead of a trial. The common desire between George, me, and the organizations we represented was the fact that we wanted the privilege of settling any differences we had, whatever they may be at any given point in time, in private. The idea of the government coming in to pick up the pieces and then claim credit for what we did to ourselves was unacceptable, if it could at all be avoided.

At the end of the day, we agreed that great effort would be made to maintain a semblance of civility pertaining to this upcoming Sturgis Run, including on the roads to and from the event. We agreed to do our best to behave ourselves in public. He gave me contact numbers of the Cleveland Hells Angels, so I could further coordinate details with them. We then shook hands again before joining the others. It was a good meeting for a good purpose. The icing on the cake for me was that I was awarded the first-place plaque in the bike show. That came as no surprise, really. I knew I had the best-looking scooter in the show. Besides, several of the judges were Outlaws!

I met several times with members of the Cleveland Angels during the months of June and July. It was an uncomfortable situation for all of us, especially at first. I must say, everything proceeded remarkably on track as far as went goes. We all had the safety of our brothers as our foremost agenda. Many of my own brothers were very leery of having any dealings with the Hells Angels at all, but I was convinced this endeavor was valid. If it could save one brother's life it was worth it to me, regardless of what anyone thought.

As the end of July rolled around, I volunteered to head up the early crew. We'd made all sorts of arrangements, from land rental to ice and beer deliveries, which needed to be solidified prior to the arrival of the Outlaw Nation en masse. I had no problem getting four volunteers to go with me, so I bought a motor home, loaded our bikes in an enclosed trailer, and headed west. We, of course, traveled incognito due to the number of guns we felt we needed to take everywhere we went. Many of us were veterans, and we just liked them, I guess. Imagine five tattooed, bearded men traveling cross-country in a recreational vehicle trying to look inconspicuous. We probably had Feds following us from the first campground where we stopped.

My crew and I arrived a good week and a half before Bike Week actually began and took possession of the property we'd rented back in January. The plateau on the high hill south of town had a single, winding road leading up to it and would be easy to secure and to defend, if necessary. After doing some routine surveillance, we settled in and began to reconnect with the different vendors with whom Taco, Dan, and I had contracted. Things were falling into place nicely and, slowly but surely, the little town began to fill up. Groups of bikers began to roll in constantly in anticipation of the fiftieth anniversary of the annual Black Hills Motorcycle Classic. Most were no more interested in the races than we were. They came to Sturgis to ride and to party. The sound of two-wheeled thunder permeated the atmosphere. At times, it seemed the very earth shook. I loved it.

Three days before the official kick-off date, Taco showed up with twenty more brothers. Our reconnaissance revealed the Hells Angels had rented a motel, also on the South side of town. As a matter of fact, our elevated knoll overlooked it. We liked that. In our favorite training film of the '80s, *The Outlaw Josey Wales*, the importance of having the high ground with the sun at your back was the utmost priority in any gunfight. Of course, we weren't here for a gunfight, especially in such a public setting so closely observed by law enforcement.

It was time to make contact with the Angels. Since I had been the chief liaison officer with them throughout this operation, Taco sent me down into the midst of a hundred or so "Red and White" to make sure we were still on the same page. I guess if I had been killed, it would have confirmed that we were not. I remember hoping Kenny from Cleveland would be there, or at least someone who was aware of our clubs' attempts to formulate this truce. If not, it wouldn't have been a very smart move to ride in there.

A faithful brother named Ed, from our Warren, Ohio, chapter, volunteered to go with me. He was a former US army paratrooper as I was, and he didn't have enough sense to be afraid of anything. Ed loved the club and had no ulterior motive whatsoever for his loyalty. Bikin' and brotherhood was what he was about, and I can't think of a greater compliment to pay the man. As he and I rode into the Angel camp, I'll never forget the looks of disbelief on their faces. They could not believe a couple of Outlaws would ride right into their midst unprotected. Many of them had never seen an Outlaw before, just as many of our guys had never seen a real Hells Angel. We had been rivals for so long, many on either side didn't even remember why. Of course, Ed and I were not without backup. I'm not talking about the Colt .45s we both carried. They wouldn't have helped very much had this situation gone wrong. Our backs were covered by twenty-plus Outlaws up on the ridge behind us with high-powered rifles, visibly and obviously capable of covering us. I remember thinking, *I hope none of these Angels have a good pair of binoculars*. The truth of the matter was, the truck with our high-powered rifles hadn't arrived yet, so Taco had the brothers find branches that resembled long guns in an effort to bluff them. I don't attribute our safety to that. I was counting on the word of George and Kenny to keep us safe. It did.

In the days to come, Sturgis transformed itself into the largest city in the state of South Dakota. Literally hundreds of thousands of bikers converged on this normally quiet, even boring, little town. Main Street was closed to all but motorcycle traffic. Bikes lined the several blocks of downtown area, and a constant flow of scooters would be going up one side of the street and down the other. The citizen biker groups would ride by, seesawing back and forth, gunning their engines, trying to attract attention.

When a procession of one-percenters, whether they were Outlaws, Hells Angels, or Bandidos, descended onto Main Street, everyone took notice. These clubs rode uniformly side by side, carefully maintaining their military-style formation. It was an ominous and intimidating sight that caused everyone on the street to stop what he was doing and watch. Many observed with curiosity, others with fear, and some even with envy, because we were what they didn't have the guts to be. We were what they pretended to be back home the rest of the year, reading their *Easyriders* magazines, memorizing the lingo, and imagining themselves to be hardcore bikers. Don't get me wrong. Many who came to Sturgis were the real deal. I never believed you had to ride with a club to be a true biker. I was one before I ever joined a club. The truth is, there was something intriguing about those of us who were *totally* sold out to the lifestyle of bikin' and brotherhood.

During the course of the next week, I spent more time with the Angels than with my own club. This peacemaker position was certainly different from what I was accustomed to. At major functions like this, my responsibility usually consisted of policing our own guys. In this situation, I diligently watched my own back because the most sincere agreements sometimes get violated when drugs and liquor work their way into the equation. As I observed these Angels, I was reminded of something George Christy told me behind the walls of the Terre Haute Federal Correctional complex. He said, "Cowboy, the biggest difference between you and me is logistical. If I lived where you do, I'd be what you are. If you lived where I do, you'd be what I am." As hard as every club tries to convince itself that it's totally superior to every other, the truth of the matter was we weren't so different after all. That was a sobering reality after all those years of thinking the other way.

My motor home was parked up on the hill, at the edge of our perimeter. If there was any problem with security or if anyone needed an executive decision, they'd wake me up instead of Taco. If I deemed it necessary, I would go to Taco myself. Such was the case the fourth night of Bike Week. One of the brothers was riding through the campsite, not paying attention, and ran into Big Moe, who was on foot. (Big Moe from Dayton was well named, for he was a huge man, strong as a bull and twice as mean if you got on the wrong side of him.) A foot peg gashed Moe's leg deeply, and it was decided he should go to the hospital. Of course, Sturgis didn't have one. The nearest medical facility was in Rapid City. Several brothers took him there for treatment where the doctor advised he spend the night for observation. Amazingly, Big Moe agreed. He was sore from the collision anyway and knew he'd have a better chance to rest there than at the campsite with two hundred Outlaws asking him how he was feeling.

About three in the morning I was awakened by one of the front gate guards, informing me the sheriff's department wanted to speak to whoever was in charge. I made my way over to them, unhappy about having been woken up, demanding to know what was going on. I knew it couldn't have been due to any trouble our people had caused. Everyone was accounted for. The sheriff's deputy informed me that Gary Elmore, aka Big Moe, had died in the Rapid City Hospital due to a blood clot to his heart. I couldn't believe my ears! I thought of all the effort that had gone into trying to prevent anyone from being hurt, and now they were telling me this beloved brother was dead. I immediately suspected foul play. I don't know whom I suspected specifically, but I knew one thing—I sure wasn't just going to take some cop's word for it.

The first thing that had to be done was inform Taco. When I headed to his campsite, I didn't know whether he would be awake or not, but it didn't matter. He had to be told right away. I hated to bear that kind of news. He took it about the same way I did. He told me to get to the hospital and verify the information personally. I immediately grabbed two Dayton brothers, and we headed to Rapid City. We got there a little after four in the morning and the place was pretty quiet. I told the information desk clerk we were there to see Big Moe, but I was informed visiting hours were long since over. Obviously, that didn't go over too well. When security showed up, they told us Mr. Elmore had died, and we would need to come back in the morning. That didn't go over too well either.

I told the guard I was next of kin and "convinced" him to let me see the body. We were escorted to the room where he lay there on a gurney, deader than a doornail. Cause of death? A blood clot in his leg broke loose, traveling to his heart. I'd known Moe since before I'd become an Outlaw. This was an unexpected and very sad turn of events. For me and for the Dayton chapter of the Outlaws, the party was over. Upon arrival back at camp and confirming to Taco that Big Moe was indeed dead, my crew and the rest of the Dayton brothers began to load up. We were heading home to prepare for another funeral. Taco would be bringing the rest of the club with him in a few days.

Hundreds of brothers came, as well as many locals. Even Big Moe's son, who was serving time in prison, was there to pay his final respects. Of course, he was in shackles, escorted by correctional officers, but we were glad he was able to make it. Big Moe's funeral was a classic: the long procession of motorcycles, the traditional gun salute at the gravesite, the ritual of taking turns at the shovel, filling in the grave. "God forgives; Outlaws don't," echoed around the cemetery. Life in the fast lane had claimed another one-percenter.

Chapter 18

What Goes Around Comes Around

*"You will spend years of your life behinds bars, die young…
or both."*

I was told up front that the life of an Outlaw had a price.
I'd seen payday for brothers come often, sometimes by
way of the prison gate; for many, it was through death's
dark door. A Detroit Outlaw named Lenny indeed had
told me the truth back in the spring of 1978.

It was the Feds who finally caught up with me.
Luckily, they came after I had crashed from a four-day
binge. At about 6:00 a.m. on the morning of October
30, 1990, they came busting through the door of the dive
I was staying at in North Dayton. It was good that the
Feds came then rather than the previous day. Had they
come while I was high, there is no telling what might
have happened to them or to me. Correction. I know
what would have happened to me. I'd have gotten my

355

wish of joining the ranks of the "Forever Chapter" out on Boot Hill, having gone down with guns blazing.

It had been a toss of the coin to see whether I would finally "reap what I'd sown" for the last fifteen years, at the hands of the cops, the street, or simply succumbing to years of substance abuse. The police were just one of our numerous adversaries. We also had enemies within the realm of organized crime, among other major motorcycle clubs, and on the streets of every city in which we had a chapter. For a multitude of reasons, there were those who were jealous of the freedom we enjoyed. Had they known the vast number of us who were in bondage to drugs and alcohol, let alone the intense scrutiny of the law-enforcement community, they wouldn't have been as envious. Others were jealous because their girlfriends left them for the apparent glamor of a life about which they knew very little. Others were just on the wrong end of confrontations they had no prayer of winning.

All these things work together to accumulate a lot of people who are happy to see you go down. Most of our enemies had better sense than to try to ambush us at a stronghold like a clubhouse or even a personal residence. Most—not all. We had some very sophisticated and daring adversaries who were capable of just about anything. It was good for me that none of them ever caught up with me when I was high as a kite. By this point in my life, I was often too messed up to make the critical judgments necessary to stay alive in the brutal world I'd chosen to be involved in for so many years.

I was awakened early that day by an unfamiliar sound. Just about the time the battering ram came through my front door, I had jumped out of bed and looked out the window. The moment the curtain moved, a handful of M16s were immediately trained on me as I realized what was going on. Cops were everywhere. I heard the familiar command, "Don't move. Put your hands in the air." I also heard cops running up the stairs toward my bedroom. The next voice I heard told me to turn around slowly. As I complied, I could see they were equipped for combat: helmets, shields, vests, and automatic rifles galore. This cavalry charge was led by a CANE Task Force agent by the name of Farrell. He looked the part too, just like General Custer, with his long blond hair and flowing mustache. His day ended better than Custer's did, though. That day, he won.

I was marched downstairs under heavy guard while his crew proceeded to tear my house apart. They emptied every drawer and closet, pried paneling off the walls, and even destroyed my vacuum cleaner looking for dope. Once they broke through the door to my office, they began to bring out weapon after weapon, hundreds and hundreds of rounds of ammo, much of it already loaded into magazines. What can I say? I liked guns. They emptied my safe of vehicle titles, several thousand dollars, and enough gold jewelry to make Mr. T proud.

With a big smile, one of the agents brought out a bag of white powder. When another came out of the room with my colors, they all realized that much more was going on here than what they expected. They were looking for the parole-jumping brother of my landlord, and their warrant empowered them to confiscate anything that could be used to facilitate illegal drug activity. They didn't expect to find a member of the Outlaws Motorcycle Club, let alone the regional boss.

It was not shaping up to be a good day for me to say the least. They were simultaneously busting the residence next door, so there were a lot of cops present, including city, state, and federal agents. The warrant to enter my residence was issued to the Bureau of Alcohol, Tobacco, and Firearms. Before the day was done, between the two addresses, they had seized over $40,000, fifty some-odd weapons, and five ounces of very high-grade cocaine. They impounded a Corvette and a couple of Harleys. As I watched all this I thought, *Easy come, easy go. I got it once, I can get it again.* Then they arrested me. I was charged with possession of narcotics with the intent to distribute, and possession of a firearm with intent to facilitate distribution of said narcotics.

Escorted to a Fed van through a maze of news channel reporters and photographers, I cursed them loudly and gave them the finger with both shackled hands, in an effort to keep this event off the evening news. It didn't work. They cropped the video, muted the sound, and successfully portrayed me as a wild man. Actually, that helped me out once I got to the Montgomery County Jail. Many of the inmates watching the news knew I was coming, and some correctly reckoned that I was not one to be messed with.

I was arraigned before Federal Magistrate Michael R. Merz that morning and when his gavel came down, so did the words, "No bond." That was attributed to my membership in an "international criminal organization with the ability to flee to avoid prosecution." He must have been reading my mind. I was still a non-felon in spite of several previous weapon arrests through the years and fully expected to make bond that morning, as I'd always done in the past. I knew bond would be high since this was a federal beef, but we had resources, to say the least. I had every intention of "fleeing to avoid prosecution" for as long as possible. I figured I'd get to make at least several guest appearances on *America's Most Wanted* before having to face the music. Besides, we were prepared for things like this, right down to researching which Central American countries did not have extradition treaties with the United States. I didn't relish the thought of spending days on a fishing trawler, not riding my Harley, or not seeing my brothers for a long time. I did have a mental picture of me lying in a hammock, sipping a piña colada on a beach in Costa Rica. That sounded great compared to federal prison. Those words, "to be held without bond," shattered that image for me and brought me back to reality. My reaction? I cursed audibly in federal court.

After the customary first night in the infirmary, I was placed in a "day side, night side" cell with eleven other prisoners. I'd never seen anything like it in any other jail in which I had ever been. Prisoners were bunked on one side of an iron bar partition with benches on the other side of the huge cell. At an appointed time in the morning, inmates were transferred from the "night side," where they slept, to the "day side," where they were expected to sit around for most of the day. I guess they didn't want anyone catching up on any beauty sleep. There was one other white guy in the cell when they put me in, but he had decided he would be better off pretending he was black too, so there wasn't much of a connection with him. I couldn't have cared less what color a person was, but I couldn't stand imposters. I had more respect on the street for a guy just being whatever he was than for someone who was pretending to be something he wasn't.

My best experience in that cell was meeting a member of the Torros MC. They were an all-black bike club located on the west side. They had horns coming out of each side of their helmets, resembling Vikings, and a big red bull on their colors. I'd seen them on the street before, but I'd never actually met one. Black and white bikers didn't intermingle much. They did their thing, and we did ours. Anyway, he was the only one in the cell with whom I made friends. The county had banned smoking in the MCJ a month before I got there, and I hadn't had a cigarette since my arrest the day before. When he offered me one, I gladly accepted. I wouldn't have cared if he was purple.

Although I didn't like the setup in my cell, at least there was a fellow biker in there with me; that made it tolerable. Until meal time, that is. When the trustee began handing in lunch trays through the slot in the door, some of the other prisoners decided to help themselves to the items on the "new guy's" tray. By the time I got my tray, it was empty. I fully understood what was going on here. Some weren't convinced by the news clip that I didn't play well with others. No problem. I began knocking other trays to the floor and announced, "If I don't eat, nobody eats." You can imagine how well that went over, especially given the odds. I didn't care a bit. I liked to fight. Suddenly the door flew open, and the cell filled up with guards, breaking up the ruckus. I was escorted out and taken to the hole, for starting a riot, no less! What a joke. It was just a good old fistfight. Anyway, I was glad to have some privacy. After a week in solitary confinement, I was transferred to what was known as a range. The range had ten individual cells opening into a common area equipped with a couple of tables, a black-and-white television with tin foil wrapped around the rabbit ears, and a payphone.

The prisoners on the E-3-North range were not in there for drunk driving or failure to pay child support.

The guy in cell number one was charged with killing his unfaithful wife in a fit of blind rage. His name was Bobby, and his background included moving hot cars from Chicago and Detroit to New York City for the black mafia. Chances are that our paths would have never crossed anywhere else. He was a serious player, not a punk or a "jitterbug." He didn't need to play games to impress anyone. He knew who he was and what he was, and he carried himself accordingly. Men like him didn't have to remind you all the time how bad they were. Bobby and I hit it off immediately.

There was another memorable black guy on the range besides Bobby. He went by Big Mac, and there was no mistaking where his name came from. He was huge, about six feet four inches tall with muscles on his muscles. Big Mac looked like he could have played in one of the old gladiator movies. By twenty-eight years old, he had already done time for killing a guy. His slick attorney got his conviction reduced to manslaughter, and he had been released for time served. It didn't take long before he got another murder beef. Needless to say, he was not a happy camper, but he was not a two-bit gangster either. He'd been around, earned some respect the hard way, and showed some too. What that means is, although he looked scary, he was predictable. If you crossed him, he'd kill you. If you didn't, he didn't mess with you. That seemed fair enough to me.

I witnessed firsthand how he dealt with idiots. Two punches and it was off to the hospital. Not the infirmary. This guy seriously hurt people. I wasn't afraid of him, but I definitely did not want a confrontation with him if it could be avoided. The problem was, in an environment like that, with everyone facing court cases, prison time, Dear John letters, and negative phone calls, tensions were always high. Most of us were detoxing from everything from heroin to cigarettes. I had been on this range about two weeks when the inevitable finally happened. Big Mac was on the phone with his girlfriend, and the conversation obviously wasn't going too well. The noise from the other inmates had risen to an unacceptable level to Mac, and he announced to the whole range, in no uncertain terms, that if it didn't quiet down immediately every one of us would suffer the consequences. I understood where he was coming from, but including me in that group was absolutely unacceptable.

I bided my time until that afternoon when Mac had stretched out on his bunk, relaxing. When this guy was standing, he was overwhelming. I knew the only way I had a chance to whip him was to get very close, within the confines of his cell. I entered quickly and before he knew what was happening I was inches from his throat. I whispered, "I couldn't care less what you do to anybody else, but I will not be grouped in with your 'All y'all' threats. We can have an understanding about that, or we can deal with it, here and now. It's up to you." He knew

I was as serious as a heart attack. He also knew that I was giving him his props as best I could, even as I was demanding mine. We came to a mutual understanding that day and never had any more trouble. I was glad. I didn't want to have to kill this guy, and I sure didn't want him killing me.

The cigarette ban just added insult to injury. I can't ever remember meeting more than one or two guys in jail who didn't smoke. As if being locked up wasn't bad enough, now you had all these people dealing with kicking the nicotine habit at the same time. I must say, it gave everyone something to focus on besides all the bad news that continually came from lawyers and old ladies. Occasionally, somebody's attorney would sneak him in a pack, and he would become an affluent person on the range. A cigarette could be traded for up to three "goodies" from the commissary list. Goodies were things like potato chips or candy bars. They were valuable commodities themselves, but they could be purchased weekly if you had money in your account. Some guys didn't. I felt sorry for them. I had more money in my commissary account than some of them needed to make bond. It made me glad I had friends. Even more importantly, it made me glad I had brothers.

If procuring cigarettes was a problem, and it was, then so was lighting them. Matches and lighters were strictly forbidden and confiscated during every shakedown. A guy who had done many years hard time in Ohio's maximum security prison in Lucasville showed me a trick that made me invaluable to the ones who did manage to find a way to get a cancer stick. He taught me how to become the "fireman"—in other words, the one they needed to light their smokes. The outlet for our TV was just outside the bars on the catwalk, controlled by a switch out of our reach. The guards used the switch to kill the power to the TV at lights-out every night. They turned it on very early in the morning, and that's when I'd go to work.

First, I would make a wick. I would run about six feet of toilet paper off the roll, separate the two plies, and then commence twisting them back together very tightly. Then I'd wedge it into the corner of the air vent high above the nifty sink/toilet/drinking fountain unit in the corner of my cell. By the way, what an efficient little invention that jewel was. I've always wondered why they haven't been introduced into the residential market.

Once the wick was in place, I began the process of getting it lit. I'd gnaw the wood off of a No. 2 pencil until about an inch of the lead was protruding. After turning the TV on, I would reach through the bars to the outlet and slowly pull the plug out until I could see the brass prongs of the plug, careful to make sure the TV stayed on. With a piece of toilet paper in one hand and my customized pencil in the other, I would gently lay the exposed lead across the prongs. It would create a blinding spark equivalent to that of an arc welder, and it would ignite the toilet paper. Of course, the outlet itself looked like it had been hit by lightning, so it had to be cleaned up before the next guard came through. Nothing an old toothbrush and some Ajax couldn't take care of. I used the burning toilet paper to light the wick in my cell and it would slowly burn all day long, the slim trail of smoke being sucked out the vent. If someone had a cigarette and needed a light, they had to come to me. For a couple of drags, I'd let them have a light off of the glowing ember at the end of my wick. Pretty clever, huh?

One day, about midmorning, they locked us all down unexpectedly. The range door opened and in came a repairman with a cart full of tools. He parked his cart directly across from my cell and began to install a mounting plate for a new payphone. He had a Harley-Davidson belt buckle on, so I asked him what he rode. The guards had evidently warned him not to speak to any of the inmates because this guy was a nervous wreck. He told me what he rode, and I told him who I was, then asked him if he knew any Outlaws. He said he had met Hambone years before, and he knew Ringo, a former member of the Dayton Outlaws prior to going to Vietnam in the late '60s.

The repair guy was preparing to put a second pay phone in on our range. He was mounting the backing plate for it, which meant he had to come back to actually install the phone. The look on his face when I told him to bring me two packs of Marlboros and a Bic lighter would have made you think I'd asked him for a pistol. He was terrified. Looking back, I understand why. Here I was talking to him through the bars of a tiny jail cell, proposing he do something that could possibly land him in a similar cell, at least in his mind. I told him to bring the items when he came back and that Ringo would pay him for them. I didn't really know if the repair guy would do it or not, or if he'd even be the one who came back to put the new phone in, but it was worth a shot.

When they locked us down again the next morning and I heard the wheels of the tool cart, I looked to see if it was the same repairman. It was. He was visibly very nervous, sweating, and resisting eye contact with me, let alone conversation. Just as he was about to finish his work, he summed up the courage to take four quick steps backwards and pulled two packs of cigarettes and a lighter out of his tool pouch. He came through for me after all. I thanked him. He nodded and wasted no time getting out of there. Normally, when I would acquire a store-bought cigarette, I would tear it open and make two hand-rolled joints out of it, but not this time. I enjoyed a whole cigarette all to myself for the first time in a long time. Little things mean a lot when you're in jail. Although forty store-bought smokes seemed like an almost endless supply, it wasn't. I was careful to return favors others had done for me and eventually they ran out. I was back to square one: trading goodies, dealing with trustees, whatever. At least I was still the fireman, and the BIC lighter made that really easy.

Every morning at 6:00 a.m., a trustee would push a cart with medications down the catwalk. Inmates who were on prescription drugs would be responsible to get up and get them at this time, as well as anyone who needed normal stuff for headaches or stomach aches. I watched a new trustee one morning as he pushed his cart, calling out, "Meds." I saw him stop and put something in his mouth, and it wasn't food. It was smokeless tobacco. I had never dipped snuff in my life, nor did I desire to, but I got out of my rack to talk to him anyway. I asked him if I could have some. He said, "Sure." He even gave me some for later.

I ripped the cardboard back off my legal pad and spread the nasty stuff out evenly, placing it under my bunk. By the time I woke up the second time, it had dried out sufficiently, enabling me to roll it up like regular tobacco. I made five tiny "joints" out of it and lit one up. That smoke hit the back of my throat like a karate kick. This stuff was strong! No Camel non-filter packed a punch like that! It definitely squelched the need for nicotine for a while. I made those last the rest of the day and was the first one up the next morning waiting for the med guy. He gave me even more that day, and more again the third day. I gave him some goodies, though he didn't ask for them, and by the fifth day, he brought me my own tin of the moist substance. For the next week or so, I had

Copenhagen drying out under my bed. Once dried and rolled into joints, it lit like any other cancer stick. It didn't smoke like it, though. It was incredibly strong. Necessity being the mother of invention as it is, it didn't take long to learn to temper each puff so as to actually enjoy it. The good news was that nobody else wanted any.

I was consumed with getting my mind off my legal troubles by figuring out how to satisfy my nicotine habit. Meanwhile, my attorney, Vic Hodge, was trying to get Magistrate Merz to set a bond for me. At my second bond hearing, I was "no bonded" again. Things were not looking good for that vacation on the beach. I was a high-profile club member, and the prospect of a lengthy stay in the county jail prior to conviction wasn't appealing. Vic had entered a "not guilty" plea for me, but the chances of an acquittal were slim to none. To make matters worse, Vic informed me that upon examination of the weapons taken from my residence, the Miami Valley Regional Crime Lab had determined that one of them, a cheap Intratec 9 mm pistol, fired fully automatically. They were going to examine it further to determine whether that was due to a malfunction of the weapon or if, in fact, it was a machine gun. If it was indeed a fully automatic weapon, the dynamics of my charges would change dramatically. Possession of an automatic weapon to facilitate the distribution of an illegal controlled substance carried thirty years federal time. I knew the Tec-9 wasn't malfunctioning. It was doing exactly what it was designed to do.

The one that was malfunctioning was me. I was going against everything I knew. In my right mind, I would never allow an illegal weapon to be where I was living and sleeping. I had arrived at a dangerous point in my career. Dangerous because, in the fast lane, breaking your own rules led to one of two things: death or prison, and sometimes both.

In the first couple of weeks I was locked up, I received several visits from others besides just my attorney. A couple of friends came to inquire about what they could do to help. I appreciated that. A Dayton brother came to ask me about what I wanted done with some of my possessions that the Feds didn't get the day I got busted. That included two Harleys, a "built" 4x4 GMC pickup, a beautiful 1978 Lincoln Town Car, and a vintage 1973 Stingray. Although the titles were confiscated from my safe, I didn't keep cages in my name. I had him contact the people whose names were on the paperwork and had them file for duplicates. My scooters were at the clubhouse, so they were safe right where they were. Just about everything else of any value at all, though, ended up in the property room, including fifteen years of photo albums. The pictures that made it into this book, though far from the best quality, were the only survivors.

Several weeks before I was arrested, I woke up with a strange tingling sensation on the right side of my face.

It resembled the numbness Novocaine produces prior to having a tooth pulled. Since I had been partying for several days with another member of the "caine" family, I figured it would wear off. It didn't. As the day went on, my face began to resemble that of a stroke victim. My right eye was stuck wide open while that side of my mouth drooped noticeably. My speech was soon impaired and I began to spit crudely when I tried pronouncing certain consonants. I would sometimes bite the inside of my mouth without realizing it, the blood trickling out of the corner as a result. A visit to a doctor produced a diagnosis of Bell's palsy. He explained that meant I had a pinched cranial nerve. He said it sometimes lasted a week or so, but in some cases, it could persist much longer. He prescribed vitamin B12, which did absolutely nothing to help. Quack.

My new hideous appearance, coupled with a terrible attitude, actually worked to my advantage when I got to the Montgomery County Jail. Not only did I act like a wild man, but now I also looked like one. I had been cautioned about the danger of my cornea not receiving the lubrication it needed from blinking, so I often had to hold it closed, as well as tape my eyelid down at night just to sleep. By this time, I had been dealing with this for over three weeks, so obviously it didn't appear to be the light case I had hoped for. When I finally got out of the hole, I requested to go to the infirmary about it.

The doctor, admittedly being no expert on cranial nerves, made me an appointment with a neurological specialist.

Because my case was federal, every time I was transported from jail, it had to be by US Marshals, who shackled me hand and foot. On the day of my doctor's appointment I was surprised that my escort would consist of one Dayton police officer. He showed little enthusiasm about taking another lowlife prisoner to see a doctor. He looked like he was just biding his time, waiting to retire. Instead of shackles connected to a belly band, he simply used a single pair of handcuffs, to the front of me no less. He obviously had no idea who I was or what I was capable of. He walked me to a police cruiser, and as we drove through downtown Dayton, I took in sights of the city. Sights I hadn't seen in over three weeks. The decorations for the upcoming annual Children's Christmas Parade were in place, the weather was pleasant, and the mood on the streets was festive, as the holiday season was now in full swing.

The medical facility we were going to was in Oakwood. That was on the ritzy side of town about which I knew little, other than the fact that Outlaws were not welcome there. Upon arrival, the patrons in the building were naturally apprehensive at seeing a handcuffed, tattooed prisoner being escorted down the hallway. I enjoyed every minute of the attention I was getting. I hadn't laid eyes on a female worth looking at for weeks, and some of those nurses were not too shabby. Once in his office, the doctor confirmed the pinched cranial nerve diagnosis, but told me an MRI would be necessary to determine how to best prescribe treatment. He informed me that MRIs were expensive and asked if I could afford one. As I sat in his examination room in a blue jailhouse uniform, I'm sure he discerned that I probably did not have insurance. He would have been correct. I had no idea what an MRI even was, let alone how much they might cost, so I responded, "No, Doc, I can't afford one." I then pointed to the officer and said, "But he can." The doctor got my drift. I was a prisoner, and a federal prisoner, to boot. The doctor looked inquisitively at the cop who responded with, "Go ahead and schedule one for him. The taxpayers can afford it."

As we again walked down the hall heading back to the car, I was presented with an unexpected temptation. As I trailed along behind him, I saw that I had easy access to his sidearm. I looked behind us, then up ahead again. The place was eerily vacant. I began to recall the Code of Conduct for prisoners of war. It was a POW's obligation to make every effort to escape captivity if he could. As we approached a stairwell door to the left, I talked myself into believing that I could secure his pistol, force him into the stairwell, and make him give me his keys. I doubt he would have even put up much of a fight. He didn't look like the hero type. With his jacket, hat, and police car, I figured I had a shot of spending Thanksgiving somewhere besides my cell up on E-3-

North. Just as I was about to go for it, the door opened and there stood a lady with her young daughter. The cop even held it open for them. As I moved out of their way, the officer stepped behind me, and we walked back out to the cruiser, this time with me in the lead. That was that. Robert Burns once wrote, "The best laid schemes of mice and men often go awry." Oh well; it was fun to think about for a few minutes.

It was becoming obvious that some decisions were going to have to be made concerning transference of leadership of the Blue Region. Wally, the boss of the Buffalo chapter, was my longtime friend, traveling companion, and reluctant vice president. It's amazing how some of the brothers strove so hard to be in charge, while others, often the more qualified, shunned positions of greater power. It's because of the responsibility that came with it. Looking back, I better understand. Looking at each other through the glass in the visitation room and talking guardedly over the old-fashioned telephone receiver, I told him he needed to take over as president of our region, and not just fill in for me while I was gone. If the Feds had their way, I was going to prison for a long time. He tried to protest, but we both knew he was, beyond the shadow of a doubt, the most qualified man for the job. I was sure Taco would agree. Finally, so did Wally. I told him to contact the presidents of my chapters and tell them to accept collect calls from me the following Saturday afternoon. When they did,

I told each of them personally that I fully endorsed Wally to be the new president of the largest and most powerful region of the Outlaw Nation. I encountered no resistance, but rather support for that decision from these men I loved, respected, and rode with for many years.

Chapter 19

Bigger Problems than Prison

Being branded a troublemaker after the problem in the stupid day/night cell, the guards wouldn't let me out of my cell to go anywhere. I requested to go to the recreation area, where I could at least pump some iron to break up the monotony. Denied. I requested to go to the library. Denied. I even asked to see the dentist. You have to be pretty desperate to get out of your cell if you are willing to go to a jailhouse dentist. Not that I'm saying some of them probably aren't good dentists, it's just that the medical environment of a correctional facility isn't famous for their liberal use of anesthetics. Anyway, all my requests were denied. Why? They said I was a menace to the other prisoners!

I filled out a slip of paper, a "kite," that read: "Spurgeon requests to go . . . *anywhere*." After several days, a jailer came to my cell on Saturday morning and said, "Spurgeon, you're going to church." I yelled back at

377

him, "No, I ain't." The prisoner in the next cell, Bobby, was going, so he yelled over, "What do you have to lose?"

My reluctance to go to the church service wasn't because I didn't believe in God. I was raised in a Christian home. I went to church as a kid. Besides, I never bought into the "accidental-explosion-in-space-fifty-billion-years-ago" malarkey. Why? I was a paratrooper in the US Army. Occasionally, we blew stuff up. The result of an explosion is destructive. What's left after the smoke clears isn't beautiful, like the aspens changing color in the Rockies in the fall, or the sun setting into the Pacific Ocean off the Southern California coast. I'd seen many very beautiful places riding around this country. Big Bang Theory? Give me a break.

Evolution? Are you kidding? It takes more faith to buy into the hogwash of evolution than to believe what the Bible says about how God created everything. My reluctance to go to the church service that morning didn't have anything to do with me not believing in God. It had to do with this: I had turned my back on Him as a young man and chose to live my life my own way. I didn't believe God would want to have anything to do with me.

Two other inmates besides me attended the church service that morning, my first in well over twenty years. Into the basement library of the old jail walked two men. One walked with crutches and leg braces, and the other carried a Bible. I remember thinking that he just looked like another cop to me. He would have taken that as a

378

compliment, as he had actually been an air force security policeman before going into the ministry. Of course, I had no way of knowing that. I just knew "the look." He may have looked like a cop, but he didn't talk like one. He said something like this, "Let's see what the Bible has to say about you men." I thought to myself, *You don't know me or anything about me.* Truth was, had he watched the evening news on television that week or read the *Dayton Daily News*, he would have known a little bit about me. I had appeared in both several times in the days following my arrest. He didn't, though. He didn't have a television. He didn't even subscribe to the newspaper. He opened his Bible and read a verse, "All have sinned, and come short of the glory of God."

Some might have been offended by that statement, but not those of us in this particular congregation. We knew we were sinners. The preacher continued, "The Bible says, 'The wages of sin is death.'" I'd seen a lot of death in my fifteen years riding with motorcycle clubs. I'd been to forty-one funerals of my own club brothers. All but one was under forty years old. All died of natural causes for us. Some were stabbed or shot in bar fights. Others were gunned down by jealous boyfriends or husbands. Several wrecked their motorcycles or cars due to being high and/or drunk; others overdosed. One was killed by police in a clubhouse raid. Some died in drug deals that went bad. Several were killed by rival motorcycle clubs. One even committed suicide. It was a lifestyle of death. I knew what this preacher said was true. After that pleasant beginning, the preacher went on to say, "I don't know what you guys are in here for, but I've come to tell you that if you die without having your sins forgiven, you've got much bigger problems ahead of you than jail or going to prison." I thought to myself, *I'm looking at thirty-seven years federal time and you're telling me I have bigger problems than that? Thanks, pal. Thanks for cheering me up.*

I remember trying to figure out what his angle was. Why was he really here? On the street, everyone has a reason for everything they do. If they are kind, or generous, or friendly, the motive behind it usually is that it benefits them in some way. I naturally wondered, *What does he stand to gain by coming to the jail early this morning to preach to us?* We sure weren't going to give him any money. After about fifteen minutes of listening to him talk about "what the Bible says," I figured him out. He wasn't there for money. He wasn't there because of any benefit it was going to bring him when he got back to whatever church he came from. Tom Gresham was at the Montgomery County Jail that morning with his Bible because he really believed what it said. He really believed people who died in their sins went to a literal hell, just like the Bible says. He really believed the only way to escape it was to trust in what Jesus Christ did on the cross of Calvary for the forgiveness of sins. Once I figured out what his angle was, I began to listen more intently to what he was actually saying. It didn't matter whether I believed him or not. What mattered to me was whether *he* believed it or not. I had no time, or tolerance, for another con artist in my life.

He opened his Bible to Luke chapter 16 and read a story of two men. One was a rich man, the other a beggar. These two guys were as different as night and day—as different as he was from me—but they had one thing in common: death. Thinking back, that preacher talked a lot about death that day. He told us about how one of these men was carried off by angels when he died, and the other went straight to hell. I had no idea where the angels carried him off to, but I had certainly heard of that place called hell. I had been taught about it as a child. I used the word frequently in my vocabulary. I told many people to go there. I stood by the graveside of many of my fallen comrades and said, "I'll see you in hell, brother." As far as I knew, that's where they went, and that's where I was going. Our notion that we were going to party there wasn't biblical, though. That preacher read passages concerning hell that morning and none of them made it sound like it was going to be any fun. It said that the one man was tormented in flames, crying out for mercy, begging for water, but got neither.

I'll never forget about being told of "weeping, wailing, and gnashing of teeth." I remember thinking, *Weeping and wailing? Not me. That's woman stuff.* That phrase "gnashing of teeth," though, I'd never heard before. However, I had seen it in real life. In mid-July 1984, the Outlaws had a national run to Oshkosh, Wisconsin. A national run meant that all members were required to be there, except for the guys left guarding the clubhouses, or going to court, or running from the law. There were always plenty of brothers on the lamb. Oftentimes at our gatherings, whether they were for parties or for one of the many funerals, law-enforcement agencies would have a national run of their own. Gang intelligence officers from all over the US and Canada would gather to photograph us and to look for those with warrants.

The day we got up to Wisconsin, a bunch of us headed to a secluded swimming hole. It was a beautiful summer afternoon, the weather was perfect, and the highway was a nice, smooth, country road. It was a pleasant break after riding through the big cities to get up there. After cooling off, we headed back to our camp, with me leading a small pack of about a dozen bikes. Everyone was refreshed and enjoying the ride. No one had been drinking yet or even getting high to my knowledge. There we were, twelve of us riding two by two, enjoying the sunshine and the wind in our faces. What could go wrong?

I could see trouble coming in an approaching car. As I watched it coming toward us that day, it was obvious the female driver was arguing with a man in the passenger seat. I could see her hands waving as she was yelling at him. She definitely was not paying attention to her driving, not to mention the pack of bikers coming toward her. Soon after she passed me, she drifted over the center line. Not a lot, but just enough. The last bike in our formation was ridden by a probationary member from Toledo named Bones. Before that lady could swerve back into her lane amid the shouts of obscenities from my guys, she caught his left calf with the bumper of her car. Not enough to knock him down right away, just enough to shove his foot into the engine sprocket of his open-primary drive train. That sprocket chewed his foot off like a meat grinder minces hamburger. It happened so fast, I don't think he knew what hit him.

I looked back over my shoulder just in time to see her cut back to her side of the road. My pack was scattered, no longer uniform. We weren't going very fast, so I was able to spin around very quickly and get back to where Bones had finally gone down. I couldn't believe my eyes. His foot had been severed, and the lower part of his leg was still tangled in the exposed double-row primary chain. I had never seen anyone lose so much blood; it was everywhere. I reached down for the stub of his leg and pulled it out of the chain, trying to apply enough pressure to stop the artery from spurting. Given our rural location, I doubted if anyone would reach us in time to save his life. I looked from his mangled leg to his face, and I'll never forget what I saw. His eyes were closed tightly. His fists were clenched. And he was gnashing his teeth in pain. I remember thinking two things about that sight. The first was that I had never seen anyone in that much pain before. That's saying something. I'd seen a lot of pain in my years with the club. I've seen men shot, and I've seen men beaten to a bloody pulp. Once I even saw a man holding his guts in after being cut in a bar fight. I've seen men in pain, but never like this. The second thing I thought looking in Bones's face was that I wouldn't want to spend one second in that much agony.

An ambulance did make it, and so did Bones. He ended up losing his left leg just below the knee. Eventually, he got a prosthetic leg, learned to ride a three wheeler, earned his colors, and the last I knew, he was a member in good standing. I ran with a tough crowd. I hadn't thought much about that day for a long time. Life goes on. Now, seven years later, I find myself in the county jail listening to a preacher tell me that I am not only going to burn forever, but I'm going to gnash my teeth in pain as well. Bones' long-forgotten expression of incomprehensible anguish immediately came to mind.

The preacher preached about sin and death and hell. That's what preachers are supposed to do, isn't it? Even I knew that. He went on to say, "The wages of sin is death, but the gift of God is eternal life through Jesus Christ our Lord." I'm glad that verse didn't stop at "death." I'm glad his message that morning went on to include some hope. He explained in detail the cost of the gift of God. He showed us from the Bible what Jesus Christ went through to make the gift of eternal life available to any and every sinner. He was betrayed by one of His own men and forsaken by the rest of them when He was arrested. He was subjected to several mock trials, found innocent in every one of them, and sentenced to death anyway. *Where was the ACLU that day?* I wondered. The preacher told us about how they beat Christ beyond recognition. I'd seen that a few times. We had guys who didn't even resemble themselves when the plastic surgeons finished trying to put them back together. They didn't take their beatings willingly, though. That preacher said Christ did, for sinners like me. At the end of the service, Tom Gresham offered to show any of us from the Bible how our sins could be forgiven. I didn't respond. I didn't take the preacher up on his offer to answer any questions we may have had. I was too proud. In the club, we considered "getting religion" in jail as a sign of weakness. I think prosecutors and jailers thought of it as a sign of weakness too. There was no room for weakness in the life I'd chosen. On the contrary. Besides, if a guy got religious, we became instantly suspicious that he may become a threat. In other words, he may become a snitch.

Interestingly enough, I was initially concerned that if I got in on this forgiveness of sins thing this preacher was talking about, I might be letting the brothers in the "Forever Chapter" down. I was actually more worried about that than I was about what my living brothers would think. The Forever Chapter was made up of brothers who had died. We went to great lengths to honor them with elaborate funerals, ornately inscribed headstones, and even memory patches sown on our colors. While I was pondering all this stuff about God and hell and Christ, I remember thinking about those close to me who had died. Hambone, Ralph, Bear, Pig Pen, Fat Louie, Big Moe—there had been so many. So much death. So many funerals. So many beloved brothers in the Forever Chapter.

In the sermon about the rich man and the beggar, that beggar went to heaven. The rich man went straight to hell, and all that wealth he accumulated didn't go with him. What he had in life didn't benefit him one bit after he died. What really provoked me to think was the fact that the rich man had five brothers. He didn't want them to come to where he was. It occurred to me while I was worried about letting my departed brothers down, according to the Bible, they were hoping I wouldn't end up there with them. They knew hell was real. They knew how bad it was.

I left the library that morning an unforgiven sinner, only now I knew it. I knew what the Bible said as opposed to what I believed or what I found convenient to believe. On my way out of the service, I picked up some of the free literature they were handing out and headed back to my cell. If that preacher ever felt like he just preached to a hopeless, hell-bound individual, it was me that day. Things were coming apart at the seams in every area of my life and, to make matters worse, now I had this sermon about a "lake of fire" rolling around in my head.

I had been told by a trustee that another Dayton Outlaw had been arrested and was in a cell on the fourth floor. I sent a message for him to sign up for the next church service, so we could talk. We sat in the back of the service while Mr. Gresham showed a video about a bank robber who had gotten saved and was living for God now. I didn't pay much attention to it. I was busy catching up on what was happening out on the street since I'd been locked up. When the service was over, the preacher asked if I needed anything. He got a surprised look on his face when I asked him for a Bible. He said he'd get one to me, and he did. On November 14, a large-print, King James Bible was brought up to my cell.

In the course of the next two weeks, I would skim through that Bible and look at the literature I got at that first church service. I reread the passage in Luke 16 about the rich man and the beggar many times. The rich man was tormented in flame, it said. I looked at a booklet I'd gotten titled "Millions Disappear" by a preacher named Peter Ruckman. It had lots of pictures. One was a very graphic depiction of people engulfed in flame. It brought that message I'd heard back to my mind, so I put it down too. Being in jail was depressing enough. I picked up the other little booklet I'd brought back to my cell. It was a little black-and-white comic book entitled "Bad Bob," written by some guy who went by the initials

JTC. It had a biker-looking guy on the cover in front of a confederate flag. Right up my alley. I got a kick out of the little story until Bad Bob and his cousin got put in jail for drugs. Then the jail caught on fire. His cousin burned alive in his cell, but Bad Bob escaped because a jailer risked his life to save him. I remember thinking, "Everything I read has something to do with fire and pain."

Tom Gresham had said the Lord Jesus went to the cross so that people wouldn't have to go to hell and burn forever. I didn't understand why He would do that for someone like me. I knew I was a sinner. I chose to be. I worked at it for a long time. I knew if the hell he preached about was real, I was going to end up there. I knew I deserved it. I was honest enough to admit that to myself. I was also honest enough to admit nothing would be worth it. Nothing I'd ever done or ever planned to do would be worth burning forever for. I wasn't worried about prison. I knew plenty of people already there. I wasn't a kid. I would survive. I wanted no part of this place called hell!

The morning of November 30 came just like the previous twenty-nine days. At 6:00 a.m., a trustee would push a cart down the catwalk calling out names, passing out meds. I wasn't awake because of him. I didn't take any meds. I was wide-awake because I couldn't get the message I'd heard three weeks earlier out of my head. I had the image of the lake of fire picture burned into my brain. Most of all, I was acutely aware that I was headed there. On top of all this, the date came over my small radio I was listening to.

November 30. That made it exactly ten years to the day since Ralph Tanner had been murdered in the alley behind the Hawley Street clubhouse. Ten years to the day since he had been gunned down by a rival club's bullets meant for me. I was always the first in the alley, but not that night. After several hours of partying at K.O.'s Lounge, I had given a couple of girls a ride up to the corner. Ralph had passed me on his motorcycle as I stopped to let them out. November 30. It had been ten years since Ralph stepped out into eternity. Only now I knew where he was and what he was doing. As far as I know, Ralph went to hell that night.

As I mulled all these things over in my head, I knew one thing for sure. If the Bible was true, I was in a lot more trouble than I thought. That preacher was right. Thirty-seven years in federal prison would be nothing compared to weeping, wailing, gnashing teeth, and being tormented in flame for all eternity. That morning I took the Bible and laid it on the floor of my cell next to my rack. I knelt down beside it and attempted to pray to the God whom I had turned my back on so many years ago, the God whom I had ignored and disrespected. The God whose name I had taken in vain literally thousands and thousands of times.

I wasn't taking His name in vain this time. I was trying the best way I knew how to sincerely communicate with Him. The conversation went something like this: "God, I'm on my way to prison for a long time, and I deserve it. I've made a mess of my life, and it's time to pay. I understand that, God. That preacher you sent down here showed me from the Bible that I've got bigger problems than going to prison. If your book is true and hell is real, I'm sure enough headed there too. You and I both know I'm a sinner, but, God, that preacher said Jesus Christ paid the price for even my sins. I believe that. I'm asking you to forgive me, Lord. I'm asking you to come into my heart and take control of my life."

I prayed that prayer sincerely. Nothing changed outwardly or immediately. I still looked the same. I was still locked up without bond. I was still headed to prison for probably the rest of my life. I had no real concept of the scope of what had just taken place as I bowed my knee and my heart to the Lord Jesus Christ and trusted Him to be my Savior. But I do know this: something changed. I knew I would never be the same.

Chapter 20

A Turn for the Better

The very next morning, the crippled man came and conducted the Saturday church service by himself. He said his name was Cleves Dodge. I recognized him from the first one I had attended several weeks before. This time, instead of sitting in the back, talking to other inmates, I sat right up front. This time I was interested in what the preacher had to say. I was fascinated by what the Bible said that Jesus Christ went through to pay for my sins. In the military, where some real heroes still do exist, if a man gave his life to save his buddy, his buddy never got over it, never forgot it. On the street, if a brother took a bullet covering your back, you owed him. I could not help but feel I owed this man Jesus at least an honest effort to learn a little bit about Him, especially in light of what I'd recently learned He did for me.

There was an inmate on my range named Tyrone, who'd been in the maximum security prison in Lucasville,

Ohio, for several years on a murder beef. He had been brought back to the Montgomery County Jail for charges he incurred at his sentencing. It seems when his trial judge sentenced him, he somehow got his hands on a policeman's pistol and threatened to kill the judge right there in the courtroom. He didn't, but he sure scared him to death. He was subdued and led out, laughing as he went. Naturally, when they brought him back to the county to await the disposition of this additional charge, they put him in the range with me. He really wasn't a bad guy to be around, street smart with a curious sense of humor. He also went to the church service I attended that morning.

When the preacher asked if anyone had ever asked Christ to save their soul, I raised my hand. It had only been about twenty-six hours since I had done it, but I figured it like this: I wasn't ashamed to be associated with motorcycle clubs, to wear their colors, to have their logo tattooed on my body. It seemed to me it would have been ludicrous to be ashamed to admit I'd prayed for the forgiveness of my sins, which were many. Tyrone, who had only known me for about a week, definitely had a surprised look on his face when he saw my hand go up. Neither my conversation nor my conduct prior to that Friday would have remotely suggested I'd ever even heard of Jesus Christ. I understood his amazement. I was amazed to find myself in church with my hand in the air too.

The preacher gave his message and then opened the service up for questions. Tyrone was well-read and began to ask the preacher about some religious beliefs different people practiced. He seemed sincere, and the preacher attempted to answer his questions from the Bible, but it soon became obvious Tyrone was only setting him up for an argument. Tyrone could be very intimidating, and he knew it. Seeing the preacher visibly shaken only emboldened him. I looked over at Tyrone and told him to shut up, or he would be dealing with me when we got back upstairs. He decided to back off. I thought to myself, *I've been saved one day and already I might get to beat somebody up for a good reason. Maybe this Christianity thing won't be so bad after all.*

I requested for the man who had sent me a King James Bible, Tom Gresham, to come to see me. I was informed he was in Texas, but would respond to my request as soon as he got back. He didn't really know exactly who he was coming to visit and looked extremely surprised to see it was me when he stepped into the visitation booth. He made his way to the chair and picked up the phone receiver that would enable us to communicate through the thick Plexiglas that separated us. I must have been a sight to behold. An unkempt, bearded, tattooed, longhaired biker in a jailhouse uniform, anxious to tell him probably the last thing he expected to hear. "I did what you said." He stared at me, wide-eyed and responded, "You did what?" I told him, "Last Friday, I asked Christ to forgive me.

I really meant it." Though we had met a month earlier when I showed up at his church service, this day was the beginning of a friendship that has lasted over twenty years.

He came back to see me again several days later. This time they let us meet in an attorney-privilege room, seated across a table from each other, without the glass or the phone. I informed him I was being held without bond on federal drug and weapons charges, for which I would most likely be doing time. He said he'd have the church he was from pray for me. I don't think I really comprehended that, but I thanked him anyway. He brought some ground-level material for me to read and said he would be back to visit again when he could.

Two days later, Tom returned, and again we were escorted to the same small room. "What am I supposed to do now?" I asked. When he asked me what I meant, I said, "I'll soon be thirty-eight years old. I have no skill and no trade. Everything I'm good at, except riding motorcycles, is illegal. All my friends are fellow club members. To top it off, I'm going to prison. What do I do now that I'm saved?" He understood my question then and opened his Bible, mumbling to himself. "Therefore any man be in Christ . . . ." He looked up at me and read the verse out loud, "Therefore if any man be in Christ, he is a new creature: old things are passed away; behold, all things are become new." Then he said simply, "It looks like God is going to have to give you some new friends."

It was right after this second visit from Tom Gresham that my attorney came to me with a plea arrangement offered from the federal prosecutor's office. If I would agree to plead guilty to possession of narcotics and of a firearm, they would drop the automatic weapons charge. They never even suggested that I rat on anyone, which I wouldn't have done anyway. Their motivation was purely fiscal. It would save the federal government between forty and fifty thousand dollars if there wasn't a trial. My maximum would be reduced from thirty-seven years to seven. Even Ray Charles could see that was a good deal. I told Vic Hodge to let them know I would accept their offer. Vic got right on it and requested another bond hearing. This time it was granted! When he came back with the news, he told me this was unprecedented in the history of the Sixth Federal Territory for a federal drug case. I remember asking myself at the time, *Did God do that for me?*

I never saw Magistrate Merz again. This time I went before a federal judge, the Honorable Walter H. Rice. Several members of the Outlaws were present. Judge Rice reviewed my case, acknowledging my agreement to plead guilty. He asked me several questions, and I responded as honestly as I could. When I saw Tom Gresham again, he assured me the church was praying for me. He emphasized the importance of coming to church should Judge Rice grant me a bond. I told him I would. I didn't realize it at the time, but he'd heard dozens of prisoners make that same promise, but none had ever followed through and actually come. I sensed his skepticism and assured him that I would come to thank the church for praying for me if I got out. That's all I promised, but I did give him my word on that.

A full week passed, and I had not heard from my attorney about anything, let alone the judge's ruling on my request. It was 4:00 p.m., Friday, December 21 now, and chances were looking very grim concerning the prospects of getting out before Christmas. Just as I was starting to get used to the idea of being in jail through these holidays as well, a jailer came and said, "Grab your stuff, including your mattress. You're out of here." Judge Rice's office had contacted my lawyer about granting a $95,000 property bond that would enable my release. Vic Hodge called the clubhouse, and by late that afternoon, the paperwork was complete. The US Marshalls escorted me to the federal building once again, and the stipulations of my release were explained to me. They were simple. No drugs, no liquor, no guns. Last, but definitely not least, no association with any members of the Outlaws Motorcycle Club. I was driven home by a non-member friend who met me with a pack of smokes, and took me directly to Red Lobster. It was time for a real meal.

A party was scheduled Saturday night at the clubhouse in honor of my release. Brothers had come from several other chapters to see me, possibly for the last time before I went to prison. If wind of me showing up at the clubhouse got to the cops, my bond, which was barely twenty-four hours old, would be revoked. I certainly didn't want that. I went to the clubhouse reluctantly, but like I expected, it wasn't the same. It wasn't them that had changed; it was me. It was good to see the brothers, to be sure, but the offers to drink, smoke pot, and snort cocaine had to be refused. That stuff had nearly destroyed my life. I now had a clear head again, possibly for the first time since the days of wrenching for Marv Yagel back at Napoleon Harley-Davidson fifteen years before. On January 11, 1991, I pled guilty to possession of an illegal controlled substance with intent to distribute and possession of a firearm to facilitate the distribution of an illegal controlled substance. The two charges carried two years and five years, respectively. I was turned over to the federal probation department for a pre-sentence investigation.

On January 25, 1991, I saw Taco for the last time. We rendezvoused at Hambone's old house in Drexel, on Dayton's far west side. We hadn't spoken since my arrest over two months earlier, and I knew he needed to make sure I wasn't in danger of rolling over. He had heard I'd been going to church, and like I stated previously, that was often grounds for concern. I knew my life had changed, though I was clueless as to how much or in what new direction it would take me, but turning on the club was never considered. Taco felt confident of that after we spoke. By the end of the meeting, he assured me he would do anything possible to help me. We wished each other well, and that was that. I turned my colors over to him that day, fully expecting to be sentenced in a matter of months. My career with the Outlaws Motorcycle Club was officially over. I knew I was a different man now, and after prison my life would follow a different course.

To my amazement, my pre-sentence investigation went on for ten months. During that time, I often visited my elderly parents in Tennessee. I got a job with a construction company, and I remained faithful to that little church that prayed for me. When my sentencing date finally arrived, I was ready to do my time. Judge Rice had other ideas. After a lengthy, detailed discourse on why he felt compelled to depart from the congressional sentencing guidelines, he did something else that had never been done before in the Sixth Federal Territory. He severed a drug charge from the accompanying weapons charge and sentenced me that day solely on the drug count. It carried a maximum of two years imprisonment, but Judge Rice chose to sentence me to five years of supervised federal probation instead. He added one thousand hours of community service and 180 days of electronically monitored house arrest as well. The probation stipulations were very similar to the conditions of the bond he had set eleven months before: no guns, no drugs, no liquor, no association with convicted felons, and absolutely no association with any member of the Outlaws Motorcycle Club. I walked into court for my sentencing on November 22, 1991, expecting to leave with the US Marshals, headed to the penitentiary. Instead, I walked out with the Pastor Greg Estep of Charity Baptist Church and many friends from the church that came to show their support.

I completed my obligation and was released from federal probation in November 1996. By that time, the United States Supreme Court had redefined use of a firearm in conjunction with a drug offense. In 1998, without even a petition from my attorney, Judge Walter Herbert Rice threw out my firearm conviction. I never went back to the deadly lifestyle that cost so many their lives and nearly killed me. I also never lost my love for the freedom of the open road.

Epilogue

The Bottom Line

For some of you, this account of my perspective on bikin' and brotherhood took an unexpected turn toward what you might refer to as "religion." You need not feel ripped off or tricked. You got enough information about Harley-Davidsons and the biker lifestyle within these pages to make whatever investment you made well worth your while. You got a candid and honest look into a world you rarely get any insight into that is not tainted by an emphasis on the negative, or downright criminal. Investigative reporters and law-enforcement personnel have written many biker books, that dwell solely on those aspects, because that's all they can see from their perspective. They do not comprehend the love of the road, or the affection for the American-made, two-wheeled thunder that gave us access to it. There are plenty of negatives when it comes to clubs, to be sure, and I've been brutally honest about them, most

401

likely to the dismay of some that may read this book. I've also tried to give you an honest portrayal that will caution you in areas of which you may want to steer clear and still enjoy your life of bikin' and brotherhood with fellow like-minded motorcyclists.

I hope you enjoyed this book, but by far, the most important information contained in what you've read is found in chapter nineteen concerning my becoming a Christian. I didn't get tired of being a biker. I didn't "get religion" in hopes of not going to prison. I have dealt honestly with how my life got completely out of control, blaming no one but myself.

I also dealt honestly with what the Bible says one must do in order to have their sins forgiven. Notice, I'm not talking about becoming religious or joining some movement. I'm talking about trusting what Jesus Christ did on the cross to be the only acceptable payment to God for sin. Maybe you weren't taught that way; maybe you don't believe that way. I'm sorry about that. All roads don't lead to heaven. In fact, all but one lead to hell. I know that sounds narrow-minded. Good. I've always been narrow-minded about most things in my life. So have you.

The Bible says in the book of Mark, chapter 8 and verse 36, "For what shall it profit a man, if he shall gain the whole world, and lose his own soul?" I gambled with my life for many years, but never considered I was also gambling with my eternal soul. So are you, every time you straddle your Harley. Until Christ becomes your Savior, you are gambling with something you cannot afford to lose. After being confronted with the fact that it was indeed possible to have my sins forgiven, I determined it would be foolish for me not to. You can call it what you will, but I call it common sense. I had made many bad choices in my life, but I am more convinced than ever, twenty years later, that trusting the Lord Jesus Christ to be my Savior was the best and smartest decision I ever made.

When I gave my sin to Jesus Christ in the Montgomery County Jail that cold November morning, I gave Him something else too. I gave Him my life. I have pursued learning about Him, and living for Him, with the same energy I applied to every other aspect of my life. I wasn't ashamed of being a biker or of being an Outlaw. I absolutely refuse to let anyone get the impression I am ashamed of being a Christian.

Jesus Christ did not make a wimp out of me when He saved my soul, nor did He require me to rat out anyone, other than myself. I am often asked, "How did you get out of the club? You can't just leave, especially if you were really such a high-ranking member." It is true that anyone determined to be a threat to the club, even remotely, would be in serious danger. Yes, there were those who were afraid that I could potentially fall into that category. There may have even been some that felt eliminating the possibility of that eventuality to be in the best interests of the club.

An Outlaw that would have certainly fallen into that category would be Wayne Hicks. No doubt you have noticed by now that there is no love lost between Hicks and me, and I have documented why. The truth is, the things about his selfish nature mentioned in this book pale in comparison to what he did in 2001, after being arrested for a dozen federal charges, including conspiracy to commit murder.

The newspapers referred to him as the "Sammy the Bull Gravano" of the biker world. Gravano was an underboss for the Gambino crime family. He is best known as the man who helped bring down John Gotti, the family's boss, by agreeing to become a Federal Bureau of Investigation witness. At the time, Gravano was the highest-ranking member of the Five Families to break his Cosa Nostra oath and cooperate with the government. The comparison was made because Hicks was the highest-ranking member of any one-percenter club in history to become a rat. Hicks went on the stand in Federal court to testify against Harry "Taco" Bowman, resulting in Bowman receiving several life sentences for a multitude of crimes. You always wanted to be famous, Wayne. You got your wish.

After all these years, I never did anything to hurt the club. No one was ever indicted because of me. I never took the stand against anyone. I didn't go on any protection program. I went to church, and I still go to church. As a matter of fact, I still pray for Taco, and for others, though many of my contemporaries are long dead.

Dope was quickly taking me off the deep end. Had I continued down the road of whiskey and cocaine abuse I was on, I surely would be long dead myself by now. Regardless of how anyone else looks at it, I know that putting my faith and trust in Christ was the right decision for me. It would be for my fellow one-percenter club brothers, and it would be for you too.

I still love to ride, and do every chance I get. In fact, I enjoy it more now than ever. Without worrying about the Feds, or rival clubs, and most importantly of all, not worrying about where my soul would spend eternity should I die in an accident. Motorcycling is dangerous no matter how long you've been at it or how good you are. A sweet little old lady, or sixteen-year-old girl with her learner's permit, could send you out into eternity in a hot pair of New York seconds. Do you know where your soul would go if that were to happen? There are only two possibilities: heaven or hell. What you do with Jesus Christ is the determining factor. You may not choose to believe that, but you would be foolish not to. My prayer is that you don't find out the hard way that what I am telling you is the truth from the Word of God, not my opinion. My opinion isn't worth a plug nickel more than yours. The Bible says, "For whosoever shall call upon the name of the Lord shall be saved." Try it. I did. It works.

Last of all, I never left the house without my mom saying, "Be careful." To my fellow bikers, I say this: Enjoy your scooter, your camaraderie with other bikers, and the wind in your face. And like a wise old Irish lady used to say, *be careful.*

GLOSSARY

Biker Terms You Always Wanted to Know
But Were Afraid to Ask

basket case: Harley completely in pieces, in dire need
of assembly.

Black and White: Slang for "Outlaws MC"

Blockhead: Name given to the head design that
replaced the Shovelhead.

Boot Hill: Slang expression for the cemetery west
of Dayton, Ohio, where the Outlaws
have their own section.

brother: Fellow patch-member of a motorcycle
club

BBT.:   Brother Bike Tramp. Outlaw MC clique
comprised of the "high-milers."

cage: Car, truck, four-wheeler.

car punk: Bike club members who were always
riding in cars cause their bikes were down,
if they even had one. (They usually wore
dirty, white tennis shoes.)

"Charlie"   Affectionate name given to the Outlaws
MC center-patch.

chopper:	Modified chassis, non-factory Harley.
chillum:	A straight dope-pipe, primarily used for smoking hashish.
church:	Official, mandatory club meeting.
citizen:	Anyone who was not a patch-wearing member of a motorcycle club.
colors:	The patch, the embroidered emblem denoting membership.
cut-off:	The actual sleeveless vest, whether leather or denim, on to which the colors are sewn.
Crunch Bunch:	Clique within the Outlaws Tampa Bay Chapter, notorious for violence.
DFFL:	"Dope Forever, Forever Loaded"
dresser:	Harley with all the bells and whistles, i.e. saddlebags, tour pack, fairing, radio, light bar, windshield, turn signals, running boards, etc.
Easyriders:	Popular cult magazine introduced in the '70s featuring Harleys, biker fiction, and Dave Mann's incredible artwork.
Forever Chapter:	Designation for A.O.A members who died in good standing.
GFOD:	"God Forgives, Outlaws Don't"
garbage wagon:	See "Dresser"
HAs:	Slang expression for Hells Angels

hang-around:	Associate. May or may not even own a motorcycle, but valuable to the operation of any club.
heat:	Pressure from the law-enforcement community
HPJ	Horsepower Junkies: Clique within the Indianapolis Outlaws, notorious for very fast motorcycles.
jonesing:	Slang expression for needing a "fix."
kite:	Request form in jail
Knucklehead:	(1936–1947) slang term for Harley's first overhead valve engine, available in 61 (EL) or 74 (FL) ci
Mother Chapter:	Original, founding chapter of a club.
National Run:	Mandatory function, requiring full participation.
OFFO:	"Outlaws Forever, Forever Outlaws"
old lady:	Biker term for female companion, regardless of age or marital status.
OLs:	Slang for Outlaws
Panhead:	(1948–1964) slang term for Harley's second overhead valve engine, available in 61 (EL) or 74 (FL) c.i.
patch:	See "colors"
patch holder:	Color-wearing member of any bike club.
Percs:	Short for Percadan. Powerful, addictive, prescription pain pill.

piglet:	Slang for Harley Sportster. Not quite a real "Hog."
probate:	probationary member
property patch:	The patch females wore on their cut-off, which included the words "Property of Outlaws."
prospect:	Prospective member (same as Probate)
Red and White:	Slang for Hells Angels MC
rice burner:	Slang for any Japanese-made motorcycle.
rice grinder:	See above
RICO Act:	"Racketeer Influenced and Corrupt Organization" provides for extended penalties for acts performed as part of a criminal organization.
road dog:	Riding partner
roadie:	see "Road Dog"
rock monster:	Crack-head
Shovelhead:	Slang term for Harley's third overhead valve head design, circa 1966–1984, available in 74 or 80 ci.
side hack:	Slang for sidecar.
swing-arm:	Motorcycle frame employing rear shock absorbers, introduced by Harley Davidson in 1958.
trick bag:	No win situation, set-up, catch 22, destined to fail.

wannabe: One who pretends to be something he's not; faker, poser.

A wannabe is the guy who uses the Harley lifestyle for his own purpose, like getting attention, or affection.

Now you "wannabe's" can memorize this list and talk like a real biker, maybe even impress a girl or two.

I must warn you. If you throw these terms around trying to convince a real biker you're something you're not, you may get more than you bargained for. 'Nuff said.

IMPORTANT NOTE:

This term does not apply to all the genuine enthusiasts who love their Harley-Davidsons and the open road, just because they don't belong to a club. Some of them are more "real" then the street gangsters who don patches, but are no more bikers than Mickey Mouse or Donald Duck.

You're welcome.